Proceedings of the National Health Lawyers Association's
Fourth Annual Program on

LONG TERM CARE
AND THE LAW

Edited by **Jonathan W. Skiba**

PANEL PUBLISHERS
division of Cantor, Fitzgerald Group, Ltd.

This publication is designed to provide accurate and authoritative information in regard to the subject matter covered. It is sold with the understanding that the publisher is not engaged in rendering legal, accounting or other professional service. If legal advice or other professional assistance is required, the services of a competent professional person should be sought.

— From a Declaration of Principles jointly adopted by a Committee of the American Bar Association and the Committee of Publishers and Associations.

Printed in the United States of America

Library of Congress Catalog Card Number: 79-89739

ISBN: 0-916592-31-6

PREFACE

The conference upon which this book is based, the National Health Lawyers Association's Fourth Annual Program on Long Term Care and the Law, attracted a whole range of health law professionals. Attorneys, accountants and administrators, together with government personnel from both state and federal agencies, met to exchange viewpoints and to hear expert presentations on pressing long term care issues.

These presentations are reproduced on the pages that follow. They were uniformly competent and enlightening. Discussion was lively—at times, even heated. As is readily apparent, much of the book carries with it a rather conversational tone. This is due to the fact that the speakers, in large part, did not rely on prepared texts.

I would like to acknowledge the assistance of Mr. David Greenburg, Executive Director of the National Health Lawyers Association, and Mr. Tom Fox, the program chairman, in preparing this book. I also wish to thank all of the speakers at the conference for their substantial contributions to the editing process.

Finally, credit must be given to the following members of Panel Publishers' production staff—Dorothy Benjamin, Carol A. Biedrzycki, Shari Davidson, Roslyn Green, Arlene Henderson, Maryanne Kerner, Deborah Love, Carol Moore, Cathy J. Muchin, Carol Rogoff, Marilyn Semble, Lori Silver, Steve Tiano—who put personalities aside and assisted me in bringing this project to a successful conclusion.

Jonathan W. Skiba
Greenvale, New York
July, 1979

INTRODUCTION

This book is based on the proceedings of our Fourth Annual Program on *Long Term Care and the Law* held in Charleston, South Carolina during February of 1979. We want to thank the faculty not only for participating in the educational program itself but also for agreeing to have their presentations recorded and subsequently edited for this book. Our particular thanks go to Thomas C. Fox, the program chairman, for taking time from his busy schedule to organize these programs for the National Health Lawyers Association. As in prior years, Mr. Fox has also agreed to chair our Fifth Annual Program on *Long Term Care and the Law* to be held in San Antonio, Texas, February 27-29, 1980. We would also like to thank Panel Publishers for producing this book.

The National Health Lawyers Association is a nonprofit association of attorneys involved with or practicing in the health care area. It publishes two monthly periodicals, *The Health Law Digest* and *The News Report*. The NHLA also conducts educational programs in other areas of health law. All of our programs are open to administrators, health executives and attorneys. These programs have been granted continued educational credits for attorneys, CPA's and nursing home administrators.

For more information on the National Health Lawyers Association, its publications and educational programs, write to:

David J. Greenburg
Executive Director
522 21st Street, Suite 708E
Washington, D.C. 20006
(202) 393-3050

ABOUT THE AUTHORS

JEROME BROWN

Mr. Brown is Vice President of District 1199, New England Health Care Employees Union, RWDSU/AFL-CIO. He has been associated with this union for ten years, beginning as a union organizer. Mr. Brown is a graduate of Iona College and holds a Masters in American History from the State University of New York at Stony Brook.

IRWIN COHEN

Mr. Cohen is the Director, Division of Planning and Development, Office of Program Integrity, Health Care Financing Administration, Department of Health, Education and Welfare. He is also designated Acting Director, Office of Program Validation, Bureau of Quality Control, Health Care Financing Administration. He has also held several other positions within HEW and IRS. Mr. Cohen received his B.B.A. from the University of Michigan and his L.L.B./J.D. from the University of Baltimore. He is a member of the Maryland Bar.

TOBY S. EDELMAN

Ms. Edelman is a Staff Attorney for the National Senior Citizens Law Center in Washington, D.C.

JOHN R. ERICKSON

Mr. Erickson, an attorney with Pierson, Ball & Dowd in Washington, D.C., is an expert on Equal Employment Opportunity matters. He is a member of the District of Columbia Bar.

THOMAS C. FOX

Mr. Fox is an attorney with Pierson, Ball & Dowd in Washington, D.C. He is a director of the National Health Lawyers Association and served as Program Chairman for the Fourth Annual Program on "Long Term Care and the Law."

ROBERT J. GERST

Mr. Gerst is a partner in the law firm of Weissberg and Aronson, Inc., in Los Angeles, California. He has been involved in the health law field for the past ten years and has extensive experience in the areas of reimbursement, licensing, acquisitions and health planning for hospitals and other health care institutions. He serves as general counsel to the California Association of Health Facilities and associate legal counsel to the United Hospital Association. Mr. Gerst is a graduate of the University of Southern California School of Law. He is a member of the California State Bar.

JOEL M. HAMME

Mr. Hamme is an attorney with Pierson, Ball & Dowd in Washington, D.C. Prior to joining that firm, he served as a law clerk to the Honorable John Biggs, Jr., United States Court of Appeals for the Third Circuit. Mr. Hamme is a graduate of Dickinson College and the University of Pennsylvania Law School. He is a member of the Pennsylvania and District of Columbia Bars.

WILLIAM HERMELIN

Mr. Hermelin is the Administrator, Government Services Division, American Health Care Association, Washington, D.C.

THOMAS E. HERRMANN

Mr. Herrmann is Legislative Counsel for Public Policy, American Association of Homes for the Aging, Washington, D.C.

MARSHALL B. KAPP

Mr. Kapp is a program analyst with the Health Care Financing Administration Health Standards and Quality Bureau Office of Standards and Certification in the Department of Heath, Education and Welfare. He holds a B.A. from Johns Hopkins University, a J.D. (with honors) from George Washington University and an M.P.H. from the Harvard University School of Public Health. Mr. Kapp is a member of the Florida Bar.

SALLY A. KELLY

Ms. Kelly is an Assistant Attorney General, Massachusetts Consumer Protection Division, Boston, Massachusetts.

JEROME T. LEVY

Mr. Levy is an attorney with Fink, Weinberger, Fredman, Berman & Lowell, P.C., in New York City. He was formerly Director of Legal Affairs for the New York Department of Health.

LAWRENCE LIPPE

Mr. Lippe is Chief, General Litigation and Legal Advice Section, Criminal Division, United States Department of Justice. Prior to assuming this position, he served as Assistant Inspector General for Investigations, Department of Health, Education and Welfare. Mr. Lippe has served with several other prosecutorial agencies; at the Department of Labor, he directed the government's investigation of the Teamster's Central States Pension and Health and Welfare Funds. He is a graduate of New York University and the New York University Law School. Mr. Lippe is a member of the New York and District of Columbia Bars. He is admitted to practice before the United States Circuit Court of Appeals for the District of Columbia and the United States Court of Military Appeals.

SHERWIN L. MEMEL

Mr. Memel is a senior partner is the law firm of Memel, Jacobs, Pierno & Gersh in Los Angeles, California, specializing in health law. He is a charter member of the Society of Hospital Attorneys and is a former member and past president of the California State Board of Medical Quality Assurance. Mr. Memel served a three-year term on the Federal Health Insurance Benefits Advisory Council. He received the 1971 Award of Honor from and lifetime membership in the American Hospital Association. Mr. Memel has been an instructor in health law at UCLA and has served as a consultant to major industrial corporations on health business matters.

JACK A. MacDONALD

Mr. MacDonald is Executive Vice President, National Council of Health Care Services, Washington, D.C.

STEPHANIE W. NAIDOFF

Ms. Naidoff is a Regional Attorney with the Department of Health, Education and Welfare in Philadelphia, Pennsylvania. She is chief counsel and manager of the Philadelphia office, which provides legal services for all HEW programs in the six-state Mid-Atlantic area. She previously held several other positions within HEW, including Special Assistant to the General Counsel, HEW, Washington, D.C. Ms. Naidoff is a graduate of Goucher College and the University of Pennsylvania Law School. She is a member of the Pennsylvania, District of Columbia and Supreme Court Bars.

GALEN POWERS

Mr. Powers is chief counsel for the Health Care Financing Administration, Department of Health, Education and Welfare, which administers, at the federal level, the Medicare, Medicaid and PSRO programs.

STEPHEN E. RONAI

Mr. Ronai is a partner in the law firm of Gitlitz, Ronai & Berchem, P.C., in Milford, Connecticut, specializing in health care and labor law. He is counsel to the Connecticut Association of Health Care Facilities, Inc.

ALAN SCHACHTER

Mr. Schachter is a Certified Public Accountant, President of Schachter & Horan, P.C., Certified Public Accountants. He represents many providers of health care as an accountant and/or consultant. In addition, he has a subspecialty in the area of investigative accounting and works with defense counsels in New York in the defense of alleged white-collar criminals. He is a member of the AICPA, New York State CPA Society Health Care Committee and the Hospital Finance Management Association Nursing Home Committee. Mr. Schachter is a graduate of the University of Pennsylvania and holds an M.B.A. from Pace University.

ELIZABETH A. TAYLOR

Ms. Taylor is Director of the Federal Trade Commission's investigation of the nursing home industry undertaken to determine the need for a trade regulation rule for the industry. She is a Consumer Protection Specialist with the FTC in Seattle, Washington. Ms. Taylor is a graduate of the University of Washington.

THE EDITOR

JONATHAN W. SKIBA

Mr. Skiba is a member of Panel Publishers' editorial staff. He is a graduate of Syracuse University and the Duke University School of Law. He is a member of the New York Bar and is admitted to practice before the United States Tax Court.

TABLE OF CONTENTS

LONG TERM CARE AND THE LAW— FUNDAMENTAL CONCEPTS

HCFA ORGANIZATIONAL CHART 2

PROVIDER AGREEMENTS
Robert Gerst 3
    Right to a Pre-Termination Hearing 5
    Other Reimbursement Issues............................. 8

OWNER-ADMINISTRATOR COMPENSATION
Joel Hamme 11
    Regulatory Background.................................. 11
    Litigation of Owner-Administrator Compensation
      Questions... 14
    Avoiding a Challenge to Owner-Administrator
      Compensation...................................... 15

RELATED ORGANIZATIONS
Thomas C. Fox... 17
    Minimizing the Risks of a Related Organization Finding 18
    Qualifying for the Exception to the Related-Organization
      Principle 19
    Proposed Regulations on Related Organizations 19

PLANNING FOR CAPITAL EXPENDITURES
Robert Gerst 21
    Conclusion 23

JUDICIAL REVIEW UNDER MEDICARE AND MEDICAID
Joel Hamme 25
    Medicare Judicial Review 25
    Medicaid Judicial Review 29

FREEDOM OF INFORMATION AND ADMINISTRATIVE PROCEDURE ACTS: AIDS TO THE HEALTH CARE ATTORNEY

Thomas C. Fox 31

Using the Freedom of Information Act 32
Disallowance by an Intermediary 32
Challenging a Medicaid Plan 33
Challenging a Program Regulation 33
Structuring the FOIA Request 34
Why Use the FOIA? 34
Administrative Procedure Act 35
Interaction of FOIA with APA 36

CONFIDENTIALITY OF MEDICAL RECORDS AND ADMIN— ISTRATIVE SEARCHES

Robert Gerst 39

AUDITS AND INVESTIGATIONS OF LONG TERM CARE PROVIDERS

Thomas C. Fox 43

Conducting an In-House Audit 45

LONG TERM CARE AND THE LAW— CURRENT ISSUES

MEDICARE-MEDICAID FEDERAL POLICIES

Galen Powers 49

Reasonable Cost-Related Reimbursement Issues 49
Provider and Patient Rights in the Termination Process 53
Miscellaneous Issues 54
Questions and Answers 55

MEDICAID REIMBURSEMENT RATE SETTING

Jerome T. Levy 59

What Is Cost-Based Reimbursement? 59
Establishing Capital Costs 60
Reimbursement of Voluntary Nursing Homes 63
Operational Cost Components 63

Imposing Prospective Rates Retroactively 66
Appeals Process in New York 67
Questions and Answers 68

MEDICARE-MEDICAID FEDERAL PROGRAM OPERATIONS
Stephanie W. Naidoff 73
HEW Regional Attorney 74
Health Care Financing Administration 74
Other HEW Agencies 81
Conclusion 84
Directory of Regional Attorneys 85

HOW TO CONDUCT YOUR OWN EQUAL EMPLOYMENT OPPORTUNITY AUDIT
John Erickson 87
Special Obligations of Recipients of Federal Financial
    Assistance 92
Why an EEO Audit? 93
Objectives of the EEO Audit 94
Employee Selection Audits 95
Uniform Guidelines on Employee Selection Procedures 97
Evaluating Selection Procedures Under the Disparate Effect
    Theory 98
Avoiding Disparate Treatment in Selection
    Procedures 101
Representing Your Company in an EEOC
    Investigation 103
Participation in the EEOC's Investigation 109
Conclusion 111
Questions and Answers 111

BUYING AND SELLING A NURSING HOME
Sherwin L. Memel 115
What Is a Nursing Home? 115
Structuring the Purchase or Sale of a Nursing Home 116
Principal Legal Concerns 117
Other Areas of Interest 126
Acquisition Checklist 126
Drafting the Acquisition Agreement 129
Questions and Answers 130

UNION ORGANIZATION OF A LONG TERM CARE PROVIDER

Jerome Brown and Stephen Ronai 133
Organizing Experience................................. 133
Organizing Nursing Homes............................. 134
Tactics in an Organizing Campaign 136
Obstacles to Organizing............................... 137
Labor Law Reform 139
Shared Concerns..................................... 140
Conclusion 140
Questions and Answers 144
Union Organizational Campaign; Supervisor's
    Checklist 146

REGULATIONS IMPLEMENTING THE ANTI-FRAUD AND ABUSE AMENDMENTS

Irwin Cohen and Marshall B. Kapp 149
P.L. 95-142—What and Why 149
Criminal Statutes—Section 4 150
Section 1909 (d) 150
Disclosure Provisions—Sections 3,8,9, and 15 151
Suspension of Practitioners............................ 153
State Medicaid Fraud Control Units 154
Medicaid Administrative Sanctions Requirement 155
Referring Cases to the Inspector General 155
Protection of Patients' Funds.......................... 156
Regulations Governing Patients' Funds 156
Questions and Answers 159

INVESTIGATION AND PROSECUTION OF PROGRAM FRAUD BY LONG TERM CARE PROVIDERS

Lawrence Lippe 167
HEW Inspector General 167
Project Integrity..................................... 170
Project Integrity II 172
Nursing Homes...................................... 173
Access to Provider Records............................ 174
Legislative Proposals................................. 174
Questions and Answers 175

ROLE OF THE ACCOUNTANT IN A CRIMINAL INVESTIGATION OF A LONG TERM CARE PROVIDER

Alan Schachter 177

White-Collar Crime 177
Accountant's Dual Role 180
What Is an Audit 181
The Investigator's Role 183
Dealing with the Investigation 185
Avoiding the Indictment 186
Referrals to Other Agencies 187
Questions and Answers 188

ACCESS TO NURSING HOME CARE FOR MEDICAID RECIPIENTS

Toby Edelman 191

State Remedies 193
Federal Remedies 196
Recent Litigation 197
Conclusion 199

APPOINTMENT OF A MEDICAL RECEIVER TO RUN A NURSING HOME AS A REMEDY IN PATIENT ABUSE CASES

Sally A. Kelly 201

Traditional Remedies for Patient Abuse 202
Medical Receivership 203
Consumer Protection Principles........................... 206
Questions and Answers 207

THE FEDERAL TRADE COMMISSION'S INVESTIGATION OF THE NURSING HOME INDUSTRY

Elizabeth A. Taylor 211

The Nursing Home Market 212
The Nursing Home Transaction 213
Nursing Home Practices 214
Ancillary Charges.................................... 217
Unnecessary Charges 219
Arguments Against FTC Involvement 220
FTC Strategies 221
Questions and Answers 223

LONG TERM CARE
AND THE LAW—

FUNDAMENTAL CONCEPTS

HCFA Organizational Chart

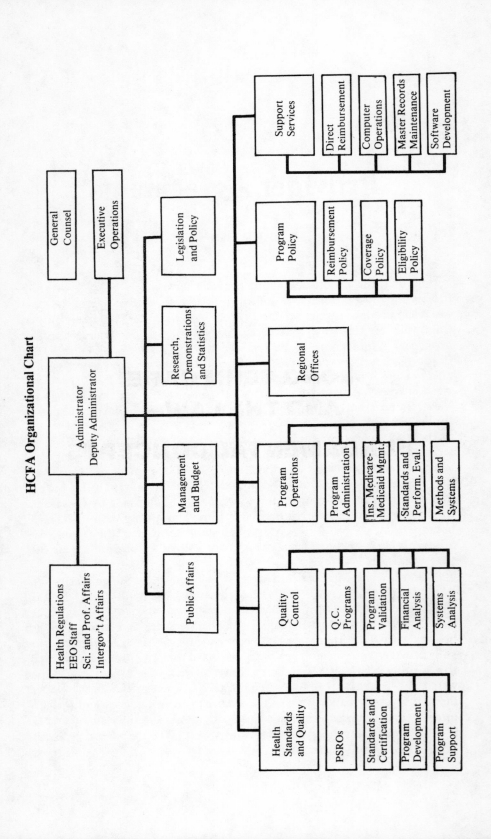

Provider Agreements

ROBERT GERST

I get to speak on the subject of provider agreements because we seem to have the most problems in California, although we don't have the most cases. One of the reasons we don't is that we lost in the Supreme Court of California on the issue of whether or not a provider whose provider agreement is not going to be renewed has the right to a hearing. The California court (*Paramount Convalescent Center, Inc. v. Department of Health Care Services,* 15 C.3d 489; 125 Cal. Rptr. 265, 542 P.2d 1) said no, we don't have a right to a hearing. It came to the conclusion that the Medicaid program was not designed in the interest of the facilities but was for the beneficiaries.

There was one line in the decision where the court said, "However, if the Department acts arbitrarily, then we would consider your having the right to try to come in and get an injunction." The Department of Health says that means they could only be considered to have acted arbitrarily if they didn't follow the normal procedure, and it has nothing to do with the question of the decision that there was something wrong with the facility, because that is not a procedural question on which they could act arbitrarily. We, of course, disagree and are waiting for an appropriate case to test the issue.

In another case, decided in federal district court by Judge Gray (*Olga Nicobatz* (C.D. Cal. 1975), CCH Medicare & Medicaid Guide ¶27,427 (1975 Transfer Binder)), it was also determined that you didn't have a right, when you were participating in both Medicare and Medicaid, to a hearing when a determination had been made by the Secretary not to renew your provider agreement. The court concluded that you didn't have a right to a hearing because (1) you didn't really have any due process rights that were being violated; (2) all that is required is a balancing—the court considers the welfare of the patients versus the welfare of the institution, and financial integrity and continuation are not really important considerations; and (3) if in fact there is any due process to worry about, under the normal procedure you get due process (as far as the court is concerned).

In Region IX we have had, perhaps, more nonrenewals of provider agreements than has the rest of the country put together. We have had about 200 cases where the provider participating in the Medicare and Medicaid program received a notice that the provider agreement was not going to be renewed. That's a rather shocking figure, really, because the rest of the country probably got fifty such notices during all of the years that this process has been going on.

On the other hand, there have been relatively few actual nonrenewals in California because when the state agency and the Secretary make the determination that the provider agreement will not be renewed, you (the provider) have the right to request reconsideration. The courts all seem to rely on the fact that, normally, you will get an inspection; you will have an opportunity for some type of conference with the surveyors; you will be required to prepare a plan of correction—so they say you have notice of what the problem is. After you prepare a plan of correction, you have an opportunity to correct any deficiencies. Then, there will be another survey. That survey may be a follow-up survey which would take place in a couple of weeks, or it could be another full survey that takes place thereafter.

If, during the later survey, you are again found to have serious deficiencies, the courts say you have already received notice and an opportunity to correct the problem. The process goes on until some licensing authority makes a decision that you have failed to meet the minimum standards and, therefore, for the protection of the beneficiary, a notice of nonrenewal goes out. The point seems to be that the courts feel due process has been given because you receive notice, you have received specific indications as to why your provider agreement is not going to be renewed and have been given an opportunity to correct it and if, in fact, you don't, you have really been given adequate notice already—so what more do you want?

The federal regulations include a provision granting a facility a right to request reconsideration. In that request for reconsideration, you identify all of the things that you think respond to the allegations in the survey that you failed to comply with the requirements. You make the best case you can. It is important that you do so. You submit that request for reconsideration and, ultimately, somebody in the Regional Office will review it and give you a notice. Normally, that notice is issued before your provider agreement is over, and they have the authority to extend the provider agreement for an additional two months if they haven't been able to make the determination on the reconsideration by that time. They frequently extend it for the two months and then give you a decision. They may say, "No, you're not going to be renewed because you don't qualify." They then are required to continue to pay for the patients in the facility for up to another month.

They pay for them for a thirty-day period, during which time you are not, in effect, participating in the program. That is the normal procedure.

The problem seemed to be what to do when you want to have some kind of a judicial review because you don't feel that the reconsideration decision has been a fair one. Many people have gone to court and tried to get temporary restraining orders or preliminary injunctions. In many cases they have been successful, but in many cases they have not.

It seems that the nonrenewal problems are the most frequent because it's so much easier for the government not to renew than it is to terminate a provider. "Termination" smacks of some complex legal proceeding that is taking away something right in the middle. But the government has come to the conclusion (and it has received support from the courts) that a nonrenewal is not something anybody can complain about. If the government has been buying all its automobiles from General Motors for ten years, does that mean that if it stops buying from General Motors, General Motors has a right to a hearing? It's only a contract. One of the judges of the Supreme Court of the State of California said to me in oral argument in the *Paramount* case: "We rent our space in this building, we've been renting it for ten years. The state has janitor service, some contractor comes in and we've been using the same person for five years. Does the landlord have the right to have a hearing if we decide to move or not to renew our lease or not to continue using that janitor service?" Of course we argued that wasn't relevant. But the point is, that was a good argument as far as the court was concerned. It had a lot of appeal to the court. It was not accidental that the government used the concept of a contract, a time-limited agreement, and one in which they would attempt to destroy any "expectancy" on your part that it would be renewed.

Right to a Pre-Termination Hearing

A number of reasons have been advanced to justify the failure to require a pretermination hearing, including all of the following: no property right in the provider, mere contract rights; no vested interest in government business; the welfare of the the patients is jeopardized; notice has already been given through inspections, as has an opportunity to correct—therefore, due process has been served; a balancing of interests, even if there are property rights, so that due process has been extended; no right to a hearing is guaranteed under Title XIX—it's up to each state to do so—and, therefore, where the argument is just under a Title XIX program, and that state does not give you any type of appeal, you have no right to get it, anyway; there is no reduction in benefits to the patient—when you remove that patient from a substandard facility, you are increasing the patient's benefits, not reducing them; post-termination or post-nonrenewal hearing, with appropriate evidentiary requirements, meets due process—it

5

doesn't have to be before the fact, after is okay; if there is a life safety code violation, it is too serious to give a hearing; if there is an emergency, you have to move the patient and stop the facility from participating; Congress wanted an agreement limited to one year if there were no compliance, and, therefore, giving a hearing which would extend it is in direct conflict with what Congress intended; there is no "liberty" or "reputation" of the facility at stake (That argument was advanced in several cases on the theory that when you are not renewed that's going to affect your reputation and shouldn't you have some ability to clear your reputation instead of being labeled "non-renewed facility"? The courts say we're not talking about liberty, all we're talking about is money and greed and the desire to keep a business that's really financially profitable.); no entitlement, a mere expectancy; and, finally, providers are not beneficiaries of this program, the patients are—therefore, providers have no rights.

On the other side, what are some of the things that have been cited by courts in determining that there ought to be a hearing? Take all those things that we just mentioned and reverse them. Those will be the reasons why you should be able to get a hearing. For example, there is a property right; it's more than a mere contract; you do have an expectancy to get this business if you meet the requirements—and so on down the line.

I would point out a couple of specific items. First, patients have a right to free choice of providers. (See 42 U.S.C. §1396 (a) (23); 45 C.F.R. §249.20.) Second, the patients, the beneficiaries, clearly have a right to a hearing before their benefits are reduced. (See 45 C.F.R. §205.10(a)(5).) That particular section and that particular approach seems to be the one that is of major consequence.

To those raising the arguments the most, the representatives of the beneficiaries, we have come full circle. Several years ago you will recall that the beneficiary representatives were screaming, hollering and doing all they could to get citation programs where you are fined if you violate regulations (ten states now have these programs). They said, "You've got to go out and enforce these regulations and don't give these people provider agreements; don't let them continue if they aren't meeting the regulations."

So, a lot of people listened, and a lot of facilities were kicked out of programs or had major problems with licensing authorities. Then, however, it turned out that there weren't enough facilities available. Now those same consumer groups and patient advocates are coming in and saying to the court: "Don't let the state kick these people out of the Medicaid/Medicare programs—because you haven't given a hearing to the beneficiaries. Don't close down facilities."

Those people are the most successful advocates for facilities. It even went so far as a case in San Francisco called *Bracco v. Lackner,* No. C-78-0471 SAW (N.D. Cal. May 29, 1978), where the facility tried to get out of business: it didn't have a license; it didn't want a provider agreement. The patient advocates went into court and were able to get an order from the U.S. district judge ordering the state and the federal government to continue the facility in business for a period of time and ordering that they pay an amount of money sufficient to enable them to stay in business. A rate was established by the state for all facilities, and the court said that wasn't adequate and ordered the governments to pay a higher rate. That decision was appealed to the Ninth Circuit, (*Bracco v. Lackner,* 78-1719 (9th Cir. Apr. 12, 1978)) which said: "Look, we really don't think you are serious and we don't think the court below was really serious about this. But, rather than just reversing the decision, we are going to put it over for about forty-five to sixty days so that you people can work this thing out." It is interesting because the patient advocates were in there saying, "You've got to take care of these patients, and don't make them move unless you are able to satisfy yourself that it won't hurt them medically; that we will be able to transfer them to a place that isn't too far away."

A final regulation was published on February 15th, 1979 (42 C.F.R. §431.151; 44 Fed. Reg. 9753 (1979)), which follows a proposed regulation (published in January of 1977) dealing with the state's obligation under the Title XIX program to give some type of meaningful review before a decision not to grant the provider status, to terminate a provider status or to refuse to renew a provider agreement under Title XIX. It says that the states must have an appeal procedure regarding those three areas—denial, termination and nonrenewal.

However, they really pass the buck on the key issues—what kind of payment will be made to facilities during this appeal proceeding, what will be done if a court orders the provider agreement extended or the state on its own extends the provider agreement, what happens in terms of a decision that reverses the determination not to give the status to that provider? Are they then able to get paid? Those items are not discussed in this proposed regulation.

The regulation says that a facility must get a full evidentiary hearing. One of the questions that is not answered, however, is, can you insist on a record being made? This regulation spells out what has to be in that full evidentiary hearing, but it doesn't say whether it has to be, or can be, on the record. If it isn't, it's going to be rather difficult to get adequate judicial review.

The hearing must be completed within 120 days of the effective date of the decision, meaning that if they decide not to renew you, within 120 days after that date you have to have your hearing. That means you are going to be without a provider agreement for four months, even under these regulations, and, therefore, you have to continue to be concerned about those cases that deal with the question of whether you have a right to a hearing.

As an alternative, the regulation provides that before the effective date of the denial, termination or nonrenewal, you can be given notice, an opportunity to respond and a review by the agency. It's not a hearing, just notice of what the problem is and the evidence upon which they are relying. You get a chance to respond and that must be finished before the effective date of the decision. So they have the choice of either giving you a full hearing or not giving you a hearing.

One of the interesting problems created by this entire process is that there seems to be a conflict with licensing laws of the state. If you are dealing with the situation where you are still going to run the risk of losing your license because there is to be a temporary suspension of a license, Medicare or Medicaid participation cannot be guaranteed (due to the fact that you don't have a license or one in effect). If the state provides a full evidentiary hearing only after the effective date, then you get this informal reconsideration.

Who is to handle the hearings? It can't be the survey agency itself. It can't be the individual directly involved. When is the effective date? Ninety days after publication—so it should be around May 17th of this year that this proceeding will be available for your Title XIX-only facility. If you participate in both XVIII and XIX, the decision under XVIII will be controlling for all purposes. It looks like those participating in both XVIII and XIX will have a distinct disadvantage because there is no set time limit under XVIII for when the hearing is to be held. Contrast this with the proceedings under XIX, where within 120 days after the decision, a final review evidentiary hearing must be completed. That means the hearing and the decision have to be made.

Other Reimbursement Issues

Claiming stock maintenance costs: If you are a public company, I would suggest that you consider claiming on your current cost reports stock maintenance costs and/or reopening all costs reports that have not been finalized by more than three years to claim these costs. I make this suggestion on the basis of the Court of Claims decision in *AMI-Chanco, Inc., v. United States,* 576 F.2d 320 (Ct. Cl. 1978).

If you have incurred stock maintenance costs—which include stock transfer fees, stockholder reports, reports to the SEC, stockholder meetings, SEC filings, attorneys' fees and accountants' fees—this decision means that you should be able to get reimbursement for these costs. You need to request that your fiscal intermediary reopen previously filed cost reports. If they refuse to do so and a pre-1973 cost report is involved, you would then file a claim in the Court of Claims. If it's a post-1973 cost report, you would then go to the Provider Reimbursement Review Board (PRRB).

The Board says that it doesn't have jurisdiction on the question of reopening. So your next step—within sixty days of that decision—would be to file in the appropriate U.S. district court or in the Court of Claims (depending on which way you want to go). You should then be in a position to collect all the money to which you are entitled—if you get a favorable judgment.

Reimbursement of physical therapist: Be sure to take a look at the way in which your clients handle reimbursement of all physical therapists and what the contracts provide. If they are going to be limited to the amount of reimbursement from Medicare, but their contract obligates them to pay on the basis of gross billing, your client is going to be adversely affected financially. The contracts should be rewritten.

Owner-Administrator Compensation

JOEL HAMME

Regulatory Background

The Medicare owner-administrator compensation regulations were formulated to prevent owner-administrators from paying themselves large sums of money for duties that they did not perform or that were totally unnecessary for the provision of health care services in their facilities. The owner-administrator regulations under Medicare are contained in 42 C.F.R. §405.426. The administrative guidelines HEW uses to assist the intermediaries and the providers in determining what is reasonable are in the Health Insurance Manual ("HIM")-15, §900 and the following sections. It is important to note at the outset that many of the states utilize Medicare principles of reimbursement for Medicaid owner-administrator compensation. Therefore, if you fall afoul of Medicare, it is very likely that you will fall afoul of Medicaid because the auditors tend to look at the same findings that are made by Medicare.

The basic rule for owner-administrator compensation is that it must be reasonable in amount and it must be for services that are necessary to the operation of the facility. What does "reasonable" mean? HEW defines "reasonable" as an amount comparable to amounts paid by similar institutions to other people who perform like services at those institutions. The judgment as to what amount is reasonable is supposed to be made on a case-by-case basis. In other words, the facts and circumstances of each particular situation are to be controlling.

When are services "necessary" to the operation of the facility? HEW says that "necessary" services are those that are essential to the sound operation or fiscal management of the facility. "Necessary" services are those services that, if the owner-administrator did not perform them, the facility would have to hire somebody else to do the job. As you can under-

11

stand, owner-administrator compensation is not to afford a means of obtaining a return on equity (which is separately reimbursed by Medicare) or withdrawing profit.

When we talk about owner-administrator compensation, it is essential to remember that this includes the total amount of benefits received by an owner—including deferred compensation—for the services he renders to the facility. It is also important to remember that individuals who are the immediate relatives of the owner-administrator are also considered to be owners for purposes of the rule. Therefore, if an owner-administrator, who owns 50% or 75% or 100% of the facility, acts as the administrator and appoints his son as his assistant, you can be sure that the son's salary will be viewed on the same terms as if he were the owner himself.

Procedures for determining reasonable owner-administrator compensation: HEW has instituted procedures by which the fiscal intermediaries are supposed to be able to determine whether owner-administrator compensation is reasonable for Medicare reimbursement purposes. Initially, HEW decided to conduct surveys, through its regional offices, of providers to determine exactly what amounts were being paid to people in the industry. From that, HEW would develop ranges of compensation to determine, for example, whether an owner, making $60,000 a year in a 100-bed skilled nursing facility in Charleston, South Carolina, was being paid a reasonable amount. When HEW first did its surveys, it decided that the intermediaries should survey all proprietary institutions in their regional areas as well as an adequate sample of nonproprietary institutions. In order to determine comparability for the salary ranges, the intermediaries took into account the geographic location of facilities, the type of facility, the range of services offered, the bed size of the particular facility, and the number and type of personnel employed at the facility to render health care services.

When the owner-administrator surveys and ranges of compensation have been challenged, HEW's main argument has always been that, despite any statistical deficiencies in formulation of the ranges of compensation, the ranges are immune from attack because HEW allows exceptions to the ranges of owner-administrator compensation. When a provider proves that it is entitled to the exception, that it is unique compared to other providers, and that the services rendered by the owner-administrator are greater than those rendered by similar owner-administrators at similar facilities, HEW will grant an exception and will allow the provider more money. In practice, this has occurred very infrequently.

To help the intermediaries determine whether exceptions are warranted, HEW has established a point system. The point system takes into account the experience of the owner-administrator, the owner-administrator's education, and the duties of this particular individual at the facility. This system also takes cognizance of the geographic location of the facility—whether it is rural, urban or metropolitan. (In this respect, rural areas get the least money; urban areas get a little more; and metropolitan areas get the most.) The point system considers how many people you supervise and the availability of assistants to you. On one hand, it is important to supervise a great many people; on the other hand, you should not have too many assistants who are aiding in the supervision because HEW will then turn around and say: "You have a lot of people performing this job, you really do not supervise that much, and you are not entitled to an exception."

There is a Catch-22 logic to the way certain of the intermediaries and HEW have applied the experience and education factors. Many people go before the PRRB or an intermediary hearing panel and argue: "I am entitled to an exception, I have a lot of experience in the area and I am very well educated." Often, the intermediary or the hearing officer simply retorts that the individual is not underpaid but over-qualified. Therefore, although you have the experience and the education, you will not necessarily warrant an exception. It may be that you should be out seeking a higher paying job that makes better use of your experience and education.

What are the problems with the surveys that have been conducted? The leading case in this area is *Hopewell Nursing Home v. Califano,* CCH Medicare & Medicaid Guide ¶28,718 at p. 10,519 (D.S.C. 1977) (1977 Transfer Binder). *Hopewell* involved a challenge to the surveys that were conducted in 1970 and 1973 in the Atlanta regional office of HEW. Those surveys resulted in the 1971 and 1974 ranges of owner-administrator compensation applied in Alabama, Florida, Georgia, Kentucky, Mississippi, North Carolina, South Carolina, and Tennessee for the years 1971-1976. There were a number of grounds on which those ranges were attacked. The main argument was that HEW simply failed to follow its own regulations in promulgating the ranges, that it had failed and its intermediaries had failed both to survey all the appropriate institutions and to make crucial distinctions between profit and nonprofit homes. The plaintiffs also asserted that HEW understated the ranges by excluding certain benefits that were paid to nonprofit personnel and that it had engaged in a statistically impermissible "double consolidation." Let me explain this "double consolidation." The intermediaries collected the data and threw out all the salaries that seemed high—the top ranges. They then transmitted the data to HEW which, in turn, threw out the top salaries on the consolidated data. Therefore, HEW had engaged in a double consolidation and, of course, the ceilings were much lower than they otherwise would have been. Finally, there were inadequate inflation factors applied to these ranges.

These allegations were accepted by the court in *Hopewell,* and the court declared the ranges illegal. The case is still pending on HEW's motion for rehearing. HEW's main contentions are: (1) that the court has no jurisdiction to review this case for pre-1973 periods and that, for periods after that time, plaintiffs failed to exhaust administrative remedies and (2) that, although HEW admits violating its own rules, the exceptions to the ranges alleviate any problem of understated salaries.

There is also a 1974 GAO report that discusses owner-administrator compensation and points out that the terms "excessive" and "reasonable" were not adequately defined by HEW at that time. (This particular report is found at ¶27,049 and p. 10,433 of the CCH Medicare & Medicaid Guide (1974 Transfer Binder).)

Litigation of Owner-Administrator Compensation Questions

How do you litigate an owner-administrator compensation question in an administrative setting—*i.e.,* where you try to settle it before going to a hearing or where you are actually involved in a hearing? First, there is a particular need for documentation. The one thing that we find especially frustrating is that people come to us saying they should get an exception and are entitled to more money because they work 60 to 80 hours a week and are performing many duties other than those of an owner-administrator. But when we ask: "Can you document this fact?" too often they reply, "No, we did not keep any records."

The whole ball game in litigation and in administrative hearings is documentation. We ask our clients a series of questions: "Do you have diaries of the activities that you engage in or a work schedule that shows how much time you put in? Are you willing to provide an affidavit attesting to the type of duties you performed and how much time you put in? Are you willing to testify to these facts? Do you have a job description which includes the fact that you are responsible for all of these other duties?" These are the important things that lawyers will request as they try to establish that you are entitled to something above and beyond what the ranges would normally allow.

Judicial review: Second, not only is it necessary, of course, to have adequate documentation, but it is also important to establish at the hearing a record which can be used on administrative appeal or judicial review. Many providers represent themselves at the hearing, lose, and then engage an attorney for court litigation. The problem with that approach is that, when a court reviews an administrative decision, it takes a look at the hearing record made at the administrative level. Often, you will find that the hearing record is totally inadequate to establish the points that you need to make to qualify for additional compensation. You are really better off having your attorney at the administrative level because you want to establish the detailed record needed to prevail at the administrative level or upon judicial review.

Avoiding a Challenge to Owner-Administrator Compensation

How can you establish owner-administrator compensation so that it will not be adjusted downward? First, you should ask, "Who established the salary?" You should try to have that salary established by an impartial body—all the other board trustees or the unrelated officers. Avoid setting your own salary. What criteria should be used in establishing your salary? Here, again, it is important to document all of this research before the salary is set. It is important to document the time spent on particular duties and the exact duties performed at the facility. Conduct your own survey of similar institutions in your locality. Determine, if you can, whether the amount of money you are being paid is comparable to the amounts paid similar personnel at other facilities like yours. If your salary is higher, establish and document why you should receive more money than others do. It is also important, when your salary is established, to look at the regional guidelines. This will give you some idea of what you will be up against and what kind of salary you are going to be required to justify. If you do all these things and the impartial third party setting your salary is relatively fair about it, you should not have too many problems with your intermediary. If problems do arise, however, you should have plenty of documentation and good factual circumstances for being able to establish that you are entitled to an exception and to greater amounts of Medicare reimbursement.

Related Organizations

THOMAS C. FOX

The regulation dealing with related organizations is at 42 C.F.R. §405.427 et seq. Further guidance may be found in the Health Insurance Manual, HIM-15 §1000 et seq. HIM-15 gives additional help to intermediaries in applying related-organization principles.

There is no specific statutory language that is similar to the related-organization principle stated in the regulation. The principle derives essentially from three statutory sections. The first is 42 U.S.C. §1302; the second is 42 U.S.C. §1395 (hh). These provisions are broad enough to drive a truck through. They give the Secretary of HEW authority to develop regulations, as shall be necessary, for the efficient management and administration of the Medicare program. The third statutory section is the basic one on reimbursement, 42 U.S.C. §1395(x)(v). This section says, "under Medicare, reimbursement or payment shall be at a reasonable cost." The Secretary's argument here is that in order to only pay reasonable costs, he is not going to allow transactions between related parties. While this is a Medicare principle, you will find that in every state the Medicaid plan and regulations have adopted, in some form, this related-organization principle.

The related-organization principle: Where a provider, a buyer, or a lessee, is related to a supplier, a seller or a lessor, and there exists what is called "significant common ownership or control," you have related parties.

What does this mean? In the case of a property transaction between buyer and seller or lessee and lessor, the buyer's cost for reimbursement purposes is limited to the cost basis of the seller—and the same holds true in a lease relationship. In the case of services, it would mean that only the cost of the supplying organization can be claimed by the provider.

There is an exception. One thing to understand about the exception is that to the extent the provider can show that a substantial part of the supplier's business is carried on with unrelated third parties—even though there may be the relationship of some common ownership of control with the supplier—the provider may be reimbursed for the charges. The important thing to bear in mind about this exception is that it does not apply to property transactions. So if there is a sale or lease, the fact that you can point to twenty-five other leases in the community where the rental is less, or any number of offers that you turned down on a sale or lease that is less, it may be to no avail.

Let me give you some factual patterns that will trigger a related-organization examination and, in many cases, a finding of a related organization and disallowance of any amount above the cost of the supplying organization, the seller or the lessor. You may have a related-organization transaction— the father selling to the son, or the mother selling to the son-in-law; sales or leases to administrators by owners of facilities; sales or leases to employees; transactions with business partners. If there are common officers and directors, rest assured that you will have a particularly difficult time trying to overcome the related-organization finding.

Another typical factual pattern would be a management agreement or management contract. Intermediaries have asserted that the rights or obligations created by the management contract may create a related organization, notwithstanding the fact that the parties initially had absolutely no relationship. In *Northwestern Community Hospital v. Califano,* 442 F. Supp 949 (D. Ill. 1977), the court indicated that you must examine the relationship that existed prior to entry into the management contract.

Minimizing the Risks of a Related Organization Finding

How do you minimize risks in this area? The easy rule is, don't engage in related-organization transactions. But there are situations in which fathers do desire to sell to their sons or daughters. If you do this and then attempt to build the case afterwards, you run an extremely higher risk of disallowance. Can you minimize the risk by doing certain things at the outset? I think you can.

In a situation where a father wishes to sell to a son, the first thing to do— before the transaction is put together—is to get an appraisal of the facility. You want an appraisal by an outside appraiser as to the market value of the facility. You should also attempt to get offers from unrelated third parties as to what they would pay to buy the facility and what they would be willing to pay to lease the facility.

Once you get your appraisal, once you find out there are four or five unrelated organizations that would be willing to buy this facility for a certain amount, you should take that information to your intermediary and indicate that you would like to sell to your son. You'll probably have to take less than the appraisal or the offer, but that's about the only way you can effect a transaction of this nature. I would strongly advise that if you are going to do it, you get the intermediary's approval up front. Intermediaries, in many cases, will give you an opinion on this or they will forward it to HEW, where you may be able to get some opinion that would approve the transaction.

Qualifying for the Exception to the Related-Organization Principle

As mentioned previously, there is an exception with respect to the supplying of services. To qualify, a substantial amount of the services must be given to unrelated third parties. To demonstrate this, you can show the revenues of the supplying party in comparison with the related organizations. By all means do it for more than the year or years in dispute because the intermediary will. You may be able to show a trend; you may be able to show that the percentage was 60-40 and, now, two or three years later, it's up to 80-20. You may be able to make the argument that the 60-40 relationship existed at that time because the business was just starting.

Many times it is best to rely on expert accounting help in this area, which, if nothing else, adds credibility to the evidence that you present. Many times the intermediaries will be more willing to accept this type of information.

The other thing you must show is that there is a competitive market for such services and the charges you are making are comparable. Here we are really talking about withstanding a prudent buyer test. But it's not sufficient just to call up a number of suppliers and ask them to give you a quote. You've got to do a little more sophisticated investigation in order to come up with the documentation that may be helpful here.

These are a few things which may give you some solace in handling the related-organization problem under the existing regulations. However, these rules are about to be changed. There has been a notice of proposed rulemaking in the *Federal Register,* and to the extent that you may envision problems with related organizations under the old rules, I think you will find there are even more difficult problems to be encountered if the proposed rules are adopted as final regulations.

Proposed Regulations on Related Organizations

You may recall that the current regulations require that there be "significant" common ownership, or "significant" ability to control two entities in order for there to be a finding of related organizations. HEW has proposed that the word "significant" be dropped from the regulations. You will be a related organization if there is *any* common ownership or *any* common ability to control both the provider and the supplier. Obviously, that's quite significant because all HEW would have to show is actual ownership of both entities.

You may also recall the exception to the related-organization rule where you have to establish that a substantial part of the supplier's business was done with unrelated entities. HEW, in these proposed regulations, indicates that "substantial" will be defined as 80%. Therefore, if you are doing 79% of your supplier business with unrelated organizations and 21% with related organizations, you wouldn't qualify for the exception.

Planning for Capital Expenditures

ROBERT GERST

Two basic laws apply to nursing homes in the area of planning. The first is Section 1122 of the Social Security Act, which provides for a limitation on the use of federal funds for capital expenditure reimbursement. This limitation applies to a provider, in a state that had signed a planning agreement with a Designated Planning Agency, who failed to get approval from that Designated Planning Agency for the capital expenditure. (A capital expenditure is an expenditure over $100,000, the addition or deletion of beds, or the addition of substantial or significant services.) There are thirty-three states that have signed an 1122 agreement as of January 1979.

This was the first attempt on a national level to control unnecessary capital expenditures. In effect, it says that if you come within the purview of the particular statute and your state has agreed to participate, you will not get reimbursement for interest or depreciation for those costs that are related to a capital expenditure—unless you have approval. In addition, for proprietary facilities, a return on equity is subject to this approval. And, if you are leasing, some portion of the lease would be disallowed unless you got 1122 approval. (For further details, you might want to check 42 U.S.C. §1320(a) and 42 C.F.R. §100.)

Certificate of Need: Under 1122, you can still build, but you won't get federal reimbursement if you don't get approval from the Designated Planning Agency. On the other hand, if you don't have a certificate of need, you can't even build. The certificate of need requirement is in P.L. 93-641—you'll find that at 42 U.S.C. §300(k); the regulations are at 42 C.F.R. §122. This requires that you get a certificate of need when you have capital expenditures. If you don't, you can't bill under your state law.

All of the states will probably be in compliance this year. Within four fiscal years after enactment, all states have to be in place or else they will not be able to get any money under the national health planning system. To give you some idea of how difficult the situation can be, consider one state that has a certificate of need law. They were the second state to be fully operational—they were a designated agency. They have a thing called SHCC, State Health Coordinating Council. They have an HSA, Health System Agency. They even have an SHPDA, State Health Planning and Development Agency. This is a state agency, and under the P.L. 93-641 rule, the state agency makes the final decision.

In that state, they were not satisfied with the way in which the certificate of need law was written or suggested by the federal government, so they added a provision indicating that acquisition for lease is an event that requires a certificate of need. Therefore, in that state, if you want to lease or acquire a health facility, you have to get a certificate of need.

What does this mean? A group was selling a facility and another group was buying it for several million dollars. Everybody was happy, except the SHPDA director. Everybody approved, down the line, until he finally said: "I'm not going to approve this acquisition, in spite of all the other things that you've got. It's going to increase the cost to the people of our state and the Medicaid program. We don't think that it should be approved the way it is. We're not going to tell you that you can't sell it, but we're going to tell you that you are not going to get a certificate of need unless you do a couple of things." Unfortunately, those people were in the position of having investors and having the deal all ready to go, and this fellow says: "If you don't think I have any authority, sue me—and two years from now, we will find out." So, the deal was made, and as you can appreciate, the buyers were a little bit unhappy. They have a return on equity and interest, and all of that is reimbursable. If you are in a state that is paying on reasonable costs without any limits and you are going in with very little money, the more your interest cost is and the more your actual cost is for depreciable assets, the more return you're going to get. These people, therefore, had to work out a compromise in the state where they are able to say "no acquisitions," "no leases," unless they approve of the terms of that transaction.

There is going to be some new legislation this year because P.L. 93-641 needs to be renewed or extended. There is a feeling that there will be some major changes in that law. You should be very aware of it because it will have an impact upon you.

State Regulations on 1122: Nebraska Methodist Hospital v. Casari, C.V. 77-L-256 (August 18, 1978), is of interest to people in a state that has an 1122 agreement. If your state has not published regulations as to how it will proceed under its own Administrative Procedure Act, this decision says 1122 should not be effective even if the state has signed the contract with the federal government. The federal regulations are not self-effectuating; you have to have state regulations. If you don't have them, then 1122 review isn't necessary.

Objection to Competing Facility: Finally, there is nothing wrong with objecting, either as an individual or on behalf of your facility or group of facilities, to somebody trying to open up a competing institution as they go through the planning process. Many people are scared of antitrust. But there is no reason that you and others can't get together to legitimately put forward your best case as to why somebody shouldn't be in competition with you. You can't undermine the process, you can't do it frivolously, you can't deny them the right to a hearing, you can't gum up the works by filing lawsuits that are not in good faith. However, there is nothing wrong in getting together and trying to legitimately beat the competitor.

Conclusion

I will close by suggesting that there is a need for effective counsel both from planners and lawyers in connection with certificates of need. That is rather clear from the tremendous number of cases under the certificate of need and 1122. It's a complicated procedure; the regulations are very difficult to understand. There is a great need to have sufficient records to be reviewed if you are going to oppose someone, or if you're trying to get your own approved. You've got to make sure that it is in the record so that it can be reviewed.

There are a lot of unanswered questions. One of them, for example, is whether an institution can avoid going through certificate of need if it has some type of a related party, separately organized, which is not a provider or a health institution, build in its own name. There seems to be support for the proposition that although a certificate of need would be required if a hospital or nursing home were to do certain things, that certificate would not be necessary if these same things were done by some subsidiary organization or some brother-sister organization or some related-party organization.

Judicial Review Under Medicare and Medicaid

JOEL HAMME

Medicare Judicial Review

We will first discuss judicial review under Medicare Part A, which includes services of skilled nursing facilities. When we talk about judicial review, the first question that comes to mind is: does a federal court have jurisdiction over a particular controversy? "Jurisdiction" is a shorthand legal term for determining whether a court has the power and authority to rule upon the particular type of claim being asserted before it.

Social Security Act: As many of you may be aware, under the Social Security Act, Section 405(g) of Title 42 of the United States Code specifies that there will be avenues of judicial revenue from adverse decisions of the Secretary of HEW. The very next subsection, 405(h), states that the decisions of the Secretary on these points shall not be reviewed, however, except as provided in the Social Security Act. It then explains that no action of the Secretary shall be reviewed under 28 U.S.C. §41. This section, which has now been recodified, encompassed various forms of jurisdiction, including the jurisdiction of federal district courts (which are the basic federal trial courts) to entertain and decide questions of federal law. Federal question jurisdiction is now contained in 28 U.S.C. §1331.

Basically, the problem boils down to the fact that until amended in 1972, the Social Security Act did not furnish Medicare providers with a clear avenue of judicial review of a decision of the Secretary. Unfortunately, Section 405(h) (which is the section which says there shall be no judicial review except as otherwise provided in the Act) is incorporated into the Medicare Act. But, Section 405(g)—which provides the mechanism for judicial review and authorizes the Secretary to establish his own administrative procedures—is not incorporated into the Medicare Act, except for some

25

very specific types of problems, including the determination of whether an institution or agency qualifies as a provider of services. (See 42 U.S.C. §1395 (ff).) Therefore, for the past five or six years in particular, HEW has consistently argued that, except for those very limited types of circumstances. Congress did not intend, at least for periods of cost reporting prior to June 30, 1973, that there should be any judicial review of Medicare reimbursement decisions.

In 1972, Congress enacted a statutory amendment which established a Provider Reimbursement Review Board (PRRB) to review certain types of Medicare reimbursement disputes. 42 U.S.C. §1395(00). As you may know, however, the PRRB cannot decide challenges to the legality of either regulations or interpretations of HEW. Under this amendment, federal district courts were given jurisdiction, upon application of a provider which was adversely affected, to review decisions of the PRRB. This type of review only applies to cost report periods after June 30, 1973 and must involve certain amounts of money. Several questions arise: (1) What occurs if you have a pre-1973 cost report that is in dispute?; and (2) What happens if you are challenging not the reimbursement, but a regulation that only indirectly affects your reimbursement? What avenues of judicial review are available to you in such circumstances?

Pre-1973 Cost Reports: HEW has contended that, as far as pre-1973 cost reports are concerned, there is absolutely no jurisdiction in any federal court to review these claims. HEW has not been particularly successful in getting that position sustained. It has been successful, however, in persuading most courts to rule that whatever jurisdiction there is does not lie under 28 U.S.C. §1331 (federal question jurisdiction—as mentioned earlier, the authority of a federal district court to decide a case in which there is an issue of federal law, whether statutory or constitutional).

The decisions on the pre-1973 reports can be classified into several categories. First, there are some decisions that say there is no *federal question jurisdiction* even in cases involving a constitutional claim. The leading case for this view is *Dr. John T. MacDonald Foundation, Inc. v. Califano,* 571 F.2d 328 (5th Cir. 1978) *(en banc), cert. den.,* 99 S. Ct. 250 (1978).

Second, there are a number of cases which hold that there is no federal question jurisdiction in pre-1973 cases in the absence of a constitutional issue. These courts take the view that, if you can raise a constitutional issue, they will listen to it under federal question jurisdiction, but otherwise they are powerless to hear your claim. This position is illustrated by a decision of the United States Court of Appeals for the Eighth Circuit, *St. Louis University v. Blue Cross Hospital Service,* 537 F.2d 283, *cert. den.,* 429 U.S. 977 (1976).

There is a third, and minority, group of cases holding that there is federal question jurisdiction in federal district courts to review all constitutional and statutory claims for pre-June 30, 1973 cost reports. There are a number of decisions taking this view. One of them is *Hopewell Nursing Home, Inc. v. Califano,* CCH Medicare & Medicaid Guide ¶27,913 at p. 9,729 (D.S.C. 1976) (1976 Transfer Binder); ¶28,718 at p. 10,519 (D.S.C. 1977) (1977 Transfer Binder). There is also *Mid-Atlantic Nephrology Center, Ltd. v. Califano,* 433 F. Supp. 23 (D. Md. 1977) and *Umedco, Inc. v. Califano,* CCH Medicare & Medicaid Guide ¶28,480 at p. 9,701 (C.D. Cal. 1977) (1977 Transfer Binder).

There are, in addition, a few courts that have agreed with HEW's argument that there is absolutely no jurisdiction in the federal courts for these cost report periods. This view has the least judicial support. One of those rulings is *James D. Inc. v. Nationwide Insurance Co.,* CCH Medicare & Medicaid Guide ¶28,402 at p. 9,431 (S.D. Ohio 1977) (1977 Transfer Binder).

It should be emphasized that, when the jurisdictional issue first arose, a number of providers sought federal court review and alleged jurisdiction not only on the basis of raising a federal question, but also under the Federal Administrative Procedure Act (APA), 5 U.S.C. §§701-706. In 1977, this approach was foreclosed when the United States Supreme Court ruled that the APA does not confer jurisdiction on federal courts. *Califano v. Sanders,* 430 U.S. 99.

Court of Claims jurisdiction: As far as the pre-1973 cost report periods are concerned, most courts have taken a position that, if there is no jurisdiction in the federal district courts to review these claims, there is, at the very least, jurisdiction in the United States Court of Claims. (This is a specialized court that considers contract claims against the United States. The jurisdiction of the Court of Claims does not rest upon former 28 U.S.C. §41—which, you will remember, is the jurisdictional basis barred by the preclusion of review contained in 42 U.S.C. §405(h).) The Court of Claims itself reached the conclusion that it has jurisdiction over Medicare reimbursement disputes for these periods in *Whitecliff, Inc. v. United States,* 536 F.2d 347 (1976), *cert. den.,* 430 U.S. 969 (1977). Court of Claims jurisdiction has also been endorsed by the Fifth Circuit in the *John T. MacDonald* case (which was mentioned earlier), by the Second Circuit in *South Windsor Convalescent Home, Inc. v. Mathews,* 541 F.2d 910 (1976), and by the Seventh Circuit in *Trinity Memorial Hospital of Cudahy, Inc. v. Associated Hospital Service, Inc.,* 570 F.2d 660 (1977).

It should be pointed out that, unlike federal district courts and United States Courts of Appeals, (which review appeals from federal district courts), the United States Court of Claims cannot issue injunctions prohibiting or enjoining certain conduct. Nor can the Court of Claims provide declaratory relief—i.e., declare a particular action or threatened action to be illegal. The Court of Claims cannot mandamus a governmental official. (Mandamus, which we will discuss next, is a means of compelling a federal official to perform a required duty.) In short, the Court of Claims simply provides money judgments. Obviously, however, there are occasions on which you want injunctive or declaratory relief to prevent monetary harm before it happens. In these instances, the Court of Claims is not a viable alternative. On the other hand, it must be noted that, in the context of cost reports filed prior to June 30, 1973, harm will generally have occurred by this juncture, and declaratory and injunctive relief may now be unnecessary.

Mandamus jurisdiction: Several courts have been presented with this issue: If they lack federal question jurisdiction to hear Medicare provider reimbursement disputes, is it possible that the type of violation that is being alleged is so egregious, so bad, so obviously wrong, that a federal district court ought to be able to rectify it (not only for the post-1973 period but for earlier periods)? A number of courts have held that, even if there is no federal question jurisdiction in the federal court, there may well be mandamus jurisdiction to compel a federal officer—in this case, the Secretary of HEW— to perform a duty which is owed to a particular person who is affected by his regulations. Under 28 U.S.C. §1361, mandamus relief is available under limited circumstances: (1) the plaintiff must have a clear legal right to the requested relief; (2) the federal officer must have an unequivocal duty to perform the act in question; (3) the federal officer must have failed to perform that duty; and (4) the plaintiff must have no other adequate remedy.

The leading cases on this point are from the United States Court of Appeals for the District of Columbia Circuit, *Association of American Medical Colleges v. Califano,* 569 F.2d 101 (D.C. Cir. 1977) and *Humana of South Carolina, Inc. v. Califano,* 590 F.2d 1070 (D.C. Cir. 1978). Both intimate that mandamus may be available in Medicare provider cases under appropriate circumstances. The Ninth Circuit has held, in a Social Security Act case not involving a provider, that there is mandamus jurisdiction. *Elliott v. Weinberger,* 564 F.2d 1219 (9th Cir. 1977), *cert. granted,* 99 S. Ct. 75-76 (1978). By implication and because the Ninth Circuit considered the preclusion-of-review effect of 42 U.S.C. § 405(h), the holding would appear to apply to a provider case. *Waitley v. Califano,* CCH Medicare & Medicaid Guide ¶29,141 at p. 10,092 (D. Kan. 1978) (1978 Transfer Binder), also ruled that mandamus is a possible basis for jurisdiction.

Exhaustion of remedies: One final question that arises concerns exhaustion of administrative remedies. Is a provider required to exhaust all of its administrative remedies before it goes into federal court? The problem here, as many of you know, is that the PRRB does not have the authority to declare statutes illegal, or to make constitutional rulings, and is required by the Secretary to follow his regulations and guidelines. In other words, even if the PRRB cannot rule on an issue and even if the Secretary is not about to overturn his own regulation, does the provider have to go through the administrative process—which will be meaningless and futile? A number of courts have said, in most instances, you will have to do this—you will have to exhaust administrative remedies. Why? Because under the statute (42 U.S.C. §1395 (OO)) creating the PRRB and providing for judicial review of PRRB decisions, federal district courts do not have jurisdiction until the PRRB has actually rendered decision. An illustrative ruling is *Aristocrat South, Inc. v. Mathews,* 420 F. Supp. 23 (D.D.C. 1976). Courts requiring exhaustion of administrative remedies have also emphasized the possibility that the Secretary might change his regulation and the benefits of establishing a record upon which a court may act. A contrary position was taken by the federal district court in South Carolina in the *Hopewell* case which was referenced earlier. That court said, if administrative remedies are futile, you can go directly into federal court.

Medicaid Judicial Review

On this topic, we will not talk about jurisdictional problems because the statutory language creating confusion about judicial review of the claims of Medicare Part A providers does not appy to Medicaid. Rather, we will discuss the types of claims that are being presented in federal courts concerning the legality of state Medicaid plans and the legality of federal regulations requiring the states to implement or adopt particular provisions or requirements in those plans.

Let me mention some basic materials that you will want to review before you make any claims respecting the illegality of state Medicaid plans as far as long term care facilities are concerned. First, there is Section 249 itself—the reasonable cost-related reimbursement requirement for nursing homes participating in Medicaid. The statute is found at 42 U.S.C. §1396 (a)(13)(E), and the applicable regulation is at 42 C.F.R. §447.272 *et. seq.* [formerly §450.30(a)(3)]. You should also read the preamble to the Section 249 regulations which came out July 1, 1976 (41 F.R. 27,300-07) and the later preamble which was issued on February 6, 1978 (43 F.R. 4861-64). You might also examine Action Transmittal HCFA-AT-77-85 (MMB) (September 1, 1977)—a series of questions and answers on Section 249.

Section 249 litigation: What are the typical issues in Section 249 litigation? The first major issue centered on the effective date of Section 249. Congress set an effective date of July 1, 1976, but HEW tried to postpone it for a period of a year and a half until January 1, 1978. All of the cases that have ruled on this issue have held that attempt illegal. (See, e.g., *Alabama Nursing Home Association v. Califano,* 433 F. Supp. 1325 (M.D. Ala. 1977).)

The issues that are being litigated now are mainly: (1) what does reasonable cost-related reimbursement mean? and (2) are ceilings imposed by the states reasonable cost-related? HEW takes the basic position that, if you pay 50% of the providers in a state at their full allowable cost, that is permissible, and you do not have to worry about the rest of the providers in the program.*

In terms of computing rates, another issue that has arisen is—can the states look to the amount of money that they have available in setting their rate ceilings? HEW says no, the providers say no, and yet from the documents I have seen on a number of states, the states have done this anyway. I have examined some very good statistical documents from two states in particular, where, if the state had done as much documentation in determining if its rates were reasonable cost-related as it did trying to fit the ceilings within its availble budget, the state's ceilings could have passed any reasonable cost-related test that a court would have imposed. Obviously, the states are quite concerned about their fiscal integrity and their authority to run their own Medicaid programs.

There are also issues involving the formulation of classes. HEW simply says classes must be reasonable, and states cannot formulate classes on the basis of whether facilities are government-owned or nongovernment-owned. Again, some of the states have ignored this, and attempted to propose Medicaid classes that are not very reasonable. In one state, HEW itself has approved a plan which is a very thinly veiled attempt to create no ceilings on state facilities while creating fairly low ceilings on privately owned facilities.

There are also significant issues regarding Medicaid treatment of property costs and inflation factors—all issues that have not really been decided yet by federal courts, but ones which we believe are going to be the subject of decisions in the upcoming months and years. Another issue which may be resurrected involves profit factors under Medicaid. Although one federal court has defined HEW's basic authority in this area (*American Health Care Association v. Califano,* 443 F. Supp. 612 (D.D.C. 1977)), new actions by HEW concerning profit limitations may prompt further litigation.

---

*   Shortly after this speech was given, a federal court upheld, as reasonable cost-related, Alabama's Medicaid plan for reimbursement of long term care facilities. This plan established certain cost limitations on individual cost centers as well as an overall 60th percentile ceiling. (*Alabama Nursing Home Association v. Califano,* 3 CCH Medicare & Medicaid Guide ¶29, 578 at p. 9,778 (M.D. Ala. Feb. 23, 1979).)

Freedom of Information and Administrative Procedure Acts: Aids to the Health Care Attorney

THOMAS C. FOX

Let me begin talking about the Freedom of Information Act by giving you two citations. The Freedom of Information Act appears at 5 U.S.C. §552, and HEW's regulations implementing that section appear at 45 C.F.R. (part 5) §5.1 et seq.

Anytime you are faced with a problem dealing with the Department of Health, Education and Welfare, one of the first things that should come to mind is the use of the Freedom of Information Act as a possible way to get access to information. The Freedom of Information Act (FOIA) only applies to federal agencies. It does not apply to states. However, most of you will find that the states have what might be called a "right to know" act, or an "open records," "sunshine," or "public records" act, which, in most cases gives you the equivalent of what is available at the federal level under the Freedom of Information Act.

Generally, the Freedom of Information Act gives you access to any identifiable records that would relate to specific requests that you've made, but there are a couple of fundamental things to bear in mind. You don't have to show cause in asking for the information. You don't have to show a need. You don't have to show any standing. Also, it is the obligation of the agency to assert any of the exemptions that the Act would make applicable to the information you have requested. In many cases, although an exemption may be available, the agency will choose to waive the exemption under the circumstances. Therefore, if you make a Freedom of Information Act request, you should ask for everything that you can conceive of as being available—including internal memoranda. Then simply wait to see what the response is from the agency.

31

Using the Freedom of Information Act

What I want to do is to explore some situations in which you, as an attorney representing a health care client, can use the Freedom of Information Act, and related state acts. Assume a long term care provider comes to you and says it is about to be decertified from participation in either the Medicare or Medicaid program. How can the Freedom of Information Act help you?

You will find it has many beneficial uses in making your requests. First of all, you can obtain inspection reports that have been prepared on the facility. This would include not only the official inspection report that you've received but also the handwritten notes. Many times you'll find that things in the handwritten notes don't make their way into the official inspection report, and often these notes can be favorable to your client.

Some other things that you might request would be the recommendations of the members of the inspection team. When you or your client get the official inspection report, what you will find is the recommendation for decertification. By requesting these current files and all the handwritten notes, as well as the recommendations of the members of the team, you may find that one or more members of the team recommended against decertification. That may give you an opportunity to make a stronger argument on behalf of your client.

Another thing we have been successful in asking for are the qualifications of the members of the inspection team. Again, this is something that you don't get in the official report, but by asking for it, you or your experts, are able to evaluate whether or not the people who are making the recommendation for decertification of your client would, in your opinion, or in the opinion of the court, be qualified to do that. You may find that the inspectors are relatively new and without any particular experience in the health care program, yet they are making recommendations having to do with patient care or other health care matters.

Disallowance by an Intermediary

Assume now that you have been retained to represent a client in the Medicare program who is faced with a disallowance of a certain cost because of the application of the "prudent buyer" concept. Under this concept the intermediary has looked at your costs (administrative costs or costs of the home office) and indicated it is disallowing a substantial amount of these costs because they are out of line with costs of comparable providers. Here, a Freedom of Information Act request upon the intermediary (and maybe on a regional office or the central office of HEW) should ask for the following: What is the type of data upon which they are basing that judgment? Have they collected data of other providers? Are those providers comparable? Have they attempted to update that data? You also should ask for any indices that may have been used and any inflation factors they may have.

Many times the intermediary will simply make the statement that the "prudent buyer" concept has been invoked and will be used to disallow costs. The intermediary often will rely on what they call their expertise in the area. Their auditor will tell you: "I've audited twenty-five nursing homes in this community and I think your costs are way out of line." It would be our position that that response doesn't sustain the burden the intermediary has in order to invoke the "prudent buyer" concept. So, by requesting this information (it can be on fee screens for physicians, suppliers or things such as that) you will, I think, obtain some very useful material.

We've requested it in a number of areas—most recently, in the area having to do with ambulance services. We found that some of the ambulance companies surveyed had gone out of existence because they were unable to meet the certification standards for participation in the Medicare program; yet the costs of those ambulance companies were being used to measure the reasonableness of the fees being charged by ambulance companies participating in the program.

Challenging a Medicaid Plan

Assume a client comes to you and wishes to challenge a Medicaid plan for payment of reasonable cost-related rates of the long term care facilities in your state. In drawing up your FOIA request, you want to find out what the state submitted to HEW to justify the Section 249 reimbursement system they are using. What plan amendments were submitted, which amendments were approved and which amendments were rejected? What information, if any, was used as a basis for any ceilings? And what information was used as a basis for any classes? You may also want the guidelines or manual provisions that the state may have submitted to the regional office. (We discovered in the State of Alabama that the manual used for the administration of the program wasn't even submitted as part of the plan amendments for approval by HEW.)

Challenging a Program Regulation

Suppose a client comes to you and wants to challenge a Medicare or Medicaid program regulation. There are several things you may want to get with an FOIA request. You should be interested in the types of comments that were filed by the parties on the regulation. You should seek information regarding the internal process that resulted in the approval of the regulation. (A regulation starts at a very low level, then goes through the various higher staff positions and, in most cases, into the Office of

General Counsel, where various comments will be made.) In a number of instances we have obtained the entire correspondence covering the initial drafts of the regulation all the way up to final approval. Sometimes you may find a conflict among some of the staff on specific provisions.

Structuring the FOIA Request

When you draw up your FOIA request you should keep two things in mind. First, you want to try to get the information. Second, you want to ask for information and have them indicate if it is not available. Many times that can benefit you. Often, you make your request by saying: "Under the Freedom of Information Act, we hereby request everything in the files relating to a specific thing." You might want to alter that a bit by identifying certain information and then say: "If such information is not in your files, would you please so indicate in your reply." At that point, if you have to go into court, you are able to say: "Look at all the things we've asked for that they apparently did not develop for this regulation."

Why Use the FOIA?

The most basic reason for using the FOIA is that it gives you a better look at the case that you may be able to make on behalf of your client. You are better able to advise your client: "Yes, I think we have a case, but you probably are going to have to invest a substantial amount of money in order to prevail." You're also able to give a better evaluation of some of the case's strengths and weaknesses. You may even find what lawyers frequently identify as the "smoking gun." That would be internal conflicts among the agency staff—possibly with the Office of General Counsel.

The FOIA many times abbreviates the discovery process. Essentially, what you're doing, if you use it correctly, is engaging in a little bit of discovery before you have to litigate the issue.

One last advantage that the FOIA provides is that it allows you to "freeze the file." You may be in court and opposing counsel may say to the judge: "Well, I'm certain that the agency considered that in their judgment and in their development of the regulation." You then stand up and say, "Your honor, we filed a Freedom of Information Act request, we asked for information such as this and it was not available. I think counsel for the government is engaging in ad hoc rationalizations which this court obviously knows cannot be considered in upholding the regulation."

Are there disadvantages to using the FOIA? We hear frequently that one disadvantage may be that it annoys the people in the agency from which you are requesting this information. In our experience, we really haven't found anybody that is offended by it. (Maybe they haven't told us.) We've found that within HEW, the Freedom of Information Act people in the central office take their jobs very seriously and will many times ferret out information from the various bureaus that the bureaus themselves may be reluctant to provide.

Administrative Procedure Act

In discussing the Administrative Procedure Act (APA), I'm going to focus particularly on rulemaking. The rulemaking provision of the APA is at 5 U.S.C. §553. Here, again, while there is a federal Administrative Procedure Act that applies to all the federal agencies, there is also, in most states, some type of state APA generally providing for the same type of rulemaking and comment requirements as are found in the federal statute.

Importance of rulemaking: What is the importance of the rulemaking process, and the importance of public notice and comment on regulations? It gives you an opportunity to try to convince the agency to revise the regulation. We have found HEW particularly receptive to what it calls "responsible and responsive comments." An interesting process you might wish to engage in sometime is to go and look at the comments that have been filed on certain regulations. There are always a number of letters that come with one or two lines claiming that the regulation is unconstitutional and will bankrupt long term care providers. These letters do not carry much weight with the agency. However, to the extent you are able to raise questions as to whether or not the language is clear, or whether or not HEW may have exceeded the statutory authority, or questions on policy considerations, we have found HEW to be very receptive and fair in attempting to deal with these considerations.

Once the regulation is commented on, it is the responsibility of the agency staff engaged in the rulemaking to determine how they are going to deal with those comments. They must, in either the preamble or the basis and purpose statement published with the final regulation, say something about how they dealt with the comments on that regulation.

A number of years ago HEW would end the preamble statement in the regulation by saying, "All comments were considered." The D.C. Court of Appeals indicated that that was not a satisfactory response for rulemaking. What the agency must do is go through what they consider to be the responsible comments and indicate, if there are problem areas, how they resolved those problem areas within the regulations.

The result of this process becomes the basis for judicial review. The court analyzes the basis and purpose statement for several things. The court looks to see if the agency really did state some reasonable basis for the decisions going from the proposed regulation to the final regulation. Also, did the agency consider all relevant issues? There is a considerable amount of case law indicating that during the rulemaking proceeding, all issues—impact upon the patients and providers, conflicts with state laws, etc.—should be addressed in the basis and purpose statement. If they are not addressed, the court may have some basis for invalidating the regulation.

Interaction of FOIA with APA

Finally, let me give you an example of how I think you can use the Freedom of Information Act, the Federal Rules of Civil Procedure and the Administrative Procedure Act. The case I want to use as an example is a lawsuit by the American Health Care Association against the Secretary of HEW. The issue was whether states, under the reasonable cost-related provisions of Section 249, were able to include in the rates some amount for profit. As you may recall, when the final regulations came out in July, 1976, the preamble seemed to indicate that the only profit opportunity available was a return on equity. The regulations were, however, silent as to any other profit opportunities. What developed was a considerable amount of confusion between the regional offices and the states, as to whether or not other profit opportunities could exist.

The first thing plaintiffs did was file an FOIA request asking for all opinions that had emanated from the central office of HEW on how it was dealing with this problem of the states that wanted to develop a prospective rate and include within it some opportunity for profit. Similar requests were made to the regional offices to see what type of information they were disseminating. This information was then taken and put into requests for admissions filed under the Federal Rules of Civil Procedure (Rule 36). The requests for admissions were filed with the Department of Justice to be answered by HEW. HEW admitted there were inconsistencies in the advice that was given. After initial briefs and supplemental briefs, HEW admitted there were six different profit methodologies that could be paid under a reasonable cost-related rate. What we then did was ask the court, as part of the relief in this case, to order HEW to engage in new rulemaking or a republication of the statement of basis and purpose, so there would be guidance for the states on the profit opportunities that were available.

Why did we do this? The plaintiff association had received a number of requests from its state affiliates as to what profit opportunities were available. They would call and ask if we had anything that would be available. We could send them the pleadings in the case but, as you know, your single state agency director is not going to read those pleadings. The strategy was that if you required HEW to republish the statement of basis and purpose and recognize the six or seven profit methodologies that it had admitted in the litigation, that would be very beneficial to the states.

The judge required HEW, sixty days after the order was entered, to publish a new statement of basis and purpose in which it set forth all the various profit methodologies under a reasonable cost-related rate that could be approved by HEW. States were then able to take that information and develop acceptable profit methodologies. This is a little different twist from what the Administrative Procedure Act is frequently used for, but it's something to bear in mind because the courts are giving more and more importance to this basis and purpose statement.

Confidentiality of Medical Records and Administrative Searches

ROBERT GERST

Medical records: Many times the client calls his lawyer and tells him that someone wants to take a look at the medical records. The request might come from a family member, the patient himself or the insurance company. Must the client release the records? Should he release them? Suppose an auditor for the state Medicaid agency comes in and says: "I want to see the medical records of all of your patients." Do you have an obligation to show medical records of non-Medicaid patients?

Suppose the administrator receives a subpoena. Do you have to turn the records over to the person that delivers the subpoena? What do you do? These are some of the things I'm going to try to touch upon.

Medical records are the property of the facility—they do not belong to the patients. The patient does not, by virtue of paying his medical bills, become the owner of his own medical records.

The facility is not supposed to disclose or release information in the medical records unless it is in accordance with your admission agreement. Here is where you get permission—you have an informed disclosure by the patient saying: "I authorize you to disclose information from my medical record with regard to billing and other aspects." Be sure, in your admission agreement, that this is covered. If the consent or authorization is not in your admission agreement, you certainly should get one anytime you are going to release information at the request of the patient. The lawyers should be sure that at each facility there is a policy, in writing, advising the administrator and others how to go about deciding when to release medical records. The authorization should be signed by the patient. (I don't think it can be signed by the responsible family member unless the responsible family member has been officially appointed by a court as the guardian or conservator.) It should specifically identify to whom it is given, it should be dated, and it should be kept.

The question of who has the authority to require release of records is important. The sheriff cannot come in, a police officer cannot come in, the district attorney cannot come in, and say: "Let me look at your medical records." You have a right to be sure that the person who is coming in has the authority to look at medical records—it's not automatic just because they happen to be part of the Department of Health or Social Welfare, etc. There are special rules in some states regarding alcoholics and mental patients, and there is an expanding role being played by advocates in connection with protecting people and their medical records from unauthorized release.

If you release medical records without authorization, it does not automatically subject you to some kind of penalty. Potentially, you are subject to an action for invasion of privacy, and, if the information is in error, perhaps some type of defamation action could be filed. There would have to be a finding that what was released, published or disclosed offended persons of reasonable sensibilities. And, of course, if you are releasing medical records and information to interested parties, the chances of your being liable for any damages are very, very small.

Administrative searches of nursing homes: In December of 1978, a decision involving a nursing home expanded the ruling in *Marshall v. Barlow's, Inc.,* 98 S.Ct. 1816. *Barlow* said that an ordinary businessman would not be subject to inspection by an OSHA inspector without a warrant. The question in the subsequent California case, *People v. Firstenberg* (No. 31550806 [App. Dept. (Los Angeles) Sup. Ct. Dec. 5, 1978]), was whether or not *Barlow* would apply to a nursing home.

The California court concluded that the *Barlow* rationale does apply to nursing homes. A surveyor came to a facility and asked to see the business records. He found some checks had been issued from the trust account into the general funds to meet payroll. He made copies of the checks and took them to the district attorney, who then got a warrant authorizing a search for the originals. The facility's operator was convicted of willful and repeated violation of California licensing regulations. On appeal of the misdemeanor conviction, the court ruled that, without a warrant, it was illegal to make that search. It said that nursing homes are not the type of business that has been so closely regulated for so long a period of time that an exception to the general warrant requirement should apply. Therefore, at least with respect to business records, you have to have a warrant—even if you are a surveyor. That case is on appeal at the present time.

Presently, we're involved in a case where a surveyor came in to look at the medical records of a patient who was no longer in the facility. They are trying to detect some sort of abuse—whether doctors' orders were carried out, failure of nurses to record injections, etc. By virtue of the case I just discussed, we are arguing that they need a warrant to come into the home. You can think of your own example where even a surveyor who comes in and tries to get hold of some records may not be able to do that if he doesn't have a search warrant. I'm not suggesting that we all of a sudden change all the rules and start to get tough and not let anybody in. Obviously, that is not conducive to a friendly, ongoing relationship. Still, you want to keep in mind that there may be some instances where you can keep people out until they get a warrant.

Audits and Investigations of Long Term Care Providers

THOMAS C. FOX

Audits and investigations of long term care providers are, as you are well aware, on the increase. It is therefore a good idea for you to prepare in advance for this contingency. Following are some suggestions for dealing with audits and investigations, procedures which hopefully will reduce your exposure to prosecution or other sanctions.

Written notice procedures: Each facility should establish written procedures to be followed by its personnel whenever the provider receives notification, by mail or in person, of any audit or investigation. These procedures should designate the responsible party or parties (the lawyer or an officer, for example) to be informed.

Why is the audit taking place? Before any audit or investigation begins, the provider representative should have a full understanding of the specific nature of what is taking place. Why are they here? Is it, in fact, a routine Medicare or Medicaid audit? Is it a licensure inspection? Is it an audit by the Office of the Inspector General for alleged fraudulent practices? Or is it an investigation by some other law enforcement agency?

The representative needs to know whether the audit is being conducted with respect to suspected criminal or civil violations. He also needs to know the authority of the federal or state agency to conduct the audit. You will want to reject the "to whom it may concern" letters because you have to be concerned with patients' rights of privacy and confidentiality. It behooves you to obtain the precise legal authority for the auditors being at the facility.

Contacts with other parties: The provider representative should also have an understanding of the extent of any anticipated contacts between the auditors or investigators and the "community." Will they contact your vendors? Will they contact past or present employees and patients? If they are going to contact past employees, this should alert you, it should raise your suspicions, because disgruntled employees are a prime source of charges against the organization.

You should make sure that a representative of the provider is present during any interviews with present employees and patients.

Auditors must respect patient privacy: The facility has an obligation to protect the privacy of the patients. Auditors and investigators should be informed that they must respect the privacy of a patient and refrain from interrogation of the patient unless his doctor is contacted and appropriate authorization obtained from the patient. If they want to examine patient or employee records, you should obtain a written statement of the legal authority authorizing the examination.

Privileged or confidential status of documents: Before any documents or records are turned over to the auditors or investigators, state and federal law should be examined to determine whether certain documents are privileged or confidential or whether there are any other reasons why a particular document or record should not be produced.

It's a good practice for a provider to have a separate file for confidential or privileged communications. You don't want to have staff members unwittingly turn over sensitive documents.

Copying documents: If the auditors or investigators want to copy certain materials, a representative of the provider should be informed of the copying before it takes place and the auditors should be required to obtain permission for the copying. Make sure you keep a complete record of every document that is examined, removed or copied.

Removal of documents and records: You should require auditors and investigators to obtain authorization from you before they remove any documents or records from the premises. Get a receipt for any material that is removed, showing the address of the place to which the documents are removed and the telephone number of the person having custody of the materials.

You also should reach some sort of understanding with the auditors and investigators to the effect that if some other state or federal agency seeks these materials, you will be notified immediately.

Audit during regular business hours: Auditors and investigators should be allowed on the premises only during regular business hours—when your staff and a competent provider representative are available. If you are subjected to an unannounced midnight inspection, simply tell the investigators to come back at 9 A.M. Normally, they will not attempt to enter the premises forcibly.

Names and addresses of auditors and investigators: It is always a good idea to get the names, addresses and telephone numbers of the auditors and investigators. If you find out one of the investigators is from the FBI, the Post Office, or the U.S. Attorney's office, you might not want to give him access to the facility.

You should also keep a logbook indicating the dates and times of the auditors' arrivals and departures. This enables you to show the court that these people have been on your premises for an extended period of time and this helps your argument that you shouldn't have to put up with any further disruptions of the business.

Familiarity with applicable laws and the provider agreement: It should be ascertained whether the auditors and investigative personnel are familiar with all requisite state and federal laws and regulations and the provider agreement. It should also be ascertained whether their supervisor has a copy of all these materials (laws, regulations and agreement).

Conducting an In-House Audit

The lawyer needs to determine his client's potential exposure to an investigation. There are a number of steps he can take in this direction as a type of in-house audit. He should conduct a review to assure that the facility's private rate is equal to its Medicaid rate and that private charges are equal to or greater than costs claimed under Medicare. He should verify all relationships with vendors and scrutinize all referral arrangements. He is then able to determine if there are any related-organization problems. A consulting agreement might be viewed as providing kickbacks.

Where discounts are received, the in-house audit needs to verify that the costs charged to the programs reflect all discounts (cash or in-kind).

The attorney should verify that ownership disclosure information is accurate. This is important because proposed regulations make the failure to supply accurate information a criminal violation. He should make sure that patient monies are not commingled with facility operating funds and that receipts are obtained from patients for expenditures.

The attorney should examine admission agreements to make sure that donations or supplemental payments are not required from either patients or their families as a condition of admission or continued stay. Otherwise, you could be subject to criminal sanctions. As part of the in-house audit, the attorney should determine whether costs are claimed which are expressly disallowed by program instructions.

As was pointed out earlier, he should also make sure there is a specific file for privileged and confidential communications, including communications subject to the attorney-client privilege.

Finally, it's good strategy to obtain the opinion of legal counsel on the propriety of particular conduct if doubt exists. Good-faith reliance on an attorney may help in the defense of a subsequent criminal prosecution.

LONG TERM CARE AND THE LAW— CURRENT ISSUES

Medicare-Medicaid Federal Policies

GALEN POWERS

Reasonable Cost-Related Reimbursement Issues

Property cost reimbursement: A lot has been written about property cost reimbursement, and it doesn't take an expert to recognize that this is a reimbursement area that presents the states with opportunities to establish reasonable incentives to avoid excessively inflated transactions relating to capital assets. (I am talking here only about *Medicaid* nursing home reimbursement.) All states, except California, have obtained federal approval of their Medicaid reimbursement plans under the reasonable cost-related reimbursement requirement. It's time, now that most states do have them, to start looking at how those plans work, and for everybody, including the industry, the states, and the federal government, to start assessing what's wrong with them and what's right with them.

Under Medicaid, nearly all of the states reimburse the cost of the use of capital assets through some form of depreciation methodology. A few states, Connecticut and New Jersey among them, reimburse at the imputed rental value of the assets.

I would like to focus on two aspects of the conventional depreciation approach—the basis and the recapture. Typical depreciation provisions of a state plan assign a basis to the owner which is usually his cost of acquisition. However, adjustments are frequently made for depreciation claimed by previous owners. In a few states, the buyer's basis is limited to that of the seller, minus his depreciation—or the seller's book value. Even where the transaction is not between related parties, all the states, except the five or six that have limited property reimbursement to the seller's book value, have adopted realistic approaches by recognizing the cost of acquisition to establish the basis.

Where the basis is limited to the seller's book value, however, the marketability of property can be unnecessarily constrained. But among the states that use buyer's cost as the basis, controls designed to minimize abuse are often lacking. These states simply recognize the sale price in determining Medicaid rates in any transaction between unrelated parties. This type of lax approach can result in inflationary trading of nursing homes, since buyers are virtually assured of Medicaid reimbursement to cover the purchase price. This problem is particularly acute where utilization levels are high and consequently the Medicaid program is paying most of the costs, inflated or otherwise, of the facility. Other states, however, do impose controls and those that do not should be required to do so. If the states don't control the spiralling escalation of property costs due to sale and resale, then I am afraid the "Feds" will have to do that.

There are numerous approaches here. A few states provide for reduction of new historical costs and the estimated useful life of assets by the dollar amount and years previously depreciated. Under this method, depreciation attributable to any asset will only be allowed once, even though the depreciation rate will vary with sales throughout the life of the asset. Some other controls used by a few states include limiting basis to fair market value (with or without subtraction of previously accumulated depreciation) or "depreciated replacement cost," which means the current reproductive cost depreciated over the life of the asset to the time of the sale. Another way to look at that is to depreciate the construction cost forward to the date of the sale and subtract the depreciation on the useful life already exhausted. This type of limitation is particularly useful in avoiding the adverse cost consequences of an immediate sale of the new facility in excess of construction cost.

Where no limitations exist, purchasers may be willing to pay a sales price that far exceeds construction costs, so long as they're assured of sufficient future property cost reimbursement. Many state plans recognize cost of acquisition as the basis without any limit, and that ought to be controlled.

The State of Illinois has developed an innovative approach for limiting excessively inflationary property transactions. Its plan reimburses capital costs based on the median of costs within classes, grouped by year of construction or acquisition and the geographic area. As facilities are resold, they remain in the same class, but the increased capital cost will translate into a higher median. This system has the virtue of creating disincentives for inflated trading of facilities without locking owners into their investments by freezing property cost reimbursement over the life of the asset.

Once basis is established, most plans provide for depreciation on a straight line or declining balance formula over the lifetime of the asset, usually determined using IRS or AHA guidelines. The sale of a facility during or after the depreciation cycle raises the recapture problem. No matter what system of reimbursement is used, the actual depreciation payments will often exceed the cost of the use of the asset. Where a state uses an allowance in lieu of actual depreciation or where basis is limited to original historical cost, recapture should generally be unnecessary. (I think that point shows the unrealistic nature of a lot of depreciation systems.) However, except in those few cases, cost basis depreciation without recapture can too often result in excessive payments and incentives for inflated sales prices.

There are numerous methods for calculating recapture, some of them quite technical. However, in simple terms, the goal of most recapture provisions is to recover depreciation payments to the extent that the sale results in a gain over the fully depreciated basis. Generally, the gross recapture amount is allocated to periods for which depreciation is claimed and the net recapture amount is calculated based on Medicaid utilization for those periods.

In many states, it is initially the seller's obligation to pay the recapture amount. But that doesn't work very well for us (HEW) and tends to lead to the recapture amount not being treated realistically in the sale price. Realistically, there may be no way to collect from the seller. From our point of view, it's a good idea to have the purchaser bear the responsibility for the recapture amount because we can offset any unpaid recapture amount against future payments to the purchaser.

Once again, Medicaid should not approve plans that do not provide for some form of recapture where there is the potential for excessive depreciation payments. I think that when we get to revising our regulations on 249, that's one of the problems we will have to address.

Reimbursement classes and opportunities for profits: I want to talk now about some of the recurring problems that we have in litigation over the 249 reimbursement formulas in the states. As a result of the decision in *American Health Care Association v. Califano,* Civ. No. 77-0250 (D.D.C., decided Dec. 7, 1977), we were vindicated in our position that it is permissible and proper to preclude profit as a separate identifiable cost item for nursing homes under Medicaid. However, we did agree that states could create incentives to reduce costs by allowing facilities to retain the difference between the payment rate and actual cost in prospective rate systems.

HEW probably has the authority to abolish all opportunities for profits under these plans, but we're unlikely to do so, however, since we recognize the need for, and the value of, reimbursement systems that contain incentives for cost saving even if it means using the lure of profits.

There are problem areas, however, where providers within a prospective payment class receive excessive profits. We think it is perfectly legal for states to impose per diem dollar limitations on the amount of profit a facility may retain, since the state need not afford any profits whatsoever. However, where federal officials have attempted to impose these per diem profit limits on the states, we have had some problems under the current regulations. No doubt we could, by regulations (with appropriate supporting data), establish a federal per diem maximum reasonable profit. Short of this, however, we clearly have the authority to take action to eliminate the underlying cause of excessive incentive payments, which is the unreasonable classification of facilities. By that I mean classes lacking criteria that reasonably group facilities with homogenous cost characteristics. Where there are a significant number of facilities that fall outside of a central range, and the differences are not solely attributable to efficiencies, reimbursement of all facilities at a uniform class rate is unreasonable. If the states are unable to establish the criteria that would reasonably group the facilities, then reimbursement at a uniform class rate should be prohibited.

Our regulations provide that states may utilize classes so long as the criteria upon which they are based are reasonable. Contrary to the indications in popular practice, this does not mean that classes are always appropriate. HEW got itself into this profit problem by approving classes for which there is no support. At the time they were approved, however, much of the data one would need to make this determination was not available. We may well find that criteria which were presumed to be logical and reasonable (such as bed size and geography) are not borne out by the actual cost data. Since most states should now have cost data going back at least two years, federal and state officials should now be able to better determine whether the reimbursement classes they have approved are reasonable.

Percentile limitations: While Medicaid has focused much of its attention on the problem of providers receiving excessive profits, the industry has been complaining about percentile limitations that result in reimbursement of less than actual costs. These issues are closely related since the extent of the problem on either end is a function of the homogeneity of the classes. The plaintiffs in *Alabama Nursing Homes Association v. Califano*, Civ. No. 77-52-N (M.D. Ala., decided Feb. 23, 1979),* have taken the position that our regulations require reimbursement of the actual costs of each and every provider that is economically and efficiently operated. Further, plaintiffs contend that the federal government must conduct studies and collect data to determine whether each and every economically and efficiently operated facility receives payment in full for its allowable costs.

Nothing could be more administratively unfeasible and undesirable. "Efficiency" and "economy" are concepts that defy precise quantification, and the statute and regulations do not contemplate that HEW will engage in

---

*The court, in its order, denied the relief sought by plaintiffs.

such fruitless exercises. We have adopted a defensible presumption that where at least one half of the homes in a class receive their full allowable costs, services will be widely and consistently available at that price, the rate will be sufficient to reimburse the full allowable cost of an efficiently and economically operated facility, and the rate will therefore be reasonable. I would add one major proviso—classes have to be reasonable in order for the system to work properly at the high and low ends of the cost spectrum. Moreover, quantification of reasonable classes is not nearly so elusive a problem as the quantification of "efficiency" and "economy." The test for classes is homogeneity, and there are relatively simple methods to determine the presence of a central tendency. Thus, if classes are reasonable, even where the upper limit is set at the median, the differences between the upper limit and the actual costs of the remaining facilities should not be great.

State budgetary considerations: During the period in which Alabama was formulating a reimbursement plan, it compiled cost data on the impact of various possible percentile upper limits on class rates. The state finally chose the 60th percentile, perhaps for reasons of cost. The Nursing Home Association contended that the state had improperly relied on budgetary considerations in selecting the 60th percentile, in violation of HEW policy.

This argument misconstrues HEW policy, which was designed to protect providers from arbitrary freezes and cutbacks that might result from budgetary constraints. However, we have never attempted to adopt a policy that would dictate or limit a state's deliberative process in developing a plan. States are clearly free to consider cost impact, or any number of factors in establishing a reimbursement rate or any other provisions of their plans—so long as in the final analysis the plan satisfies the statutory and regulatory requirements.

Provider and Patient Rights in the Termination Process

Pre-termination rights of nursing homes: What kind of relief is available to the provider who is threatened with termination? New, final HEW regulations, 42 C.F.R. §431.151 *et seq.* (44 Fed. Reg. 9749-53 (Feb. 15, 1979)), provide for hearings for nursing homes that are terminated in the Medicaid program.

These regulations really provide for one of two processes, at the state's option. First, the state can have a full formal hearing prior to termination, if it so desires. As an alternative, it can give the nursing home, prior to termination, a reconsideration—a sort of informal reconsideration. All that is required there is that it indicate to the nursing home the reasons for the impending termination and allow the home an opportunity for rebuttal. (A full-blown evidentiary hearing will take place within four months after termination.)

These regulations do not address two important topics. One is, what are the matching consequences for the state vis-a-vis HEW, if it is under a court order, or otherwise tied up in some state administrative or judicial process? We are going to issue a separate regulation on that. There will be a notice of proposed rulemaking on that problem.

Patient's right to hearing: The other question the regulations don't address is the right of the patients to a hearing. We were going along for a couple of years, litigating the nursing home's right to a hearing, and suddenly, the patient's right to a hearing crept up on us. We are trying to establish the principle that a nursing home has no right to a full, oral, evidentiary pretermination hearing. I think we've now come to a place where we've got a conflict in the circuits on that, but I think we'll eventually prevail on that point. What has caught us by surprise really is the issue of the patient having a right to a hearing before the nursing home is terminated. We're convinced he doesn't. However, the courts aren't convinced of that—and the Third Circuit has held that they (the patients) do have a right to some sort of hearing before the nursing home is terminated. *Town Court Nursing Center v. Califano,* 586 F.2d 280 (3d Cir. 1979); *Klein v. Califano,* 586 F.2d 250 (3d Cir. 1979). We're not seeking certiorari in that case because we are going to publish a regulation that involves patients in the survey, certification and termination processes. I don't know exactly how they're going to be involved—it will not be a full evidentiary hearing—but some account is going to be taken of the patients' views of how the home operates, and if there is going to be a termination, what their desires are in the matter as to where they want to go.

Miscellaneous Issues

Functional integration: There is an awful lot of talk about so-called "functional integration," the integration of Medicare and Medicaid requirements and procedures. The parts of it that we are slowly getting into focus are common billing procedures, common audits, and uniform cost reporting. There is a proposed regulation on uniform cost reporting for hospitals, with an enormous manual—which will be followed by one for long term care. We hope, through uniform cost reporting for SNFs and ICFs, to get comparable cost data for purposes of cost and policy analysis, health planning, and an assessment of how the reasonable cost-related reimbursement systems work.

Grant Appeals Board: When the old Social and Rehabilitation Service was abolished, there were something like 180 pending disallowances of state funds in Medicaid, involving over a billion dollars—maybe two billion dollars. Many of those dated back to 1969, 1970, 1971, and they were never decided. The responsible official was the Administrator of the Social and

Rehabilitation Service, and whoever he was (we passed one through about every 18 months), he never got anything decided. He wanted to run a very efficient and economical program, but he also wanted to expand services, get the states to bring in more providers, and cover more beneficiaries, and it's kind of hard to do that when you are taking money away from the state.

Some people had the idea that the way to get these disallowances resolved was to transfer them to the Departmental Grant Appeals Board, which had been established originally to handle cost disputes in small discretionary grants. Most of those cases have been transferred; it's been about a year now and we're still awaiting the first decision by the Departmental Grant Appeals Board. They are working, though, and I hope they will make some decisions soon.

There's one aspect of their procedures that I want to point out to you. Under their regulations, interested parties are entitled to participate in the proceeding upon approval of a petition for intervention. If I were a nursing home owner being disallowed funds by the state because HEW was disallowing them to the state, I might want to intervene in such a proceeding.

Provider Reimbursement Review Board: The last thing I want to mention is the Provider Reimbursement Review Board (PRRB), which handles provider cost disputes in Medicare, including nursing home disputes. That Board has problems, as you know if you've had to deal with it. It needs strengthening and improving. There is an effort now to strengthen and improve it; one idea under consideration is the naming of a lawyer to the Board. Also, we need to limit the review process so that issues and evidence before the Board are all that are reviewed by the administrator. We got some help in that regard from Judge Sirica in a recent case in the District of Columbia. He said, in dicta, that the administrator had inherent authority to remand a matter to the Board for the taking of additional evidence— authority we didn't think he had. We are going to establish a procedure for the administrator to remand matters to the Board—so if he's not satisfied with the record, instead of taking additional evidence at this stage, he can remand the matter for further proceedings.

There will be a notice of proposed rulemaking about procedures for review of the Board's decisions fairly soon, and it will give you all an opportunity to comment on various ways in which those procedures can be improved. In all probability, it will also propose that the Medicare Bureau be the party to the hearing before the Board, rather than the intermediary, as is now the case.

QUESTIONS AND ANSWERS

Thomas C. Fox: In the July 1, 1976 regulations, HEW indicated that it was not prescribing any rules for property cost reimbursement. This led a number of states to develop proposals for reimbursement of property costs based upon some appraisal of the property. However, there seemed to be advice out of both the HEW regional offices and the central office that an appraisal-type system that would assign some value to the property was not permissible under the regulations. Would you care to comment on this?

Galen Powers: Assuming there were reasonable ways to arrive at some appraisal, it is hard for me to see why that system wouldn't be acceptable. I don't personally know of any plans that were disapproved for that reason, though a lot of things go on out in those regional offices. I assume you are talking about a system in which, instead of a sale price, there is some appraisal value given the property, and that appraisal value is then depreciated over whatever the term of years is. On its face, I don't know why that system would be unacceptable.

Jerome Levy: Let me ask you a question with reference to your comments on the reasonable cost reviews that the state or the federal government were doing. To what extent does HEW plan to get involved in the details of each state plan, in terms of the determination of what is reasonable cost for reimbursement purposes? Specifically, do you anticipate that HEW will get involved with individual complaints of providers that some application of an otherwise approved plan is somehow violative of the federal law in a particular situation?

Powers: We have a responsibility to get into the details of those plans, to take a statement like, "there will be periodic updates of reimbursements to take account of inflation," which used to be sort of the acceptable thing, and look into it. We have to say, "what do you mean by periodic updates, how periodic and how are you going to do that and what are the details of your method for that?" We should not be approving plans that have those general commitments to do "good" things.

Once you understand the plan in detail and find it approvable, then there has to be some resistance to the tendency of providers to come to the federal government first before they go to the state. We need to tell them, you've got to go talk to your state and see if you can't work it out with the state. But, if they can't, I just can't see us ignoring the problem and saying it's a state problem.

Levy: As a provider representative at this point I might encourage you.

Fox: With respect to the Provider Reimbursement Review Board, one of the frustrations that counsel representing providers have is the inability of the Board to pass any judgment on the propriety of a regulation or a policy that's before the Board. However, we are under the requirement, as a result of several decisions, that we must go through the Board, however futile that review may be. Is there any thought being given to the Board's having broader authority to actually pass upon the validity of a regulation?

Powers: No, I don't think that's going to happen. I think the Board will always be bound by HEW regulations. It's not realistic to think that the Board is going to be able to upset regulations. Inherent in your question, though, are some real problems that can be addressed in other ways. It is silly to run a provider through the Board, year after year, on the same problem that the Board is turning down, or on which the Board has been reversed by the administrator. That is really a great waste of time and effort and resources, and there ought to be several ways to avoid that sort of problem.

The Supreme Court said some pretty interesting things in *Mathews v. Eldridge,* 424 U.S. 319 (1976), about the futility of review and the exhaustion of administrative remedies. I think it's within the power of HEW to have a regulation that recognizes the futility of certain kinds of reviews before the Board. We have not done that yet. Personally, I would like to see that done, because that would relieve a lot of these frustrations.

There are probably other practical ways to get at that problem, if you can get some understanding between the intermediary and the provider that they'll just sit on the matter until the one that is in court is resolved. That may not work in a lot of cases because it may take so many years to resolve one in court that a provider doesn't want to wait anymore. But if you've got that kind of problem in a particular case, I think you ought to talk to me or my office and maybe we could work out something so that you don't have to go through the Board on a relatively futile matter.

Fox: It's really a cost-benefit argument since the Medicare program is paying for all these legal fees. What we are doing is trying to save you money if you give us a direct right to challenge the matter in federal court.

Powers: Speaking of legal fees and cost-benefit, we had a decision against us the other day in the District of Columbia. I was delighted by it on policy grounds, not on legal grounds. The case was *Good Luck Nursing Home v. Califano,* Civ. No. 78-863 (D.D.C., decided December 27, 1978). Everybody chuckles in my office about Good Luck Nursing Home because we could all visualize the physician sending the patient over there and saying, "good luck." In any event, the court held that the legal costs of the Good Luck Nursing Home in pursuing its appeal before the Provider Reimbursement Review Board were direct costs of the Medicare program. So, we have to pay all of it, unless we get the thing upset on appeal.

As a policy matter, where we (the government) lose before the Provider Reimbursement Review Board or in court, it makes a good deal of sense that the program bear the legal costs of the providers—we were wrong and they were right. On the other hand, if they lose before the Board or the court, it wouldn't make any sense at all to pay them anything, either as a direct or an allocated cost.

Audience: Could you give us the names of some of the members of your staff who specialize in Title XIX issues?

Powers: I have about thirty-five lawyers on my staff and a few of them tend to do more of this Title XIX reimbursement work than others, but most of them touch on it once in a while, one way or another. One of the people who works a good deal in this area is Eugene Tillman. Another person on my staff in Washington who works a great deal on these issues is Jeffrey Golland.

Medicaid Reimbursement Rate Setting

JEROME T. LEVY

Nationwide, the system of reimbursement for long term care providers in the Medicaid program has moved towards cost-based reimbursement. Federal law (P.L. 92-603), now codified at 42 U.S.C. Section 1396a(a)(13)(E), mandates a cost-based reimbursement system. It is questionable, however, as to whether this is the best method, or whether it is, in fact, the only method that should be employed to pay for care rendered to Medicaid recipients in residential health care facilities. New York State, which is obviously the state with which I am most familiar, went to a cost-based reimbursement system in the early days of the Medicaid program and has had many cost control elements in place since 1969.

What Is Cost-Based Reimbursement?

Essentially, cost-based reimbursement is a process by which the facility's costs attributable to patient care are identified and broken down into components (with perhaps some of the costs being disallowed by reference to "ceilings"), with the reimbursement then being computed on the basis of some relationship to those costs, allowing for a return on equity or some other profit margin if the facility is proprietary.

Costs can be assigned on various bases. A "per discharge" base is one currently under discussion. "Per month of stay" is a base that is used. Generally, though, the prevailing method under which costs have been attributed is the "patient day." You divide your total costs of the production of services by the number of patients multiplied by the number of days in the year that you have had patients in your facility. The resulting figure is the base for determining what you will be paid for each day of treatment to each patient in the facility.

Advantages of cost-based reimbursement: If a provider is operating in a system where he is being reimbursed on the basis of his costs, he should, theoretically, never "lose money" because his costs should be covered fully by all the range of patients in accordance with the rates paid by the various sponsors. If you should have some Medicare, Medicaid, maybe some private insurance or Blue Cross patients, and private paying patients in a facility, and if all are reimbursing on a cost basis, 100% of the costs should be recovered. (In practice, we know this does not always occur, however.)

Another theoretical advantage is that the payor—the state in the case of Medicaid or the federal government in the case of Medicare—is protected from charges in excess of costs.

The patient is also protected because cost-based reimbursement, in theory, mitigates against cost cutting, which would lead to a reduction in service. In fact, the practice does not conform to this theory. One of the problems for the patient under a prospective rate system, where the amount of income is assured to the facility, is that there is incentive on the part of the provider to cut costs by cutting services. The provider knows that he is being paid $29 per patient day for each Medicaid patient in the facility. If he provides $27 worth of services, he gets $2 in his pocket. If he provides $28.50 worth of services, he may only retain 50¢. Thus, the prospective rate system has led to skimping on care.

Establishing Capital Costs

Costs related to the production of services are divided into capital costs and operational costs. Costs of services attributable to capital investments are established by the various states in a number of ways.

The present New York State method for reimbursement to proprietary facilities requires a determination of historical cost. (Bear in mind that in New York State, there is a difference in reimbursement for capital costs depending on whether a facility is proprietary or voluntary. This raises some very interesting constitutional questions which have yet to be litigated, but which lurk in the background.) For the proprietary facility, the historical cost is determined by finding the cost of construction of the building, whenever constructed, or by examining the costs on an arbitrarily selected date for certain older facilities. Essentially, you go back in time, the facility is examined, and the records of the corporation 'that originally constructed the facility are audited. If there have been changes in title, there is no reference to the costs of the present owner; rather, the cost to build the facility is examined.

To determine the annual reimbursement amount, a 40-year useful life period is selected. This is established by regulation—it is not a rebuttable presumption. One of the challenges to this system has been that in most situations, it is impossible to get financing for 40 years. Nonetheless, the system has been set up so that arbitrarily there will be a 40-year useful life. This results in a recovery of 2.5% of the historical costs in each year. Under the present New York system, all interest paid on the mortgage will be reimbursed (provided that the mortgage is with a commercial lending institution or privately placed at a "reasonable" interest rate). (No one is quite sure what a "reasonable" interest rate is these days.) All real estate taxes are also reimbursed. In addition, there is a system allowing for a return on equity that is established using the figures employed by Medicare, with an adjustment. The return is computed without regard to unamortized principal, i.e., only on the equity actually invested.

Fair rental system: A method of reimbursement previously used in New York State is the fair rental system. This system still is in existence in Connecticut and New Jersey. New York did away with fair rental because it had some very harsh results.

The depreciated book value of the facility was taken as it existed at the time the system began. An amount assigned as the valuation for the land on which the building was constructed was added. The sum was divided by a 40-year useful life period—again, that same arbitrary period in a situation where most financing is based on a much shorter period. Forty years was used for a new facility. For an existing facility, the actual age was subtracted from the number 40. So, if you had a facility that was 13 years old, the divisor under the fair rental system was 27; i.e., there were 27 more years to go. You would start with your net depreciated book value, which presumably took into consideration the 13 years of depreciation, and you would divide that figure (after adding in the land figure) by 27 to determine the annual amount to be reimbursed. This figure, multiplied by a percentage designed to include a rate of return on equity, was the fair rental figure. Reimbursement for property costs was paid on this basis, with no departures permitted.

Unlike the present New York system, actual interest was not allowed under fair rental. Instead, a debt service factor was imputed, equal to the Medicare rate of return. This factor was applied to the depreciated book value to yield a system for determining the imputed interest payment.

Rationale behind these systems: The rationale behind both the existing New York State system and the previously used fair rental system is basically very simple. *The State of New York did not wish to pay for any facility more than once.* In New York (and probably in most of the other states) skilled nursing facilities are almost entirely supported by their

61

revenue from Medicaid. It is not uncommon for facilities to have an average of as high as 95% of their patient days attributable to Medicaid patients. (Some of the facilities' rates are lower but there are some that have 98-99% Medicaid patient days.) Accordingly, if the state is providing capital cost reimbursement in a Medicaid formula, it is actually underwriting virtually the entire amount of depreciation that any facility is going to have in a given period of time. If increases in the sale price are reflected in the basis for depreciation of a subsequent owner, a facility which costs, say, $2,000,000 to build, will end up being sold for $5,000,000 and depreciated on the books of the acquiring individual or operator at $5,000,000. The state, which paid perhaps as much as $2,000,000 for depreciation to the original owner, will now find itself paying anew, at a higher rate, for this facility. Since, in theory, if the state purchased the facility outright and provided the services itself it would have paid only historical cost, the state maintains that it should pay no more than the historical cost of the building during the life of the building.

There are problems with this approach. It is a very serious restraint on the alienability of the facility. One cannot sell a facility for higher than its net depreciated book value (under fair rental) or its historical cost. States are coming to realize that they are faced with operators who no longer want to be in the business (or who perhaps die), and that these operators are left without anyone willing or able to purchase and operate these facilities because the purchase prices are just so far below the value of the building for other purposes.

To illustrate, consider a situation where individuals who, in effect, are descendants of the original operators become the owners of the facility and have no interest in or ability to operate the facility. This type of situation has led to the closing of nursing homes in New York State. A second illustration of the problem (though fortunately for the state, it hasn't occurred too often) may be seen where the use of the building for another purpose becomes exceedingly more profitable than its use for a nursing home. The nursing home will close. On Long Island, there was a facility where the capital cost reimbursement was considerably lower than the fair market value of the property and the owner of the facility closed the nursing home, over the state's objection, and turned it into a restricted-diet resort for overweight individuals. The result was an alternative use for a facility that state officials assumed had no other use. The operator turned the facility into what is euphemistically referred to as a "fat farm," resulting in the loss of 90 skilled nursing facility beds in an already under-bedded county. It is this kind of situation that the states are going to have to face up to because it is one of the consequences of placing severe limitations upon capital reimbursement.

Reimbursement of Voluntary Nursing Homes

The method used to reimburse voluntary (nonprofit) nursing homes seems to work very well. In fact, New York State has had no complaints with respect to the reimbursement of such facilities. Payment for depreciation is made as determined on the books of the organization. Any facilities that own their property subject to a mortgage will have their interest expenses paid. Where the voluntary agency owns the building, you are not concerned with real estate taxes, so there is no reimbursement for taxes. This system works very well, as I indicated. It may well be that some modified form of this system should be used as a solution to capital cost problems of the proprietary facilities.

Operational Cost Components

There are two major approaches to computing the operational components of rates: the "retrospective" method and the "prospective" method. The retrospective method is used in Medicare (Title XVIII). Under the retrospective system, the facility submits the data upon which an estimated rate per patient day is calculated. The facility is paid at this rate for each patient day during the cost year. It submits a bill for the care it renders and is paid at this interim rate. At the conclusion of the year, the facility will submit its cost report, which is then audited by the paying agent of the program (a fiscal intermediary in the case of Medicare). After the audit, a revised per-patient-day charge is computed, based upon actual costs incurred during the rate period. If there is an amount due the facility, it will be computed and will result in an increase in the projected rate for the next year. If, on the other hand, there is an amount due the program—i.e., the costs turned out not to be as high as originally estimated by the facility, or there are disallowed items on audit—then the rate for the following year is adjusted downward. That, very briefly, is retrospective rate setting—which, in fact, results in a cost-based rate being paid to the facility after the audit is completed.

Prospective rate setting: Again using the example of New York State, the facility submits a cost report for the prior year. Based on the cost report for this year, called the base year, the next year's rate is computed. For example, the cost report for the year 1976 was submitted. This base year cost report (actually filed in 1977) was used as the basis for promulgating the 1978 rates.

Inflation is accounted for by means of what is called a trend factor (sometimes referred to as a projection factor). It is an economically determined index of increase in the elements of the cost of providing care. The New York State system looks at several broad-based economic indicators to determine the percentage of increase in the system. For example, the 1976 base year costs were trended forward to 1978 by the inclusion of a projection factor of approximately 11%. That was determined by the State Division of Health Care Financing to be the trend factor for the two-year period between 1976 and 1978. Accordingly, the facility's rate for 1978 was the 1976 base year cost multiplied by 1.11.

There is no auditing to determine whether the facility's costs in the rate year (e.g., 1978) were more or less than the reimbursement rate. The program seeks to encourage efficiency in the delivery of the health care system by allowing the facility to keep the difference. Accordingly, if the facility has a $40 rate for 1978 and it delivers services at $38 a patient day, the facility gets to keep the $2 difference as profit. If, on the other hand, the facility, through mismanagement, does not deliver care at $40 but in fact has costs of $42 a day, the facility is, in theory, supposed to bear the loss. What actually happens often is the facility appeals its rates. If there are unexpected cost increases or if there are changes in the kinds of services performed in the facility, a rate appeal is allowed. The Health Department will determine whether the changes that caused the increased costs were due to inefficient operation or whether they were, in fact, due to bona fide increases in costs beyond the facility's control. If it is the latter, some rate increase will be permitted. If it is determined that inefficient operation or some other nonallowable cost increase was the cause, there will be no increase in the rate.

Obviously, the question of whether the increased cost is a legitimate cost that the state ought to bear or whether it is a cost resulting from some fault of the operator is going to be a subject for litigation—and there is already a good deal of litigation going on. One case involves a determination, made in 1975, that an increase in labor costs resulting from collective bargaining agreements would no longer be grounds for this special appeal treatment, and that any labor cost increases in excess of the projection factor had to be borne by the provider. This is presently in litigation, and we ought to know in about a year whether New York State was correct in its determination on this issue.

Rate ceilings: When we talk about operational rates, one of the things that has to be considered is the existence of ceilings. A ceiling is the level of costs above which there will be no reimbursement even if the cost of production of the services in question exceeded that amount. There are a number of ways to determine ceilings. New York State had a system with a 60th-percentile ceiling—which meant that if your costs were above the 60th percentile for facilities in your group, you would not be reimbursed fully but would be reimbursed only up to that 60th percentile level. This resulted, in effect, in 40% of the facilities having ceilings imposed.

Presently, there are two commonly used methods of imposing ceilings. Ceilings can be imposed either on total operational costs or on cost centers.

The determination of cost centers can vary from state to state, but there are generally certain basic cost centers. "Administration," for example, is a cost center. "Nursing services" is a cost center. "Dietary" and "housekeeping" are cost centers. In the New York State system enacted in 1976, each of the six cost centers delineated in the regulations was examined and arrayed against the 60th percentile limit for the group. Disallowances would be made if the costs in any of these systems were in excess of that 60th percentile amount. This system was revised for 1978 and an "aggregate of costs" system was employed.

One of the problems that surfaces immediately with this system is that one person's "dietary" might be another person's "housekeeping," or one person's "administration" might be another person's "nursing." Where, for example, do you report your Director of Nursing Services? In some circumstances, a person will say, "Well, that's Administration. She's non-union and if I put her in my nursing costs, my union is going to come after her and try to sign her up and I can't have that. So, I'll call her Administration." Couple that with the administrator and his nephew and several other people, along with legal expenses and accounting fees, and suddenly we reach a ceiling on administrative costs and certain costs are disallowed. But while this particular operator might report very high administrative costs, his nursing cost figure is very, very low—because certain nursing expenses, such as salary for individuals involved in the management of the nursing services, were not reported in the nursing costs where they perhaps belonged.

The cure for this is either aggregation of cost centers, or requiring a uniform system of accounting, though the uniform system has its problems and results in a lot of complex appeals. New York State is presently implementing such a system, which will go into effect, I believe, July 1, 1979, with the guidance and assistance of HEW. Facilities will be required to report in a uniform way, making the application of costs into ceilings far easier.

An additional method by which ceilings, or rather disallowances, were imposed has to do (in New York State) with what is called a "linkage to quality of care." There were, essentially, three categories for quality of care statewide. While there were five or six different types of ratings one could get on various aspects of quality of care, these were collapsed into essentially a "very good," a "good," and a "needs improvement" category. "Very good" facilities are allowed reimbursement of all their operational costs without regard to ceilings. The theory is that if the operator is running a home that state surveyors say is "very good," the state will allow the operator 100% of his costs because he is efficiently producing those services that are in considerable excess of the standard. The "good" facilities are allowed reimbursements up to the group average, formerly the

60th percentile ceiling, as I have described. Facilities found in need of improvement were given a *10% rate cut;* i.e., they were penalized.

Obviously, the question comes along, if a facility "needs improvement," how do we insure that it will improve if we take money away from it? There is now less money available to provide care for the patient. There is, of course, an incentive for a facility to stay above the "needs improvement" level because it doesn't want rate penalties imposed. The difficulty is that if the facility should fall to the "needs improvement" level the system is, in effect, guaranteeing that the facility will never be able to come back up to standard. What happens is that as soon as the facility comes into the "needs improvement" category, a rate appeal is filed. It becomes obvious to the accountant who views this situation that the facility cannot long survive.

Given the fact that the facility is probably needed, there will then be a "war" between the "rate people" and the "quality people." The quality people say this facility is bad; we insist it be punished, so the rate people lower rates. But then the rate people say this facility has to remain viable; we have to find a way to grant a rate appeal to raise its rate back up to a level where they can provide acceptable care. And we have the administrative dog chasing its tail.

Imposing Prospective Rates Retroactively

What is happening with the question of imposing prospective rates retroactively? Let me give you an example of what happened in New York State. In 1975, we had, as many of you may know, something of a scandal in nursing homes. The result of this public interest in the system was a series of new laws designed to affect the state's rate-setting methodology. On the date appointed for the promulgation of the 1976 rates, November 1, 1975, the Commissioner of Health was forced to issue a letter to all facilities which in effect said that the state had not had time to implement the law passed by the legislature. The letter went on to say that since the state had not had an opportunity to develop acceptable statistical data, the rates promulgated at that time were interim and tentative. Lo and behold, they were identical to the 1975 rates. So for the year 1976, 1975 rates were enacted without change. The letter to the facilities states clearly that the rates promulgated were *interim* rates. The facilities billed and operated on the basis of these interim rates for a period of ten months. On November 1, 1976, about the time that the 1977 rates were due, the state came out with a press release and attached to it was a folder containing revised rates for residential health care facilities—prospective rates, computed according to 1976 methodology. These rates were put into effect retroactive to January 1, 1976.

Well, needless to say, litigation quickly erupted over this action. Some, about one third, of the facilities came out very well. They discovered, for example, that their 1975 rate had been $34 while their 1976 rate, as recomputed, was, say, $37. Accordingly, these facilities were owed money for the ten months they had been providing care at the old rates.

For the majority of facilities, however, the 1976 rates, computed as a result of the new methodology, were lower than the 1975 rates (largely as a result of changes in the capital cost system). A lawsuit was filed, asserting that it was unconstitutional and a violation of the reasonable cost statutes to impose a retroactive cut on rates after services had already been rendered. The Supreme Court in Albany County agreed with the providers, but the Appellate Division reversed. The Court of Appeals, in a very brief and non-illuminating opinion, upheld the right of the state to retroactively revoke a rate and promulgate a lower rate, provided that notice is given that the earlier rate was tentative and interim. (See *Kaye v. Whalen.*)

The *Kaye* experience is instructive because, as cost control spreads and other changes are implemented by HEW, states could be required to change their state plans—and many states may be tempted to change them retroactively. When this happens, bear in mind that the New York Court of Appeals has held that it can be done, provided there is notification at the beginning of the rate period that the rate being promulgated is tentative and subject to this kind of adjustment.

Appeals Process in New York

Another item on my agenda is a description of the appeals process. All nursing home cost reports are subject to audit. New York State has been relatively selective in recent years as to which providers are audited, although proprietaries are usually prime candidates. The procedure is as follows: First, the state goes in and does an initial audit. After the initial audit is completed, there is a conference at which the field auditor sits down and discusses with the provider the adjustments that will be made. If the provider objects to any of these adjustments, he has the right to request what is called a "bureau review," performed by an administrative staff composed of auditors independent from the auditors who did the field audit. These review auditors will look at the paper documentation submitted by the facility. They will also have extensive conversations with the field auditor who made the audit, and they tend to rely upon that field auditor's interpretation in resolving the complaint of the provider. At the conclusion of this "bureau review," if the provider is still not satisfied, he is entitled to a formal hearing. At the formal hearing, attorneys can be present, a record is made, cross-examination of the auditors is allowed—it is a full, on-the-record hearing very much akin to the post-determination hearing for provider agreements under Title XVIII.

The problem in New York State is, how does one get such a hearing? The requests are backlogged and the state lacks sufficient lawyers, hearing officers and auditors to handle the number of hearings that are requested. So, there is a tremendous problem there, and very often, of course, justice delayed is justice denied.

At the conclusion of the hearing, a recommended decision is made and court review is permitted. This system is probably similar to systems in effect in most states, with perhaps one important exception—i.e., many states do not have full evidentiary hearings. I would suggest to you, however, if your state does not presently have a full evidentiary, on-the-record hearing, this is the wave of the future.

QUESTIONS AND ANSWERS

Galen Powers: Jerry, one of the things that bothers me with this whole problem of government reimbursement of these facilities is that we don't seem to know very much about the effects of these different systems. I was wondering if any conclusions have been drawn about the effects of New York's abandoning the fair rental system and substituting its system for property reimbursement. Did the number of beds go up or down? Did the costs rise at a faster pace? Did ownership turn over faster? How does the state feel about the merits of what it accomplished by that change?

Jerome T. Levy: The state, at this point, is satisfied with the change away from fair rental, but it is really too early to tell since the system only went into effect approximately one year ago. (It went into effect with the January 1978 rates.) It is too early to tell what the actual long-term effects will be.

For example, we can't really judge whether there has been a slackening of closure of proprietary facilities because of the fair rental system's repeal. The one thing that was clear about the fair rental system was that it resulted, in many cases, in an inadequate reimbursement of debt service. It was, therefore, not a matter of stopping windfall. Rather, it was clear that the facilities had obligations to institutional lenders that were not being met. Some 47% of the facilities that were under the fair rental system received an amount which, even when the supposed return on equity was included, did not equal the amount of their present debt service. The reason for that was not always the result of what people sometimes call "venal overmortgaging." It resulted from the fact that the mortgages were for shorter periods, and therefore had a quicker payback than 40 years. Also, where a facility had been in existence for awhile, its depreciated base was so low that if it acquired a perfectly legitimate 80% fair market value mortgage, the amount of amortization just plain exceeded the fair rental calculation. So, about 50% of the facilities were not being reimbursed adequately.

I think that the change would not have come about by virtue of the pressure from the nursing home industry alone. I believe that the interest group that tipped the balance in this was the savings banks in New York State. Savings banks were very concerned because they were very heavily invested in this industry. Without savings bank pressure and, let's say, explanation of the issues to the state legislature, I doubt very much that we would have had the kind of change that we ultimately got.

The system that we have now didn't intend to continue with this cardinal principle of not paying for a facility more than once and at the same time insuring that a legitimately constructed financing arrangement can be paid off. It is really too early to tell, though, whether it will stop providers from going out of business. It has not, because the reimbursement is always based on historical costs, remedied the evil of the unmarketability of nursing homes. This continues to be a problem. The state has been lucky—most nursing homes are single-use buildings and cannot readily be used for anything else. But, there are situations, as out in a desirable section of Long Island where a facility was turned into a reducing salon, that may be repeated in other parts of the state. There is discussion in Manhattan now of converting some nursing homes into apartment hotels. If this happens, we may see a very serious shortage of beds—it's a possibility.

Alan Schachter: On January 1, 1975, the Office of the Special Prosecutor for Health in New York State was formed. I know that there are Medicare and Medicaid fraud units being established throughout the country. I am wondering if you can give us some insight into how that office affected the Health Department in terms of (1) the appeals process; (2) the interchange between the fraud unit and the Health Department; and (3) the audit procedures. I think it would be interesting to find out how the special prosecutor impacted your office in those areas.

Levy: This is a very difficult question to answer because there are a lot of nuances involved. Obviously, the Health Department was a rate-setting agency and also the standards-and-quality agency, but not the single state agency. We had responsibilities for procedures for dealing with audits and for dealing with settlement of civil suits, if necessary. The existence of the Office of the Special Prosecutor to some extent created a duplicative structure, and the problems were largely what you might call "intragovernmental tensions"—the kinds of things that exist when different agencies are set up with similar purposes in mind.

The Office of Special Prosecutor, as it started off, had the vigor that many young agencies have, and it was not prepared to see some of the problems that existed in making audits and in making determinations on civil recovery. There were differing methodologies with respect to how an audit was to be made. This naturally created an amount of tension between the auditors. Disagreements would result as to whether a particular item of claimed cost was allowable.

There was a memorandum of understanding signed very early where OSP and the Health Department attempted to carve up the area and times of audits, with certain years being done by the special prosecutor and certain years being done by the Health Department. This, however, didn't work because when the Office of Special Prosecutor got interested in a case, it would decide that it had to do all the audits for that provider. The Health Department was either forced to give up the books that it had for those years or, what was more often the case, OSP got the books first and then wouldn't release them to the Health Department. I don't believe that these problems have gone away.

As the more obvious instances of fraud are disposed of, the OSP is starting to get into things that it probably never intended to get into. OSP appears to be getting more and more involved in what I would regard as ongoing programmatic auditing functions. In my view, the way the federal government has seized upon the model of an Office of Special Prosecutor, first for HEW itself (the Office of Inspector General), and then encouraging it in other states, is only going to create more duplication and HEW is going to end up underwriting, with federal Medicaid dollars, the cost of two agencies doing the same thing.

Schachter: Another question I have deals with new institutions. In New York State, as an example, a start-up facility, one that goes into operation, say, this year (particularly in the Level 2, ICF health-related facility area), experiences a relatively low occupancy rate and usually has, for the first year, a substantial operating loss. In New York State, reimbursement is based on the assumption of a 90% occupancy rate, with no methodology for recouping these costs that are subject to low occupancy. In some states, however (Vermont, for example), there is a methodology for recouping some of these low-occupancy-type costs. My question is (1) What was the thinking of the state in establishing that rule? and (2) Is there any movement towards recognizing total cost when the low occupancy is not due to the provider but is due to the economic situation involved?

Levy: I can't answer the first part of the question because I wasn't involved in the decision. When I began working for the state, the decision had already been made not to recognize the start-up costs that were attributable to low occupancy.

At times, it has been suggested that these costs should be allowed. There are problems, though, practically speaking, in defining for what period you are going to allow them. A facility should not be permitted to delay its filling-up beyond the optimum point. A facility should be encouraged to reach the 90% occupancy level as quickly as possible.

When the state starts agreeing to pay certain other costs, in advance of reaching the 90% occupancy level, you run into substantial problems. Suppose the facility doesn't reach that level for four years because it knows it is getting some kind of additional factor built onto its rates during the period that it is under 90%? (This is related to the question of volume adjustment, which is probably more seriously debated in the hospital setting than in the nursing home setting.) One of the serious questions that the state is reckoning with, but doesn't have a good answer for yet, is how to deal with the costs when the occupancy runs below the suggested level.

Audience: My question deals with the system of capital reimbursement. You stated that because of the system, many facilities became unmarketable and, eventually, trustees and executors may become the operators of a facility. However, New York has a regulation that prohibits trustees from qualifying as operators. If that regulation is upheld and the trustees must then liquidate the facilities at a potentially large loss, do you think they would have a right of action against the state for an involuntary conversion?

Levy: To give you a very simple answer, I think it would be worth a try. I don't think, though, that you are going to see that happen (i.e., liquidation) in any large number of cases. What's going to happen is that the practicality of the situation will force a change in the system—as it did in destroying fair rental in New York. (The fact that 47% of the facilities were not being reimbursed for their current mortgage payments forced a change.) I think in this situation as well, there will have to be a change in the system. In New York, there are presently rumblings within various parts of the state machinery to deal with this severe problem. The executive is pushing for legislation to change the system to allow for fair market value purchases under certain circumstances.

I should explain that in New York a publicly-owned corporation may not operate a hospital or nursing home. The nursing homes are either closely-held corporations, individual proprietorships, or partnerships. You then have a situation where, if an individual proprietor or a partner dies, a testamentary trust is supposed to take title to the facilities. There is, however, this regulation you mentioned that prohibits operation of a facility by a fiduciary, and you come up with what might be regarded as a "Catch-22" situation. A legal void is created in terms of who in fact is the appropriate operator of that facility. It is happening in one or two cases around the state now. When it happens in half a dozen or a dozen, the state will have to sit up and listen. There will have to be some changes.

We may see a situation where the legislative remedy enacted in New York may have a number of problems getting approval, if HEW is serious about including, as a requirement for acceptable state plans, some kind of depreciation recapture or some kind of variation of the fair market value concept. New York State may be retreating from this system at just about the time HEW is imposing it.

71

Medicare-Medicaid Federal Program Operations

STEPHANIE W. NAIDOFF

When Robert Benchley was a student at Harvard he took a course in international law. The final examination confronted him with a question something like this: "Discuss the arbitration of the international fisheries problem with respect to hatcheries protocol and dragnet and trawl procedure as it affects (a) the point of view of the United States and (b) the point of view of Great Britain." Benchley, who had not studied, was somewhat desperate, and wrote as follows: "I know nothing about the point of view of Great Britain in the arbitration of the international fisheries problem, and nothing about the point of view of the United States. Therefore, I shall discuss the question from the point of view of the fish."

Today I would like to discuss long term care from a different perspective, that of an HEW Regional Attorney.

Some of you may not even know we exist; many of you probably are not fully aware of what Regional Attorneys do. But all of you should get to know us. The Office of the Regional Attorney is a valuable source of information and assistance for health lawyers and their clients.

HEW is an umbrella to a number of important agencies; the Social Security Administration, Health Care Financing Administration, Public Health Service and Office of Education are the most familiar. The Office of General Counsel provides all legal advice and representation to these HEW components with certain exceptions, primarily in extensive trial cases and some appellate work which is done by the Department of Justice.

The Office of General Counsel, headquartered in Washington, D.C., has a division for each of HEW's principal operating components (for example, the Health Care Finance/Human Development Services Division, the Public Health Service Division, the Food and Drug Division, the Education Division, the Civil Rights Division, etc.) and divisions dealing with administrative areas such as Regulation Review and Business and Administrative Law.

HEW Regional Attorney

The Office of General Counsel also has an office headed by a Regional Attorney in each of its regional centers. Our office in Philadelphia is one of those. We have twenty-one attorneys, reflecting the size of Region III, which covers the mid-Atlantic states. It encompasses Pennsylvania, Maryland, Delaware, Virginia, West Virginia, and the District of Columbia. Our region represents 12% of the nation's population squeezed into about 4% of its land area, and has a disproportionately large share of health care providers. Our HEW client agencies handle certification and reimbursement for 3,000 health care providers and suppliers, including more than 1,200 extended care facilities. The size of our workload in this area is constantly growing, and our style has been changing as well.

Although Regional Attorneys once acted as "solicitors" do in the British system, working with the Department of Justice and the United States Attorneys as their "barristers," we have pressed rather successfully in the past several years to present oral arguments and conduct much of our own litigation. In addition, we have been emphasizing preventive legal practice, and have been heavily involved in program advice, coordination, and resolution of disputes between program staff and the provider community.

Health Care Financing Administration

The major client I want to talk to you about is the Health Care Financing Administration, which was created in March 1977. It is primarily composed of four components: Medicare, Medicaid, Program Integrity, and Health Standards and Quality.

The Health Standards and Quality Bureau: Under the reorganization of health functions, some Medicare functions belonging to the Bureau of Health Insurance and some long term care functions belonging to the Office of Long Term Care Standards Enforcement were shifted to the Health Standards and Quality Bureau. This bureau is primarily responsible for the monitoring and review of survey and certification functions for Medicare and Medicaid.

In most states, there is a state survey agency, usually the Health Department, to which survey responsibility and certification recommendation authority for Medicare providers are delegated by the Secretary. But the final authority for certification of all Medicare providers and for all joint Medicare-Medicaid facilities resides with HEW.

For Medicaid facilities, the state survey agency relays its recommendation to the state welfare agency which is responsible for the administration of that joint federal-state program.

In both cases, HSQ professional staffers conduct validation surveys to ensure that federal standards are properly and uniformly applied by state surveyors. In this area, the Regional Attorney staff advises on both program and procedural issues, and reviews proposed termination or non-renewal files to determine the sufficiency of the evidence. We are also responsible for presenting the Department's case at the provider's administrative hearing, and for defending that hearing decision in federal district court, if necessary.

The *Town Court* cases, with which many of you are familiar, were handled in our office. In *Town Court,* 586 F.2d 280 (3rd Cir. 1978), we attempted to decertify a skilled nursing facility in Pennsylvania which participated in both Medicare and Medicaid. A complaint was filed by the provider and some patients challenging that termination action as violative of their due process rights since it was effective prior to the administrative hearing on the merits of the decertification.

After protracted district court and circuit court proceedings, the Third Circuit Court of Appeals ruled that the provider had no right to a prior hearing, since the procedures already provided—such as the exit interview, statement of deficiencies and plan of correction, and reconsideration—were sufficient to protect the provider's interests. However, the court ruled that since termination is tantamount to an order of transfer, Medicaid *patients* have a right to be heard on conditions in the facility and on whether transfer is in their best interests.

This decision, which we understand is being appealed to the United States Supreme Court by the Commonwealth of Pennsylvania, presents numerous problems for HEW and for the state survey and Medicaid agencies. For example:

On what conditions are the patients to be heard and what weight should their comments be given?

Are their comments on such matters as Life Safety Code compliance or medical records requirements relevant since most C/Ps require professional medical or engineering judgments?

Are their comments on nursing care controlling?

What weight should be given to the opinion of one patient over another?

How are they to be consulted?

What if a patient is incompetent?

The list goes on and on.

HSQ also administers the Professional Standards Review Organization program. Some PSROs are already performing utilization reviews in long term care facilities, although full implementation of that program in the long term care setting is some time off. We have rendered program advice, relating, for example, to questions of a PSRO's continuing participation in the program, and have engaged in defensive litigation in this area. We also expect some role in the administrative processing of appeals from PSRO denials.

One of our recent PSRO cases involves a Freedom of Information Act request by a hospital provider for all PSRO records on delegation of review to other hospital providers. This came on the heels of another case, *Public Citizen Health Research Group,* 449 F. Supp. 937 (D.D.C. 1978), which raised the question of whether a PSRO is a federal "agency" within the meaning of the Freedom of Information Act. This was decided in the affirmative last year in the District Court for the District of Columbia; the case is now before the District of Columbia Court of Appeals.

Other interesting Freedom of Information Act issues we have faced include whether survey reports or provider cost reports must be released under the Freedom of Information Act.

The Medicare Bureau: Since the reorganization of the health care components of HEW, the Medicare Bureau's primary responsibility is handling provider reimbursement through its contracts with fiscal intermediaries and carriers. Our staff renders advice on program issues, participates in the preparation of civil fraud actions, and conducts litigation, including overpayment recovery actions.

A description of some specific issues we have been involved in may be of interest to you. In one case, *Langhorne Gardens,* 371 F. Supp. 1216 (E.D. Pa. 1974), a provider of services had established an outpatient physical therapy service program in a series of nursing homes throughout Pennsylvania and Maryland. The provider had contracted with several physical therapists to provide these services; however, the services were being provided in such volume that in most cases an assistant actually performed them while the physical therapist was not present in the facility and was not supervising the assistant.

Pursuant to an administrative hearing decision on the issue, the absence of the physical therapist was held not controlling since the requirement that the therapist be on the premises when the services were rendered was set out in the Health Insurance Manual, but not in the regulations or statute. The case resulted in the remedial action of an amendment to the Medicare regulations requiring the presence of a physical therapist on the premises when the services are rendered in order to be reimbursed under the Medicare program.

Still another area in which questions are presented to us is that of assignments—whether an assignment of Medicare accounts payable by a provider is permitted. Of course, since the passage of the Medicare-Medicaid Anti-Fraud and Abuse Amendments, assignments have been even more strictly limited, but we have just recently been faced with a case which raises an interesting assignment matter: *North East Emergency Medical Services,* C.A. No. 79-581 (E.D. Pa.). This company contracts with hospitals to provide physicians for emergency room services. We recently advised them that we could not reimburse them for their services—that payment had to be made directly to the physicians. North East sought a temporary restraining order (TRO) to prevent our implementing this decision but withdrew it when we agreed to postpone our decision for one month.

Another class of questions posed to us involves change of ownership of long term care facilities and whether a particular transaction constitutes a change of ownership. New regulations have been proposed at 44 F.R. 6958 (2/15/79) which will address this and coordinate the disparate approaches taken until now by Medicare and Medicaid. But in recent years we have been asked by Medicare to consider other ownership changes such as the sale of assets by one chain to another, lease-purchase agreements, and the creation of new corporations by the principals of the old owner. Each case is determined on its own facts and on general principles of local corporate law.

We have also recently dealt with the problem of the Medicare concept of certified *beds.* The Medicare statute speaks of certified facilities, not beds, except for the concept of the Medicare distinct-part skilled nursing facility. But Medicare has traditionally operated with a concept of certified *beds.* If a provider has a distinct part of its facility certified for Medicare purposes, Medicare patients may only be placed in beds that are located in the Medicare-certified part of the facility.

We have recently discovered several situations where providers have placed patients, either purposefully or inadvertently, in uncertified beds and then charged the Medicare program for services provided to these patients. It is our position that these services are not covered by the Medicare program and they result in overpayments to the provider which must be recovered by Medicare when the cost report is finalized.

In a related area concerning Medicare beds, we have recently approved the concept of dually certified Medicare/Medicaid facilities. In other words, a single facility may fully qualify as both a Medicare/Medicaid SNF as well as a Medicaid ICF. The basic concept is that the entire facility meets both the SNF and ICF requirements for participation and, therefore, when and if a patient's level of care requirement changes from skilled to intermediate, there is no need to move that patient from one bed to the other, as is usually the case. This concept will be a key one in the State of Maryland's new reclassification of nursing homes, which I will mention again later.

We also defend the decisions of the Provider Reimbursement Review Board at the district court level. Issues arising in the cases handled by our office include reimbursement of legal fees and malpractice insurance premiums, and, of course, cases dealing with recapture of accelerated depreciation. One pending Board review matter (*Oakmont,* C.A. No. 78-563 (W.D. Pa.)), dealing with recapture of accelerated depreciation involves an interesting case of decreased Medicare utilization. The decrease in utilization resulted from the intermediary's decision to include in earlier cost years certain "waiver of liability" days, thus inflating the provider's utilization rate in that year but causing a decreased utilization in the subsequent year, which triggered an action to recapture the accelerated depreciation.

In other PRRB matters, an interesting conflict has arisen with respect to treatment of administrative and general (A&G) costs. In *Goodluck Nursing Home,* Medicare and Medicaid Guide (CCH) ¶29,450 (D.D.C. 1978), the court reversed the Board and held that legal fees directly resulting from Medicare program participation can be charged 100% to Medicare and not spread with other A&G costs. This approach is in interesting contrast to that taken by the Board in *Mercy General Hospital,* 410 F. Supp. 344 (D. Mich. 1975), in which it held that a hospital's malpractice settlement, relating to an incident which occurred long before the inception of Medicare, could be included in the A&G cost center and spread so that Medicare would absorb a share of the costs.

Another interesting PRRB case in our region is the *Beverly Enterprises* group appeal on the issue of allocation of standby costs, where utilization in the noncertified parts of facilities is significantly higher than that in the certified parts. In that case, the Board required allocation on a patient-days basis rather than on a square footage basis. (See 446 F. Supp. 599 (D.D.C. 1978); 432 F. Supp. 1073 (D.D.C. 1976).)

The Medicaid Bureau: I should first point out that providers have less contact with the Department in this area because the Medicaid program is administered primarily by the states. In our monitoring of a state's performance, however, several serious long term care problem areas have been uncovered.

The failure of some states to survey and issue provider agreements in a timely fashion has plagued us, since the Medicaid statute prohibits payment of the federal share absent a valid provider agreement. That problem reached critical proportions in Pennsylvania and resulted in HEW bringing suit against the Commonwealth of Pennsylvania for failure to conduct adequate or timely Life Safety Code surveys. After several years of litigation, we entered into a consent order under which the state is bound to specific timetables for conducting its survey activities. Under the terms of this agreement, Life Safety Code surveys of skilled nursing facilities should be completed far enough in advance of provider agreement expiration dates to allow for proper evaluation of the surveys by HEW as well as timely notice to the facility concerning any enforcement action.

Regulations have recently been proposed to solve another serious problem area, that of Medicaid payments to an extended care facility pending appeal of its decertification. The proposed regulations, and indeed the present ones, would allow federal matching payments for thirty days after the expiration of the provider agreement. But the recent regulations are new in that they will *require* a state to provide a hearing before a facility may be terminated from the Medicaid program, and they will give the state the option of conducting the hearing within the time span of four months before the expiration of the provider agreement or four months after.

Several states in our region have been particularly disturbed by our position that we will not pay federal financial participation pending the appeal beyond thirty days after the expiration of the provider agreement—in the face of this requirement which condones the providing of a hearing up to *four* months after the expiration of the agreement. These states have been compelled by state law and state court decisions to continue paying the nursing homes, pending the appeal decision, out of 100% state funds.

A related area of activity for us is that of hearings before the Grant Appeals Board. When HEW discovers a situation where a state has put in claims for federal financial participation (FFP) for nursing homes undergoing an appeal beyond the thirty-day limit, we have disallowed these monies, requiring repayment.

When we disallow FFP in this manner, the state agency has the right to request reconsideration of the decision, followed by a hearing before the Department's Grant Appeals Board, and ultimately obtaining review in federal district court. Presently, there are several hundred disallowances pending nationally on a wide variety of issues. Thus, while a nursing home may be unaware of it and unaffected by it, protracted proceedings may be going on between the state agency and HEW over federal Medicaid reimbursements to the facility.

Perhaps the most controversial provider-related aspect of Medicaid today is the alternative reimbursement and reasonable-cost-related reimbursement schemes being proposed, attacked, and defended in various forums.

We have been involved with the Department's consideration of several of these. As I mentioned earlier, we have been working closely with the State of Maryland, since it has established a new classification system for nursing homes based mainly on its cost-related reimbursement plan for SNFs and ICFs. Maryland has, in effect, established a three-tiered system of nursing home care under the Medicaid program by establishing a so-called "super-skilled" level of care. Under the reasonable-cost-related legislation, this would be reimbursed at a higher level than Medicare skilled care due to the intensity of care provided. Maryland also has a comprehensive care rate, which includes both skilled care and intermediate care.

Initially, we believed that Maryland was establishing Medicaid conditions of participation which were higher than the Medicare standards. This would, under Section 1864 of the Act, require Medicare to adopt the same higher conditions. In the alternative, it appeared that Maryland was establishing different levels of skilled care in the Medicare and Medicaid programs, which is prohibited by the statute. After much negotiation, Maryland agreed to amend its regulations to establish a uniform definition of skilled nursing care for both the Medicare and Medicaid programs and to assure the access of all Medicaid patients to skilled nursing facility services in the state.

Another of the few tools we have to assure quality care in nursing homes participating in the Medicare and Medicaid programs is the use of the so-called "look behind" provision of the Medicaid regulations at 42 C.F.R. §442.30. Under this provision, if the state survey agency fails to follow the proper procedures for surveying and certifying nursing homes or fails to apply the proper standards for determining compliance, HEW may "look behind" the state's determination and make its own determination as to whether the nursing home qualifies to participate in the Medicaid program.

Again, however, HEW's remedy is against the state. If the Regional Office personnel determine, with the concurrence of the Regional Attorney's Office that the nursing facility does not meet the program requirements, federal matching payments to the state are terminated for that facility and improper payments are recouped. Again, the state has a right to reconsideration, a Grant Appeals Board hearing, and record review in federal district court.

The Office of Program Integrity. This HCFA component is responsible for the investigation and prosecution of Medicare and Medicaid fraud and abuse. You all know, I'm sure, of the initiatives established by the President and the Secretary to root out fraud, abuse, waste and error in the HEW programs.Our goal is to eliminate unnecessary expenditures amounting to $2.5 billion. Directing our energies and our efforts to this goal has resulted in a tremendous increase in activity in the regional investigative offices.

The Regional Attorney offices are beginning to participate more frequently in the development of these criminal and civil fraud cases, as well as the exclusion process under Section 1862 (d) and (e) of the Social Security Act. In our office, for example, we currently have several exclusion cases pending, one of which is particularly thorny since it involves a provider who was convicted, but *before* the effective date of this provision. In another interesting exclusion case, one of my colleagues is grappling with the question of how to proceed where the provider's conviction has been expunged under state law.

In both instances, we are proceeding under Section 1862 (d)—the intent-to-defraud provision—rather than the newer route of subsection (e), the criminal-conviction section. We also expect to work with the Program Integrity staff in the development of penalty cases under Sections 1877 and 1909 of the Act and in examining certain arrangements that raise questions under the kickback provision. I might also mention here that we are involved in assisting the Bureau—and some private attorneys as well—in examining certain possible conflict-of-interest situations. One involved an arrangement where the members of the board of a provider group were also doing business with the individual facilities.

Thus, while the Program Integrity people can and have historically worked directly with the Department of Justice, it is now becoming an area in which the Regional Attorneys are playing more of a role.

Other HEW Agencies

While HCFA is one of the Regional Attorney's major clients and certainly the HEW agency most directly relevant to the concerns of lawyers attending this conference, long term care questions also come to us from other HEW agencies; I would like to describe some of those to you.

Public Health Service: The Public Health Service's regional activity centers around the administration of grants, and only one major area significantly affects long term care providers. That area, as those of you who have proposed construction of new facilities must know, is, of course, health planning. Under Section 1122 of the Social Security Act, added in 1972, Medicare and Medicaid reimbursement for costs related to capital expenditures in excess of $100,000 is available only if those capital expenditures have been approved by state and local health planning agencies. These agencies were restructured by P.L. 93-641 into a series of local health systems agencies, together with state health planning and development agencies.

Although the federal role in Section 1122 approval is limited to insuring that prescribed review procedures have been followed, we also engage in legal advice on the broader health planning issues such as HSA governing board composition, and have been responsible for defending the Department in several major pieces of health planning litigation, including the pending case involving the Southeastern Pennsylvania HSA, and another matter, *Wilmington United Neighborhoods,* 458 F. Supp. 628 (D.Del. 1978), which challenged the Department's Section 1122 policies.

Certificate of need: We also review proposed state legislation on the certificate of need program. All states must have such legislation in place soon or face loss of substantial federal funding. Although the Hill-Burton program was replaced by a new construction assistance program in P.L. 93-641, we are also engaged in significant activity relating to monitoring compliance with the uncompensated care and community service assurances

81

made by recipients of Hill-Burton assistance over the past twenty-five years.

The Office of Human Development Services: This office administers the Older Americans Act of 1965, recent amendments to which will impact on the provision of long term care in the future. The amendments fund state long term care ombudsmen and legal services for the elderly, and provide for a variety of studies of alternatives to institutional care for the elderly. (See P.L. 95-478 (Oct. '78).) Many of you know the *Pennhurst* case, 446 F. Supp 1295 (E.D. Pa. 1977), which arose in our region and which has prompted this office—OHD—and ours, working with HCFA and others, to consider with particular urgency the problem of de-institutionalization.

Another OHD area in which the Regional Attorneys have played an important role is the development of government-wide regulations on age discrimination. The 1975 amendments to the Older Americans Act contain the Age Discrimination Act. This directed HEW to develop regulations for use by all government departments in rooting out age discrimination in any program or service that receives federal financial assistance.

This past December, in response to this mandate, HEW issued its proposed regulations. (The delay was caused by the need to await the findings of the Civil Rights Commission study on the scope and extent of age discrimination in federal programs.) These HEW proposed regulations have recently been the subject of ten public hearings across the country, conducted by the Regional Attorneys, intended to solicit comments and views on our approach to the implementation of the Age Discrimination Act. Working with the General Counsel's Staff, we will now consider the suggestions we received and issue final regulations by July of this year. Efforts to root out age discrimination in federal programs will then really get underway.

Regional Office of Facilities, Engineering and Construction: The Regional Engineer and his staff play an important role with respect to long term care providers since they are responsible for recommending granting or denial of Life Safety Code waivers for Medicare and Medicaid facilities. One specific problem we've had to deal with is the failure of the Medicaid regulations to provide for any administrative appeal of Life Safety Code waiver denials to facilities participating in the Medicaid program only. In recognition of this problem, we have developed an *ad hoc* hearing procedure that provides for a hearing before an Administrative Law Judge. This general procedure was upheld in *Case v. Weinberger,* 523 F.2d 602 (2nd Cir. 1975).

An interesting and related development is the proposed "point" system for evaluating the safety of buildings under the Life Safety Code, which will make the process somewhat more objective and precise.

Another ROFEC matter in which we are involved is a case in litigation in Pittsburgh. In this case, we are providing a ROFEC employee as an expert witness on the Life Safety Code of 1967 for a hospital which has sued its architects because of the hospital's failure to meet LSC requirements. The hospital was one of innovative design. It opened in 1974 and applied to the Regional Office for Medicare and Medicaid participation. The Department determined that the hospital did not meet the requirements of the LSC and, therefore, could not participate in the programs unless a sprinkler system was installed throughout the building.

The hospital reacted vigorously since its architects had apparently assured them that the building could meet the LSC. They sued us over our decision and obtained a TRO. However, when the court indicated that it would not issue a preliminary injunction, the hospital reluctantly agreed to install the sprinkler system, in return for HEW's providing an expert witness who would testify to our position on the Life Safety Code in a lawsuit brought by the hospital against the architects.

The Office for Civil Rights: OCR is responsible for enforcing the provisions of Title VI, Title IX and Section 504—the civil rights legislation relating to discrimination against minorities, women and the handicapped. As most of you know, each long term care facility that participates in Medicare and Medicaid must file an assurance with us that evidences the facility's agreement not to discriminate in the provision of services.

Much of the Department's activity in this area has been centered on discrimination in educational institutions—elementary and secondary schools and our nation's higher education facilities. But, increasingly, discrimination in health and social service institutions is receiving closer inspection and review.

Our office, for example, handled the compliance reviews and litigation involving Wilmington Medical Center. In that case, a group of Wilmington residents—minority and handicapped—attempted to block the efforts of the Medical Center to relocate to a suburban site. We performed a comprehensive review of the matter which resulted (after extensive negotiations over assurances we required of the Center) in a finding that the Center would be in compliance with the civil rights provisions. That finding was upheld by the district court, but is now on appeal to the Third Circuit.

Of specific interest to long term care providers are the questions on which OCR seeks our assistance involving admissions to nursing homes where the admissions policy results in no minority patients residing in the home. In one case, the facility was religiously affiliated and only accepted patients of that religious faith. In another case, we reviewed the admissions policy of a Masonic home, and still another involved a facility that refused to take Medicaid patients—both of which resulted in no minority patients.

We also have helped OCR in several Section 504 complaints involving handicapped individuals in long term care settings. One recent case involved a patient denied admission to a nursing home because the facility claimed it could not treat his particular illness. And, of course, I should mention the recent Fourth Circuit decision in *Trageser,* 590 F.2d 87 (4th Cir. 1978), a case involving the firing of a nursing home employee whose eyesight was failing. The district court had held that Medicare and Medicaid payments did not constitute "federal financial assistance" within the meaning of the civil rights provisions and thus refused to find jurisdiction under Section 504. The circuit court also ruled that there was no jurisdiction, but not because it found no federal financial assistance; it held that Section 504 simply does not cover discrimination in employment.

Conclusion

As you can see, in addition to HCFA, there is PHS, OHD, ROFEC and OCR—all pieces of the HEW long term care puzzle. The Regional Attorney works with all of them and can help you in your interaction with the Department on long term care issues. I invite and encourage you to use this resource. Following is a list of the names, addresses, and phone numbers of all the HEW Regional Attorneys. I offer that to you and want to leave you with the thought that I know my colleagues share—if we don't know the answer to your question, we'll try to find it; if we find more than one answer, you'll have your choice; and if HEW doesn't have an answer we'll offer you lots of sympathy and understanding.

Medicare-Medicaid Federal Program Operations

REGIONAL ATTORNEYS

U.S. Regional Attorney	Address	Phone	States in Region
I—Samuel C. Fish	Room 2407 JFK Federal Bldg. Boston, MA 02203	(617) 223-5843	CT, MA, NH, ME, RI, VT
II—Borge Varmer	Room 3914 26 Federal Plaza New York, NY 10007	(212) 264-4610	NY, NJ, PR, VI
III—Stephanie Naidoff	P.O. Box 13716 Philadelphia, PA 19101	(215) 596-1242	PA, DE, MD, DC, VA, WV
IV—Carl Harper	101 Marietta Tower Suite 201 Atlanta, GA 30323	(404) 242-2377	AL, GA, FL, KY, MS, TN, NC, SC
V—Marvin E. Gavin	300 S. Wacker Dr. 18th Floor Chicago, IL 60606	(312) 353-1640	IL, IN, MN, MI, OH, WI
VI—John Stokes	1200 Main Tower Suite 1330 Dallas, TX 75202	(214) 729-3465	AR, LA, MN, OK, TX
VII—Paul Cacioppo	Room 601 601 E. 12th St. Kansas City, MO 64106	(816) 758-3593	IA, KS, MO, NE
VIII—Ronald Ludemann	1961 Stout Street Room 1106 Federal Office Bldg. Denver, CO 80294	(303) 327-5101	CO, MT, ND, SD, UT, WY
IX—Sara Green	Room 420 50 United Nations Plaza San Francisco, CA 94102	(415) 556-5642	AZ, CA, HI, NV
X—Andrew Young	M/S-624 Arcade Plaza Bldg. 1321 Second Ave. Seattle, WA 98101	(206) 399-0470	AK, ID, OR, WA

How to Conduct Your Own Equal Employment Opportunity Audit

JOHN ERICKSON

Let me first talk briefly about EEO audits in general and then turn to a particular consideration of audit selection procedures. EEO auditing deals with accounting about people, as distinguished from accounting in other areas, particularly financial areas. I think this is a relatively new concept for employers—to have to work at an accounting system for personnel as well as their balance sheets.

The audit itself really has two aspects. The first involves figuring out which laws and regulations apply to the institution with which you are concerned. There are laws that apply to employers generally—for example, Title VII of the Civil Rights Act of 1964, the Equal Pay Act of 1963 (equal pay for equal work), and the Age Discrimination in Employment Act. Virtually all employers are going to have to contend with these statutes.

Title VII of the Civil Rights Act of 1964: Any company "engaged in an industry affecting commerce" and having 15 or more employees working each day in 20 or more work weeks during the current or preceding calendar year is subject to Title VII. Any company employing 15 or more employees will almost invariably have such a direct influence on interstate commerce as to "affect commerce" within the meaning of the Act.

Title VII states that it shall be an unlawful employment practice for an employer

- to fail or refuse to hire or discharge any individual or otherwise to discriminate against any individual with respect to his compensation, terms, conditions, or privileges of employment because of such individual's race, color, religion, sex, or national origin;
- to limit, segregate, or classify his employees or applicants for employ-

ment in any way which would deprive or tend to deprive any individual of employment opportunities or otherwise adversely affect his status as an employee because of such individual's race, color, religion, sex, or national origin;

- to discriminate against any individual because of his race, color, religion, sex, or national origin in admission to, or employment in, any program established to provide apprenticeship or other training;
- to discriminate against any of his employees because he has opposed any practice made an unlawful employment practice by the Act, or because he had made a charge, testified, assisted, or participated in any manner in an investigation, proceeding, or hearing under the Act; or
- to print or publish any notice or advertisement relating to employment by an employer indicating any preference, limitation, specification, or discrimination based on race, color, religion, sex, or national origin (except that such a notice or advertisement may indicate a preference, limitation, specification, or discrimination based on religion, sex, or national origin when religion, sex or national origin is a bona fide occupational qualification for employment).

Note that these provisions prohibit with equal force both unintentional discrimination and deliberate discriminatory practices. This fact was demonstrated in *United States v. Medical Society of South Carolina,* 298 F. Supp. 145 (D.S.C. 1969), where the health care employer recruited workers by word-of-mouth and usually hired relatives of current employees. The court found that this hiring system effectively limited the number of black workers, so that a Title VII violation resulted. Similarly, the courts have demanded strict compliance at all levels of an employer's business. Thus, even where upper management was believed to have treated workers fairly, a court found Title VII discrimination because management listened to complaints about an employee by his fellow workers which may have been racially motivated. *Anderson v. Methodist Evangelical Hospital,* 4 FEP Cases 33 (W.D. Ky. 1961) *aff'd.* 464 F.2d 723 (6th Cir. 1972).

It can truly be said, therefore, that if your company falls within the scope of the Act, Title VII imposes upon it a broad requirement to prevent, at every stage of the "employment experience," all discrimination because of race, color, religion, sex or national origin.

Equal Pay Act of 1963: Congress enacted the Equal Pay Act in 1963 as an amendment to the Fair Labor Standards Act (FLSA). Its coverage parallels that of the minimum wage and overtime provisions of the FLSA. Although employees working in a bona fide executive, administrative or professional capacity, or as outside salesmen, are specifically exempted from the FLSA's basic coverage, they are *not* exempt from coverage under the Equal Pay Act.

The Equal Pay Act prohibits differentials in wages based solely on sex. An employer violates the Act if he pays wages to employees of one sex in an establishment "at a rate less than the rate at which he pays wages to employees of the opposite sex in such establishment for equal work on jobs the performance of which requires equal skill, effort and responsibility, and which are performed under similar working conditions."

Jobs need not be identical in order to be equal, since the law requires only substantial equality. Thus, the courts have usually held that maids and porters perform equal work entitling each to equal pay. (See, e.g., *Brennan v. Anco Hospital,* _____F. Supp. _____ (S.D. Tex. 1973), where the court found that maids and porters each spent substantially all of their time doing routine cleaning.) On the other hand, some wage differences have been permitted with respect to female nurses' aides and male orderlies, though the case law is by no means consistent on the issue. Health care employers have claimed that only orderlies perform such tasks as lifting or subduing patients, setting up traction or catheterizing male patients. Where the employers have proved that their orderlies spent almost all of their time in such work, as in *Hodgson v. Golden Isles Nursing Home,* 468 F.2d 1256 (5th Cir. 1972), greater pay for the orderlies has been upheld. Otherwise, courts have found differing pay scales to be violative of the Equal Pay Act. (See, e.g., *Brennan v. Prince William Hospital,* 503 F.2d 282 (4th Cir. 1974), where the additional "heavy" tasks performed by the orderlies were only secondary to the primary job of patient care.)

Aside from permitting different wages for jobs requiring different skills, effort, or responsibility, the Equal Pay Act specifies exceptions to its general standard of equal wages for equal work, regardless of sex. Where it can be established that a differential in pay is a result of a wage payment made pursuant to a seniority system, a merit system, a system measuring earnings by quantity or quality of production, or that the differential is based on any factor other than sex, the differential will be allowed. Thus, wage differentials may be justified, even as between employees of opposite sexes performing equal work in jobs which meet the statutory tests of equal skill, effort and responsibility.

Courts have closely scrutinized the numerous attempts by employers to justify wage differentials based upon "factors other than sex." Consequently, employers must establish a true relationship between the asserted factor and the differential. Such relationships have been successfully proven with respect to bona fide training programs and temporary reassignments, but not for alleged differences in the costs of employing men and women and not for higher wages to heads of households. In any event, the fact that the "system" relied upon to justify a wage differential is not reduced to writing will not necessarily invalidate the system where the essential terms of the informal or unwritten system or plan being used have been communicated to the affected employees. The facts necessary to show that a wage differential falls within one of the exceptions are particularly within the knowledge of the employer, so he should be prepared to prove their existence.

Age Discrimination in Employment Act: The Age Discrimination in Employment Act (ADEA) covers employers who are engaged in an industry affecting commerce and employ 20 or more employees for each working day in each of 20 or more calendar weeks in the current or preceding calendar year.

As amended in 1978, the ADEA protects employees who are at least 40 but less than 70 years of age. It is unlawful under the Act for an employer

- to fail or refuse to hire or to discharge any individual or otherwise discriminate against any individual with respect to his compensation, terms, conditions, or privileges of employment because of such individual's age;
- to limit, segregate, or classify his employees in any way which would deprive or tend to deprive any individual of employment opportunities or otherwise adversely affect his status as an employee because of such individual's age;
- to reduce the wage rate of any employee in order to comply with the Act;
- to publish or cause to be published any notice or advertisement relating to employment by such employer indicating any preference, limitation, specification, or discrimination based on age;
- to require or permit the involuntary retirement of any individual under age 70 (phase-in dates for the application of this provision are specified in the Act); or
- to discriminate against any current or prospective employee because he has filed a charge, testified or participated in any ADEA proceeding.

A different upper age limit restriction is applicable to two categories of employees:

- Compulsory retirement at age 65 of employees working in the capacity of bona fide executives or in high policymaking positions who are entitled to pensions of at least $27,000 per year is permitted.
- Colleges and universities are permitted to require the retirement of their tenured employees at age 65 until July 1, 1982.

It is not unlawful for an employer to take an action otherwise prohibited by the Act (other than retaliation against current or prospective employees) where the difference in treatment is based on reasonable factors other than age. It was not the purpose of Congress in enacting the ADEA to require the employment of anyone who is disqualified on grounds other than age from performing a particular job. The reasonableness of a differentiation is determined on a case-by-case basis, not on the basis of any general or class concept, and unusual working conditions are given weight according to their individual merit.

Where age is a bona fide occupational qualification (BFOQ) reasonably necessary to the normal operation of the business, differentiations based on age are permissible under the Act. Whether a BFOQ is established will be determined on the basis of all the pertinent facts. The BFOQ defense is narrowly construed, and the burden of proof to establish it rests on the employer.

Physical fitness requirements reasonably necessary for the specific work to be performed which are uniformly applied may result in a differentiation based on factors other than age. However, a claim for a differentiation will not be permitted on the basis of an employer's assumption that every employee over a certain age in a particular type of job usually becomes physically unable to perform the duties of that job. Evaluation factors such as quantity or quality of production, or educational level, would be acceptable bases for differentiation when, in the individual case, such factors are shown to have a valid relationship to job requirements.

The ADEA permits employers to observe the terms of bona fide seniority systems or employee benefit plans which are not subterfuges to evade the purposes of the Act. Although a seniority system may be qualified by such factors as merit, capacity or ability, to be bona fide it must be based on length of service as the primary criterion. Unless the essential terms and conditions of the system have been communicated to the affected employees, it will not be regarded as bona fide.

An employer is not required to provide older workers who are otherwise protected by the law with the same pension, retirement or insurance benefits as are provided to younger workers, so long as any differential between them is in accordance with the terms of a bona fide benefit plan which is not a subterfuge to evade the purposes of the Act. A retirement, pension or insurance plan will be considered in compliance with the ADEA where the cost incurred in behalf of an older worker is equal to that incurred in behalf of a younger worker. Additionally, an employer may provide varying benefits under a bona fide plan to employees within the 40-70 age bracket, when such benefits are determined by a formula involving age and length-of-service requirements.

The 1978 amendments to the ADEA changed the law regarding involuntary retirement. Formerly, the Act authorized involuntary retirement irrespective of age, provided it was pursuant to the terms of a bona fide retirement or pension plan. In *United Air Lines v. McMann,* 16 FEP Cases 146 (1977), the Supreme Court ruled that a bona fide plan established before enactment of the ADEA under which the employer could compel retirement at age 60 was not a subterfuge to avoid the purposes of the Act and was lawful. The 1978 amendments to the ADEA had the effect of reversing the *McMann* decision. Thus, the ADEA now forbids the involuntary retirement of an employee below the age of 70 pursuant to the terms of a seniority system or employee benefit plan.

Special Obligations of Recipients of Federal Financial Assistance

There are also requirements that are particularly applicable to recipients of federal financial assistance—a category into which most long term health care providers fall. The principal equal employment obligations of recipients of federal financial assistance are set out in three statutes: Title VI of the Civil Rights Act of 1964, Section 504 of the Rehabilitation Act of 1973 and the Age Discrimination Act of 1975. Title VI prohibits discrimination based on race, color or national origin; Section 504 prohibits discrimination based on handicap; and the Age Discrimination Act prohibits discrimination based on age (without specifying any age limits for coverage). The operative language of the three statutes is identical, with the exception of the prohibited bases of discrimination:

> No person in the United States shall, [on the ground of race, color, national origin or age; or solely on the basis of handicap] be excluded from participation in, be denied the benefits of, or be subjected to discrimination under any program or activity receiving federal financial assistance.

Litigation under Title VI, Section 504 and the Age Discrimination Act has been relatively limited, so that many questions as to their application remain. One such question is their applicability to the employment practices of recipients of federal financial assistance. According to the Court of Appeals for the Fourth Circuit, a private action alleging employment discrimination under Section 504 may only be maintained where the primary objective of the federal financial assistance is to provide employment. See *Trageser v. Libbie Rehabilitation Center, Inc.,* 590 F.2d 87 (4th Cir. 1978). In this court's view, Medicare, Medicaid, and Veterans Administration reimbursements to providers were not designed to furnish employment. Nor did employment discrimination on the part of providers of these funds necessarily result in discrimination against patients. In the Fourth Circuit, therefore, health care employers cannot be sued under the above-mentioned financial assistance provisions, though Title VII and other equal employment laws may apply. Nevertheless, the *Trageser* case is not binding outside the Fourth Circuit, and the Supreme Court has not yet ruled. Hence, employers potentially subject to the financial assistance laws should be aware of their potential applicability to employment practices.

The statutes do not define "federal financial assistance," so that the regulations of each agency with respect to its programs should be consulted. The following definition contained in the regulations issued by the Department of Health, Education and Welfare in connection with the implementation of Section 504 is generally representative:

> "Federal financial assistance" means any grant, loan, contract (other than a procurement contract or a contract of insurance or guaranty), or any other arrangement by which the agency provides or otherwise makes available assistance in the form of:

(1) Funds;

(2) Services of Federal personnel; or

(3) Real or personal property or any interest in or use of such property, including:

    (i) Transfers or leases of such property for less than fair market value or for reduced consideration; and

    (ii) Proceeds from a subsequent transfer or lease of such property if the Federal share of its fair market value is not returned to the Federal Government.

Determining whether your institution is a recipient of federal financial assistance can sometimes be a difficult endeavor. The Justice Department is presently compiling a list of all federal financial assistance programs, but it is not anticipated that the list will be completed until next year. One point worth noting, however, is that in the government's view federal financial assistance can be received indirectly through another recipient. If payments are made to an individual which are dependent on that individual's participation in a particular program, the employer will be deemed to be receiving federal financial assistance. A common example of this is veteran's education payments. The "recipient" issue, too, is one on which the law is unclear.

State and local laws: You also have to contend with state and local laws. Too often overlooked, these are laws that tend to create unique problems. Many statutes and ordinances at the state and local level have prohibitions that extend beyond federal prohibitions. For example, in the District of Columbia, homosexuals are a protected group—discrimination against homosexuals is prohibited. Often there are more extensive remedies available under state and local laws. Also, you will find state and local laws accompanied by particular regulations in many areas. There are question and answer books showing what to ask an applicant, and what not to ask an applicant. Remember, if you don't look at the state and local laws, and focus entirely on federal laws, you are going to wind up caught behind the eight ball when some state person comes around.

Why An EEO Audit?

Once you have identified all the laws and regulations applicable to your company, the next step in the EEO audit is "suing yourself." Lawsuits aren't much fun, but what you have to do is take the position of a plaintiff's attorney. Look at all your employment practices, standards and procedures and decide where you are vulnerable. Having done that, having identified the problem areas, your next concern is what is your answer going to be? Why do you want to do this? Why do you need to find this answer? There are several reasons.

This conference alone is evidence of the fact that nowadays employers don't really run their own businesses. The government is running your business; other individuals are running your business. You can think of the equal employment opportunity laws as a government grievance procedure for employees, allowing an employee or rejected applicant or terminated person to complain about what's been done, to claim it was discriminatory. The right to complain is not limited to the individual harmed. For example, in certain circumstances, labor unions can file charges on behalf of employees. Civil rights groups can file charges on behalf of employees. One employee can file a charge on behalf of another employee. So there is always somebody looking over your shoulder as an employer, trying to tell you that you are going to have to do something that you don't want to do.

A second reason you should conduct one of these audits is to minimize your liability. A current advertisement pretty well explains the type of problems we have in this area. A mechanic is standing in front of two cars, saying one car is in to have the oil filter changed and the other car is in for a new engine. He extolls the virtues of a certain brand of oil filter and says at the end, "You can pay me now or pay me later."

That is really what we are talking about here. Either you figure this out for yourself, or some plaintiff is going to come along and figure it out for the institution. If he finds out what you are doing wrong, it can lead to back pay, attorneys' fees (not only the fees for the institution but also for the plaintiff), and the possibility of an additional damage award, depending upon the statute being used. There is an indirect cost of the litigation—since the court can tell you what to do, somebody else can wind up running your personnel function. That can have financial ramifications. Those of you who read the article about AT&T in a recent issue of *Fortune* magazine (January 15, 1979) saw that their top management felt that as a result of the consent decree they were operating under, their costs were increased. This stemmed from the fact they were not always able to place the person best qualified to do the job in the job. *Note*—there were real financial considerations involved in noncompliance.

A final rationale for the EEO audit is that if you are an employer, or if you represent employers, you must have an innate feeling that you and your clients are not bad people and, in fact, if they can figure out what it is that the law requires in this area, they will do it. Today, most enlightened employers feel that advancing minorities and women in employment is an important part of their business.

Objectives of the EEO Audit

There are several objectives in doing any audit. One is to figure out if you are not doing something you should be doing. This is usually pretty simple. The statutes in this area are going to be worried about simple things—like posting notices.

More important is identifying problems with things you are already doing. Are you doing something that is unlawful? This requires an overall review.

If you identify problems, you have to figure out what to do with them. Look at them prospectively and retrospectively. You may conclude that for the last five years your client or institution could have been discriminating against some particular group of people. What are you going to do about that? Well, one thing you can do is pay them; but not many people do that. Another thing you can do is determine what the limitations period is going to be and decide whether you are going to just try to wait it out. Still another alternative is to try to stop the discrimination at that point in time so that liability doesn't accrue into the future.

Another objective of the audit is to figure out how you can respond to lawsuits. If you have ever been involved in a Title VII case, you know that you usually get a set of questions asking you everything that has ever happened to any of your people over the last ten years. The embarrassing thing is that the judge may order you to answer the questions and you can't. It leaves you in a very difficult position in defending the case. It is hard to say that you didn't discriminate while not really knowing what happened. One of the things that you should be able to do is figure out what has been going on in your personnel system for a long period of time.

The last thing you want to do in conducting an audit is to establish systems within the organization so that you can continue to keep track of what is going on. There is no sense in making this a one-shot deal. There is also no sense in seeing it today on file and having someone come along five years from now and say, "Well, in that intervening period you have done something wrong." You want to be in the position of continually monitoring what is happening.

Employee Selection Audits

Selection procedures are procedures used to make employment decisions such as hiring, promotion and selection for training. They may be based on things such as job requirements, education requirements, experience requirements, filling out an application form, employment interviews, probationary evaluation, tests and things of that nature.

There are really three questions that you have to answer about any selection procedure. First, is it inherently discriminatory?

That is usually a very easy question. Even today there are organizations that have jobs, for example, that are men's jobs or women's jobs. It doesn't take a lot of insight to know that any plaintiff could come along and attack on that point and you would probably lose. The other questions are a little more complicated. One is whether or not selection procedures are applied in a discriminatory manner—now you are talking about the "disparate treatment" theory of discrimination. The other question is, what is the impact of the selection procedure? Here you are talking about what is called the "disparate effect" theory of discrimination.

Employment decisions aren't evaluated in the abstract. The disparate treatment theory is really what most people think of as discrimination. It talks about purposeful discrimination, an intention to do something to a person because of that person's race, sex, national origin, or some other characteristic. The way to show disparate treatment is by comparing similarly situated individuals and seeing how they have been treated. For example, in the abstract it might seem reasonable to fire somebody who was late for work ten days in a row. But if that person is a woman and it appears that in the past men have been absent ten days in a row and have not been fired, that sort of a decision becomes suspect under the disparate treatment theory.

The other theory of employment discrimination, disparate effect, also goes under the name of adverse effect or adverse impact. Understanding and applying this theory of discrimination is really at the heart of the EEO audit, and, you will find, probably at the heart of any litigation the institution is involved in. According to the disparate effect theory of discrimination, liability attaches even in the absence of an intention to discriminate. What we are talking about here is a neutral policy, neutrally applied, that has an effect on a protected group of people that is different and adverse as compared to some other group.

The leading case in this area is *Griggs v. Duke Power Company,* 401 U.S. 424 (1971). In this case, the employer required that applicants who transferred to certain positions either have a high school education or pass an intelligence test. These requirements were not intended to discriminate against anyone; they were fairly applied. However, the plaintiffs were able to show that in the area where the case arose, 34% of the white people had a high school education and only 12% of the black people did. They showed, with respect to the test, that 58% of the white people passed the test while only 6% of the black people passed the test. The Supreme Court concluded that application of the test and high school education requirement was discriminatory and set down a rule: Employer policies and practices which have an adverse impact on any race, sex or ethnic group are illegal *unless* they are justified by business necessity.

How far does **Griggs** *go?* **Griggs** has been the heart of the development of employment discrimination law since 1971. Later cases have applied its principle in other contexts. In *Dothard v. Rawlinson,* 433 U.S. 321 (1977), the Alabama state prison system had a rule that persons who wanted to be prison guards had to be at least 5'2" tall and weigh 120 lbs. A woman applied to be a prison guard. She was 5'2" but she was not 120 lbs. They rejected her. The case went to the Supreme Court and her position was vindicated—but only on the question of whether that policy was discriminatory. The Court said it was clear that the height and weight requirements had a disparate effect on women.

The Court pointed out that that particular requirement would exclude about 22% of the women who might apply but only about 3% of the men— a clear disparate effect. The assertion of the Alabama Prison Authority that a person has to be strong to be a prison guard was accepted by the Court but it observed that no proof was offered that being 5′2″ and 120 lbs. makes you strong enough to do anything. (The employer ultimately won the case on the ground that the job required close contact with prisoners in certain situations (such as taking showers), so that sex was a bona fide occupational qualification for the job.)

In another Supreme Court case, *City of Los Angeles v. Manhart,* 435 U.S. 702 (1978), the city had a contributory pension plan which made women contribute more than men—the rationale was that women live longer—in order to fund increased benefits for them. I think the important thing about this case is that no one (including the Supreme Court) disputes the fact that women live longer than men on the average. Yet the employer lost because, once again, this was found to be a classification which discriminated against women—even though the classification was true.

Now, how far does this theory go? There is at least one case where this theory has not led to the plaintiff's prevailing. The plaintiff in *Smith v. Olin Chemical Corp.,* 555 F.2d 1283 (5th Cir. 1977), had applied and been hired for a job that required manual labor. At the conclusion of his probationary period, he was given a physical examination (like everyone else). The physical revealed that he had a degenerative back condition and the doctor said he was not fit to do manual labor. He was fired. This individual was black, and he said, "Well, I do have a degenerative back condition but that is attributable to the fact that I have sickle cell anemia." (Sickle cell anemia is a disease of the blood found almost exclusively in blacks.) "This requirement that you have a good back—insofar as it is applied to people with sickle cell anemia—has a disparate effect on blacks. As a consequence, you've discriminated against me by firing me."

He lost in the district court, but a three-judge panel in the Court of Appeals ruled in his favor. That was overturned by an en banc decision of the Court of Appeals, saying that at some point this disparate effect theory has got to stop and this is it. But you can see that just because a particular selection procedure seems to be a reasonable procedure, that doesn't mean it is lawful.

Uniform Guidelines on Employee Selection Procedures

In the selection area, the federal government has issued Uniform Guidelines on Employee Selection Procedures. (*See* 43 Federal Register No. 166, page 38290). These guidelines are the product of about six years of "negotiation" among various government agencies to come up with a uniform federal position on selection procedures. They are often called testing guidelines.

Don't be misled by that—they apply to all selection procedures, not just employment tests. Their purpose is really to serve as a guide for prosecutorial discretion by the government in pursuing employers. They are not intended to state a rule of law. The important thing about them is that if you can satisfy the guidelines, the government will probably let you alone.

Based on disparate effect theory: The guidelines are based on the disparate effect theory of discrimination. They tell employers they first have to determine (by comparing selection rates) whether or not their selection procedures have a disparate effect.

There are two possible answers to that question. One is "No, there isn't a disparate effect." If there isn't, the guidelines say fine, that's the end of the inquiry. On the other hand, if there is a disparate effect, you have two options. The first is to change the procedures so they don't have a disparate effect. The second is to justify the procedures by a showing of business necessity—which is a difficult task.

Business necessity: A justification potentially applicable to all forms of discrimination is "business necessity," which is defined in terms of the safety and efficiency of operation of the company's business. This is a judicially created defense. It has been narrowly construed, and its application is dependent largely upon the particular facts of each situation. Many employers have advanced this theory to justify particular employment practices, but few have succeeded in convincing the courts. Accordingly, an employer who raises the justification of "business necessity" must prove an irresistible demand rather than mere management convenience. In addition, the challenged practice must carry out its alleged business purpose and there must be no acceptable alternative available.

Evaluating Selection Procedures Under the Disparate Effect Theory

How do you figure out if a procedure has a disparate effect, i.e., if it has an adverse impact? The government uses what they call the 80% or four-fifths "rule of thumb." A selection rate for any race, sex or ethnic group which is less than 80% of the rate for the group with the highest rate will generally be regarded by the federal enforcement agencies as evidence of adverse impact.

That's not a legal test of discrimination, it's just the guide that they are going to use in enforcing their guidelines.

To give you an example of how this rule of thumb works, let's suppose you have 120 applicants for hire. Eighty of them are men, forty are women. Out of that group, sixty people are hired. Forty-eight are men and twelve are women. The first thing you have to do is calculate the rate of selection for each group. When you do this, you are talking about men and women, or whites and blacks, or Hispanics or some other group—you are not talking about white males against black males (i.e., mixing groups), and you are not talking about minorities against nonminorities. Take the forty-eight "hires," divide by the eighty male applicants. The rate of selection for males is 60%. Then take the twelve female "hires," divide by the forty female applicants. The rate of selection for females is 30%.

Next you have to figure out which group has the highest rate of selection. In this case it is obviously the men. From that you calculate the impact ratio. You divide the selection rate for women, 30%, by the selection rate for men, 60%, and you get 50%. The government says this figure suggests discrimination because it is less than 80%. (That is why we call it the 80% rule of thumb.)

This is obviously a very simple rule to apply—it's probably the simplest thing to do in the whole process. The question you really have to ask yourself is where did the numbers come from? Supposedly, they are based on the employer's records. But, you may say that your client or your institution doesn't have those records. Well, you are going to have to have them now because the government says you must. There are simplified reporting requirements for employers with fewer than 100 employees, but as a general proposition, the government says that for every job, you must, on an annual basis, be able to say how many people applied for each job and how many people were selected for it. You have to be able to divide that up by race, sex and ethnic category.

This calls for internal accounting. If you haven't got a system like that yet, one of the key aspects of your EEO audit is going to be to set up this system to generate the numbers the government says you have to have. Of course, you might say, "Well, suppose I don't do that. It sounds like too much trouble." According to the regulations, what the government will do then is draw an inference that your selection procedures have an adverse impact—and this puts you behind the eight ball from the start, at least at the administrative stage of any proceeding.

Definition of "applicant": One of the interesting things about this whole process is that the government wants you to compare applicants to something else, but they don't tell you what an "applicant" is. The definition of "applicant" is still up in the air. For example, suppose an institution decides they need a registered nurse and they put an ad in the paper which says, "We want a registered nurse." A person comes down to apply and says, "I'm here to apply for the registered nurse's position but I am not a registered nurse." The person then fills out an application. Should we count that person as an applicant? How about the type of situation where people just come in off the street and say, "I was just walking by and need a job. Can I fill out an application form?" They fill out a form and leave. Are those people applicants? The government doesn't say, but obviously the way the institution defines applicants is going to have a very substantial impact on the way the numbers come out.

Assume that you start counting those people as applicants. They will probably be rejected and, therefore, will probably be "bad numbers" from the standpoint of your EEO audit.

The "bottom-line" concept: Inherent in these examples is another notion called the "bottom-line" concept. What we did was compare "applicants" to "hires." When you think of your hiring process, you know that something happens in between the application and the hire. Applicants fill out an application form, and are probably screened by somebody. There may be an employment interview and some kind of a test. There may be a further interview by another manager of the organization that this person would work for, and then some kind of medical checks. And finally the person gets hired. You can see that every component of the procedure has the potential for having an adverse effect. The government takes the position in their guidelines that they don't care about the stuff in the middle—all they care about is the stuff down at the end—how many came in and how many got hired.

However, just because the government is only concerned about the end result *doesn't* mean that plaintiffs are only going to be concerned about that. In fact, plaintiffs don't like that at all. They say that in evaluating selection procedures, every component has to be evaluated because no employer has the right to use a procedure that has an adverse effect on a protected group of people. Note that if it turns out that the selection procedure does have an adverse effect, the government says you are going to have to go on a component basis in assessing adverse effect.

They will want to know, for example, the selection rate at the screening of the application form stage, the selection rate at the first interview stage, the selection rate on the typing test, and the rate with respect to subsequent interviews.

Again, where do those numbers come from? They come from the employer. Part of the audit is setting up a system to account for people— to show how they went through the process and the effect of the process on them.

Self-nomination factor: There is something that I call the "self-nomination factor" that has an important bearing on the audit of your selection procedures. It makes a lot of sense, without even thinking about it, that in the example I gave you the only people who were counted as applicants were people who came in and applied. However, the institution said that to be counted as an "applicant" people had to come in and do something. But suppose you have a promotion situation. People are promoted to Job B from Job A. As it happens, Job B is a higher-paying job and is also a job that requires a substantial degree of strength. Now assume that 50% of the people in Job A are women and 5% of the people in Job B are women. The plaintiff comes along and says, "Look, you have 50% women on Job A but only 5% on Job B—you obviously discriminate in promotions." The employer's probable response would be, "Well, you know Job B requires great physical strength and most women wouldn't want that job in the first place." That is a really good argument, but that's all it is, an argument. You don't have any facts.

How are you going to be able to prove that it wasn't your selection procedure that discriminated, but that it was, in fact, a "self-nomination" decision by the women, saying that they didn't want this job. The only way you can do that is to have some sort of system through which vacancies are generally made known so that people can apply for them. When you do that, the institution removes itself from any blame for the decisions of the people who do not apply. An awful lot of employers don't have self-nomination systems for promotion, for selection for training or for anything else. It seems like a big pain in the neck, but it is certainly easier than trying to go back later and explain why it is that women (or blacks, or some other group) are not in certain jobs. If people are going to elect not to want a job, be sure you can show that they made that election.

Avoiding Disparate Treatment in Selection Procedures

Everything we have discussed so far is based on the disparate effect theory—the theory that says that without any bad motive at all, the numbers just didn't turn out right, and the employer is held accountable for that. But even when the numbers turn out right, the employer can wind up in trouble. The fact that the numbers look good does not provide any insulation with respect to an individual selection decision. What that means is that in addition to having good numbers, you have to have good procedures overall.

Well-defined selection standards: There are several elements that I think will help to strengthen any type of selection procedure and make it, if not totally immune, then more immune from attack than it would otherwise have been. First you have to have well-defined selection standards. It is always nice to know how people get picked. In many organizations, individual managers may select people on different bases. You are asking for trouble if you allow this to occur because it leaves you in a situation where disparate treatment is easy to prove. You want to have a procedure or a set of standards for selecting people. In a unionized organization, seniority is an obvious standard for selecting people. You may conclude that physical fitness or experience or education is a selection standard.

Formal system for evaluation: Once you have the standards, you have to have a way to apply them. What we are talking about here is a formal system for evaluating people. It can't be a hit-or-miss thing; it's got to be a real set of procedures so you can show that this is the way you always do it.

Specific guidelines to be used by evaluators: You also need guidelines for the people who are involved in the system—the evaluators. For example, you may conclude that for a particular job, appearance is important. In any type of a health care institution, slovenly people project a bad image to the public. This image hurts business and reduces confidence in your ability to provide good care. Since you can't have people looking that way, that might be one of the things that is going to be evaluated when a person comes in to apply for a job.

I suppose you can put a blank on the form that just says "appearance," but depending upon who's doing the evaluating, you are going to get a different judgment as to how the person looks. Somebody might say, "Well, the person is overweight." Another person might say, "This person is wearing a Pierre Cardin suit with an orange tie." There are all kinds of things written on forms. If you are interested in whether or not the person has a neat and well-kept appearance, there should be guidelines so that people applying the standard all have the general idea of what it is you are looking for. If you are sued, the plaintiff is going to want to know what "appearance" means, and how you figured out whether he met your standards.

Group decision making: To the extent that decisions are made by whites and males in most of these employment discrimination situations, the decision is going to be suspect just on the basis of who made the decision. One thing that helps is a "group" decision. For example, it is generally felt that if three white males make a decision, it is less likely to be a discriminatory decision than if one white male made the decision—the thinking being that any prejudices are going to be submerged in the evaluation process and the group decision is going to winnow out all improper considerations.

Well-documented decisions: The next thing you need is good documentation. As I said before, if you can't figure out what happened, you are likely to lose. Of course, if you have bad numbers in a case, it isn't the end of the world because you can still go back and try to show, on a decision-by-decision basis, that your actions were correct and not discriminatory. Obviously, though, you cannot even make the attempt if you have no real records of what happened.

Remember, too, that the discrimination case has two stages—a liability stage and a damages stage. Even if you are unsuccessful at the liability stage, you may be able to show that the specific plaintiffs claiming damages were not victims. For example, if it is established that as a general proposition you have discriminated against women in promotions, it's still possible for you to show that the individual women making claims for money were not discriminated against. But, again, you can't provide any information at that stage of the trial unless you have some kind of records regarding the decision making processes in which these women were involved.

Evaluating the evaluators: There are certain people in every organization who have responsibility for making decisions about employment matters. Those people ought to have, as a part of their evaluation, an evaluation based on their performance in providing equal employment opportunities. Salary adjustments should be affected by equal opportunity performance. If, for example, a particular manager in a particular department gets a raft of complaints about discrimination, that's a person who doesn't need a raise—that's a person who needs to get straightened out.

There should be some kind of reward for good performance. Though not generally a very popular idea, evaluating managers on their equal opportunity performance is very effective. You will find that if you use it and can show in litigation that evaluators are evaluated themselves based on equal opportunity performance, you are going to stand a much better chance of prevailing on any claims of disparate treatment—because in those circumstances, the individual's inclination is not to give disparate treatment.

Representing Your Company in an EEOC Investigation

The filing of a charge of discrimination against your company with the Equal Employment Opportunity Commission (EEOC) marks the onset of an administrative process that could have far-reaching implications in terms of financial liability and changes in well-established employment practices. Litigation in this area is generally complex, protracted and expensive. Liability for back pay and attorneys' fees, as well as potentially costly restrictions on management prerogatives, are virtually assured if the employer loses the case. Even if a company prevails, it is likely that it will be required to bear the burden of its own expenses incurred in defending against the allegations. Consequently, it is important to strive to avoid discrimination charges and, if such charges are filed, to handle them properly from the outset.

As we've seen, the best way for a company to protect itself against EEOC charges is to eliminate their root causes through effective "preventive maintenance." Every employer should make a strong commitment to provide equal opportunity in employment. This commitment should be effectively communicated to employees at all levels and to the community. All persons making decisions affecting employment should understand what the law requires, what the company is doing to comply with the law, and the nature of their own responsibilities. Finally, an ongoing audit should be conducted to ensure implementation of the company's policy of providing equal employment opportunity. This audit must include an inquiry into systemic (unintentional) forms of discrimination as well as into situations potentially involving the influence of purposeful bias.

Despite your best efforts, however, a charge of discrimination may be filed against your company. This will trigger an investigation by the EEOC which, from the employer's standpoint, is the most critical stage in the processing of a charge of discrimination. Improper handling of the Commission's investigation may needlessly propel your company into further administrative proceedings or litigation. It is essential for the company to conduct its own investigation to uncover the facts and make a realistic assessment of its position in order to participate meaningfully in the EEOC's investigation. In those cases where the dispute between the parties requires formal adjudication, failure to gather all the facts at the earliest possible time, while memories are fresh and records are intact, may seriously hamper the presentation of the company's defense in later proceedings. It is foolhardy to wait until a lawsuit is filed before devoting serious attention to a charge.

The importance of the investigation: Once a charge is filed, the investigative stage of the proceeding assumes critical importance for the employer. A train of events which may culminate in litigation has been set in motion. Now is the time to stop the train, or at least to get ready before being hit. Your company is headed for trouble if it is not properly represented in the investigation.

The investigative stage may be concluded in several ways. First, the company may agree to settle the case. Possible reasons for settlement include a simple desire to avoid further proceedings, inconsequential demands for relief from the charging party, or a decision that, based on the facts and law and the anticipated effectiveness of the company's witnesses and evidence, the company's chances of prevailing in litigation are not good.

On the other hand, the charging party and/or the Commission may conclude that the charge lacks litigation merit. If the EEOC is so convinced, administrative proceedings will be stopped with a "no reasonable cause" determination. Should both the charging party and the Commission be convinced, both litigation and further administrative proceedings will be avoided. Even if only the charging party feels that the charge is not worth pursuing, the matter will probably be concluded. However, the charging party and the Commission may be convinced that discrimination has occurred while the company may be convinced to the contrary, so that the dispute can only be resolved through litigation.

Aside from determining the direction of future proceedings, the investigative stage is important in those instances where litigation ensues, as this stage provides the company with its first opportunity to find out something about its opponent's side of the dispute. The best time for determining the facts is immediately after the events in question. Title VII litigation generally does not commence until long after the events giving rise to the dispute have occurred. In the intervening period memories fade, records may be lost, and the participants in the events tend to take sides. Thus, the time to begin preparing for litigation is while the charge is being investigated.

Effective representation of a company in an EEOC investigation requires the ability to find the facts, to determine which facts are significant and marshall them into arguments, and to critically evaluate the company's position. An understanding of Title VII law is essential. Thorough, well-thought-out preparation is the rule.

Limit the investigation to the specific harm alleged by the charging party: In years past, employers have often been confronted with broad investigations based on rather narrow charges. For example, a single charge of racial discrimination in hiring might trigger an inquiry into whether racial discrimination played a role in any of the company's employment practices. Every effort should be made to avoid such sweeping investigations. Under the EEOC's new procedures, your chances of doing so are dramatically improved. The legal authority of the Commission to conduct far-ranging investigations is reasonably well-established. Courts frequently have upheld the right of the EEOC to conduct such investigations on the theory that the Commission should be empowered to look into aspects of discrimination "like or related" to those alleged in the charge.

With this broad mandate, the Commission in the past "made a federal case" out of many charges. Titanic struggles between employers and the Commission concerning the breadth of their investigative demands often ensued. This had two predictable results: A vast backlog of charges accumulated and individual charging parties often obtained no relief. As part of its plan to expedite the processing of charges, the Commission has decided that it will ordinarily limit its investigation to allegations of violations which will directly affect the charging party.

Since the EEOC is now predisposed to limiting its investigation to the allegations of harm affecting the charging party, your efforts to do the same should meet with greater success. However, care should be exercised to avoid inadvertently providing more or different information than the EEOC requests in its investigation or more information than is actually relevant to the charge. This additional information could provide the basis for a determination of liability. For example, in one case, the EEOC uncovered evidence of sex discrimination in its investigation of a race discrimination charge and sued the employer for discriminating on the basis of both race and sex. The company argued that the Commission's suit should be dismissed insofar as it alleged sex discrimination, since no charge of sex discrimination had been lodged against the company. The court rejected this argument, stating:

> The EEOC has the right during the investigation to compel the production of any material or evidence that has relevancy to any claim made in the charge.

105

> If the EEOC uncovers during that investigation facts which support a charge of
> another discrimination than that in the filed charge, it is neither obliged to
> cast a blind eye over such discrimination nor to sever those facts and the
> discrimination so shown from the investigation in process and file a Commissioner's
> charge thereon, thereby beginning again a repetitive investigation of the same
> facts already developed in the ongoing investigation...[so] long as the new
> discrimination arises out of the reasonable investigation of the charge filed
> it can be the subject of a 'reasonable cause' determination, to be followed by an
> offer by the Commission of conciliation, and, if conciliation fails, by a civil
> suit...*EEOC v. General Electric Co.,* 532 F.2d 359, 364-66 (4th Cir. 1976).

The message of the *General Electric* case is clear. Careful analysis of
requests for information is mandatory.

Convince the charging party and the EEOC not to pursue the charge:
Your company wants to prevail in the case. The easiest way to accomplish
this is to convince the charging party and the EEOC not to pursue the
matter further. Providing the facts which establish that the charge lacks
merit is a big step in the right direction. Remember, however, that it takes
more than just facts to be convincing. The facts must be persuasively
presented. This involves not only advancing a clear, understandable
argument, but pitching it so as to avoid antagonizing the investigator and
the charging party as well. Every person involved in the EEOC's
investigation on the company's side should be aware of this role as a
persuader.

If necessary, negotiate a favorable "no-fault" settlement: For any one of
a variety of reasons, the company may wish to terminate the processing of
the charge as soon as possible. The "no-fault" settlement is an excellent
device for accomplishing this. Although the investigator will offer
assistance to the charging party in the negotiation, the employer should be
able to achieve a reasonable settlement in virtually all instances.

Commence preparation for trial: Every charge represents a potential
litigation vehicle for either the charging party or the Commission. The
investigative stage presents the company with an opportunity to get the facts
while they are fresh in the minds of witnesses and to identify relevant
records that should be preserved. It is frustrating, to say the least, to
attempt to justify employment actions in court when no one can recall the
circumstances.

Preparation for the Commission's investigation: Sometimes it is possible
to commence preparation for the Commission's investigation even before
the charge is filed. This occurs when someone in your organization has
anticipated that a particular employment action may produce a charge,
either because of the individuals involved or because charges have been filed
in similar circumstances in the past. In these situations, the groundwork for
responding to the potential charge should begin immediately.

More frequently, however, the company's first inkling of discontent is the receipt of the charge itself. An active role should immediately be assumed in the handling of the charge. Do not simply respond to the EEOC. Start your own investigation immediately. Then, with facts in hand, play your role in the Commission's investigation.

Ascertain the facts concerning each allegation: Before launching your investigation, determine what it is that the company is accused of. To do this, you must read the charge carefully. Note when the discrimination is alleged to have occurred, the basis (race, sex discrimination, etc.) of the charge, and the particular facts the charging party states to be true. While doing this, take note of anything in the charge which may be helpful to the company. Now you are ready to investigate the truth of the facts alleged and to ascertain whether all the pertinent facts have been presented.

Start your investigation by conferring with any management personnel who were involved in the incident raised by the charge. Even those indirectly involved should be questioned. Get their versions of what happened. Have them identify persons, management or otherwise, who may have knowledge of the facts and records that may be relevant. Note any apparent gaps or inconsistencies in their statements. Above all, get *facts* ("She was absent without excuse on February 2, 6 and 8 and the week of the tenth"), not conclusions ("Her absenteeism was excessive"). While talking to these people, also make a judgment as to their effectiveness as witnesses before the Commission's investigator or in the court.

In many instances, company records contain information relevant to the charge. The personnel files of the charging party and any potential witnesses, including management personnel, should be examined. Other records, such as payroll records, absence calendars, newspaper ads and disciplinary action forms, may be relevant, depending on the facts of the case. Analyze these records and consider their relationship to the anticipated testimony of witnesses.

It is also possible to interview the charging party and/or non-management witnesses. Caution should be exercised if this is done. It is an unlawful employment practice for an employer to discriminate against any employee or applicant because the person has filed a charge or participated in an investigation, or because the person has opposed practices made unlawful by Title VII. Additionally, it is possible that, by talking with persons other than the charging party about the charge, they will be encouraged to file charges of their own or to take the side of the charging party. Whether to interview the charging party or nonmanagement personnel is a matter of judgment to be exercised on the facts of each case.

Finally, it may be possible to obtain information from the EEOC. The charging party may have provided more information to the Commission than is contained in the charge. Witnesses may also have provided statements. Even the mere fact that there is more information available in the investigator's file than is contained in the charge is useful. The difficulty is getting this information. While attorneys for charging parties frequently are granted access to the Commissioner's files, the Commission has generally been reluctant to open its files to respondents. A call to the investigator may be productive, particularly if the charge gives you insufficient information to respond meaningfully.

Develop the company's position: Having determined what the allegations are and investigated the facts surrounding them, you are ready to develop the company's position. Some facts may be undisputed. With respect to those facts that are disputed, be prepared to establish that the company's version is correct. If the charging party has omitted relevant facts, you should be able to explain why they are relevant and to prove that they are true. The facts are the building blocks of the company's position.

To use the facts effectively, you must understand the law. In the context of an EEOC investigation, this means that you must have an appreciation of what Title VII requires and of how violations are established. Knowledge of Title VII law will enable you to marshall the facts into a powerful argument as to why the company is not guilty of the discrimination alleged, if this is, in fact, the case. Knowlege of the law should also aid you in identifying situations in which the company has made a mistake.

Anticipate the probable reactions of the charging party and the Commission's investigator when developing your position, particularly the charging party. Sufficiently antagonized, the charging party, with a totally meritless charge, may nevertheless press onward. In the final analysis, however, you must "tell it like it is."

Preparation of the company's representatives for the investigation: Persons involved in the investigation on the company's side should understand what is happening, why it is happening and what their responsibilities are. They should be thoroughly familiar with the company's position. The significance of the EEOC's investigation and the company's representatives' role should be made clear to them. Once they are sensitized to the proceedings, you can prepare them to play an active role.

Contact between management personnel and EEOC investigators often occurs during an investigation. (The fact-finding conference in the new rapid charge processing system is an obvious example of this.) The company's representatives should be prepared for these encounters. This preparation should include instruction not only in what to expect, but in how to respond. The investigator's decision on disputed issues of fact may well turn on the demeanor of the company's witnesses. The whole case may hinge on an offhand remark by a loquacious first-echelon supervisor. In addition to discussing matters such as demeanor and responsiveness with management personnel, you should advise them to talk to the EEOC's investigator only in the presence of the person representing the company in the investigation. They should be assured of your moral support.

Based on the facts as you understand them, the law, your evaluation of the effectiveness of the company's witnesses and evidence, and practical considerations, develop a preliminary position regarding settlement: The EEOC encourages the settlement of charges. No matter how strong or weak the company's case is, the Commission will try initially to resolve the matter through settlement. Since settlement overtures will be made, the company should be ready to respond.

The preliminary position regarding settlement adopted by the company should be tentative only. More information may come to light which will change the situation entirely. During the predetermination interview, for example, the company will be informed of the investigator's recommendation regarding a finding of reasonable cause in the case as well as the reasoning behind it. The posture of the case may shift even at the conciliation stage. As an alternative to litigation, settlement is often an attractive prospect. At this early stage of the proceedings, you should plan to "wait and see."

Participation in the EEOC's Investigation

The company's participation in the EEOC's investigation begins when it responds to the Commission's request for information. The investigation should be viewed as an adversary proceeding.

Exercise caution in providing information: We have already touched upon the need for caution in providing information to the EEOC, but this is a point worth focusing on. The company is, of course, required to provide such information relevant to the charge as is requested by the Commission. The Commission's right to the information may be enforced through the subpoena process. However, whether or not particular information is relevant to a charge is frequently subject to debate. When the company provides information, it tacitly admits that the information is relevant. Hindsight may prove such an admission to be ill-advised in some instances. Furthermore, any information provided can become the basis for a lawsuit against the company.

The information the company provides becomes part of the Commission's investigative file. This file may be made available to the charging party, an attorney representing the charging party, other persons who have filed similar charges against the company or their attorneys, or attorneys who review EEOC files under special arrangements to identify litigable cases. Although the point is not yet settled, some information from the file may be available to interested members of the general public through the Freedom of Information Act. Finally, the EEOC has an information-sharing arrangement with the Office of Federal Contract Compliance Programs (OFCCP), so that OFCCP Equal Opportunity Specialists generally are aware of charges outstanding against the companies they review. Thus, the information the company provides to the EEOC may not remain confidential and may, in fact, be used against the company.

Submission of a statement of position: The Commission will invite the company to submit a statement of position as part of its investigation. The company's right to put its position before the Commission is also protected under the EEOC's procedural regulations. It is a mistake to submit a poorly thought out statement, however. Once your position is on record, the investigation will tend to focus on whether it can be substantiated. If the statement of position is vulnerable to attack, either because it is legally insufficient to establish a defense or because it contains misstatements of fact, the company's chances of securing a determination of "no reasonable cause" are greatly diminished.

The statement of position can be a valuable tool, however. First, merely by preparing it, the company is compelled to focus on contentions made in the charge and the facts surrounding them.

Secondly, the statement should provide direction to the investigation. The process of determining which facts are disputed will be facilitated. Finally, if the statement of position outlines a meritorious defense and the company is able to establish the truth of the matters it asserts, it should prevail with respect to the charge. Assuming that the statement of position is properly prepared, it generally will be advisable to submit one.

The representative's role at the fact-finding conference: The EEOC's investigator is in charge of the fact-finding conference and will want to run it. This should present no problem, as long as the investigator does not become overzealous and convert the conference into an inquisition. The company's representative must prevent this from happening. To the maximum extent possible, the representative should act as spokesman for the company.

The purpose of the fact-finding conference is to get the facts on the table. Although it is the EEOC's role to investigate, there may be facts which the company would like to discover. For example, the charge may state that an unidentified friend described company policy in a particular way, which the company believes is a misstatement. Knowing the name of the friend may provide an additional avenue for the company's self-investigation. The company's representative can seek such additional information at the conference.

The fact-finding conference also provides an opportunity to size up the charging party. Just as the demeanor of the company's witnesses may be crucial in the disposition of the case, so may be the demeanor of the charging party. Additionally, the response of the charging party to the contentions advanced by the company at the fact-finding conference can be evaluated and factored into the company's thinking regarding settlement.

The company's representative should also play a leading role in any settlement discussions. Of all the company personnel present, the representative should have the fullest understanding of the company's position. The representative's skill as a negotiator should serve to offset the tendency of the investigator to assist the charging party in securing a favorable settlement.

The representative's continuing role: Investigations may extend over a considerable period of time. Even in those cases in which a fact-finding conference is conducted, the investigation may continue. The representative must remain active on the employer's behalf throughout the entire course of the investigation.

As the investigation proceeds, the need for further self-investigation may be indicated. New facts may require alteration of the company's position on the merits or with respect to settlement. Additionally, the Commission will continue to urge settlement, and the company will have to reevaluate its position even if no new facts emerge. Finally, it may be necessary to submit additional information in response to the predetermination interview.

Conclusion

From the company's standpoint, the EEOC's investigation is the most crucial phase in the administrative processing of a charge, since it determines the course of further proceedings. An investigation cannot be handled "by the numbers," for too many matters of judgment are involved. Nevertheless, it is hoped that observing the basic principles for handling the EEOC investigation outlined here will aid your company in avoiding the time and expense of Title VII litigation.

QUESTIONS AND ANSWERS

Audience: Is there a legal definition of the term "minority group?"

John Erickson: Not of minority group, that I know of, but there is a definition of race/ethnic categories. The Office of Management and Budget divided all of us up into five groups: white (not of Hispanic origin), black (not of Hispanic origin), Hispanic, Asian or Pacific Islander, and American Indian or Alaskan Native. The definitions are contained in the set of instructions to Standard Form 100 (EEO-1), the form which employers of more than 100 employees must file each year.

Audience: What about asking people: "Out of these five groups, which do you belong to?"

Erickson: This is one of those areas where state and local laws touch you. Many states (and many local laws) prohibit asking people what their race is and what their sex is. There are other states that don't prohibit that. The

EEOC, in its guidelines, says as a general proposition that it doesn't like the idea of asking applicants about race and sex information—the reason being that there are suspect uses to which that information could be put.

Fifteen years ago, the notion of asking about race on an application form raised a spectre of discrimination in the mind of enforcement agencies. For example, the federal government completely took that sort of question off their applications. When it turned out nobody could figure out anybody's racial background, the federal government changed these forms back, asking people to identify what they are, with a disclaimer explaining the reason they are asking.

Those of you who are acquainted with the regulations under Section 503 of the Rehabilitation Act know there is disclaimer language regarding inquiries about the handicapped status of people, saying in effect that it will only be used for the appropriate purposes—it's confidential, used for the purpose of making employment decisions. I think that probably the same type of language could be included on an application form to justify an inquiry as to race, sex, etc. (in a state that doesn't have any law prohibiting it). The great virtue of self-identification by applicants is that you don't have to guess anymore about what people are—they tell you. As I say, though, you have to use that with some degree of circumspection in terms of who it is that has access to such information.

Audience: To what extent, if any, does the mandatory use of a union hiring hall insulate an employer from EEOC liability?

Erickson: None.

Audience: Prior to the selection process, there are job categories that have to be examined. In the health care institutions, is it legal to try to recruit the category of orderly? I suggest that this is always considered a male.

Erickson: There are job titles that themselves indicate sex, such as a sales*man* or press*man*, so you get the notion that it should be a man for the job. As a general proposition, under federal law at least, they would like you to think of job titles as if there were no sex designation. Some state laws also prohibit using sex-designated job titles.

What you are talking about is simply an understanding in this particular industry about the types of people that fill certain sorts of positions. There is nothing wrong with advertising for orderlies. If no women apply (remember I spoke of the self-nominating process) you are going to be in a position where you say: "I made the offer, it was open to all and this is what I got in the way of applicants."

One of the hookers in the self-nominating process is that it can always be argued that because of, in this case, an industry's reputation or general practices, an apparent invitation to all who apply is understood to be only a limited invitation—that only men are supposed to apply to be orderlies.

In that circumstance, what you have to try to do is, in the recruiting process, make it apparent that you are also looking for applicants of both sexes.

One way is to advertise in newspapers as an Equal Opportunity Employer. Some people put Equal Opportunity Employer and then put the M/F at the end. If you use an employment agency of some type, make it clear to the agency that you are looking for people without discrimination. One thing that is always a good idea is to seek applicants through the State Employment Service. But there is nothing wrong with advertising for an orderly if that's what you want somebody to do.

Audience: Inasmuch as there is no real definition of "applicant," can you provide us with one? For example, where you have people walking in off the street looking for a job, is it legitimate to define "applicant" only as a person responding to the announcement of a position being open?

Erickson: From a plaintiff's standpoint, those people who just walk in off the street and fill out application forms are supposed to be counted as applicants. My advice is that until some court or the federal government tells you differently, what you should do is not count as an applicant a person who is obviously not qualified for the position. The example I gave about the registered nurse—that's the type of thing that I mean by "obviously not qualified."

As far as those just walking in off the street and filling out an application form are concerned, I wouldn't count them—but I also wouldn't allow that to happen. One of the things that I tell clients is not to let people apply unless there is a vacancy, and then make them apply for a specific vacancy. To give you an example, I represent a hospital which has about 1,600 employees. They always have vacancies. They post them in their personnel department—what vacancies exist. If a person walks in and wants to apply for a job, they tell him, sure, you can apply for any one of those on the board. If it's not there, you can't apply. They keep a file for each job. They have a form in each file for everybody who applied and another form which tells them who got the job and why. Admittedly, the reason they do all this is because they were sued, but this is a great way to keep track of things.

So you can limit applications for vacancies. Another way you can do it is to take applications on certain days. You may find yourself in the position of having people walking in every day to fill out application forms, and you are accumulating a tremendous amount of applications. The implication is that when you do get a vacancy, you should go back over all those forms and pick somebody. In fact, most employers I know put them all in a drawer and never look at them again. One day one of those applicants is going to complain, so it makes sense to at least cut down on applications by saying that if you want to apply for a job here you must come in Wednesday morning. Something like that makes sense.

Audience: In some parts of the country, we have a new minority, the Spanish-speaking person who doesn't speak any English at all. Has there been any decision regarding discriminatory hiring practices with respect to whether or not a person speaks the language of this country?

Erickson: One case that comes to mind involved a hotel with an employee who spoke some English but not a whole lot. A front-desk-type job opened up and the employee applied for it. He was rejected on the grounds that his English capability was limited to such an extent that they did not think he could do the job. He sued and he lost—the language capability requirement was found to be justified by business necessity.

You have to look at the type of job involved. For example, in a hospital or nursing home, if you have an employee who is supposed to be dealing with patients, either responding to their requests to bring things or helping them in some way, that person would have to speak and understand English. On the other hand, if you are talking about a laundry in a hospital, that employee doesn't see anybody. As long as somebody is around to communicate sufficiently with the employee so that the employee knows what to do, there is no reason not to employ him there, regardless of his language limitation.

Buying and Selling a Nursing Home

SHERWIN L. MEMEL

What Is a Nursing Home?

The first thing that you have to look at when you are involved in a purchase and sale transaction is, what is a "nursing home"? It is a generic term. We used to call them ECFs, extended care facilities, under the Title XVIII and Title XIX programs, but that's been changed. We have SNFs now, which are skilled nursing facilities delivering extended care. Then you have ICFs, intermediate care facilities—and you have what are really non-health facilities, i.e., residential and social-care-type facilities.

Licensing considerations: The licensing laws vary tremendously from type of facility to type of facility. So, in a purchase and sale, you must know what you are doing with respect to licensing considerations. These considerations all vary from state to state. You may find that in some of the states where you have less intensive regulatory schemes, some of the facilities below the level of intermediate care will not require any type of licensure. And in other states, there will be a very strong regulatory program affecting each type of facility, each one requiring some separate type of licensure.

Licensure also, of course, implies that certain types of code requirements have to be met with respect to square footage, for example, or services within the institution. It is important that you know what you are buying because you have to make sure you are not walking into a problem area. You need to know that there isn't going to be some upgrading required because a prior owner was in

© Copyright 1979 by Sherwin L. Memel. All rights reserved.

115

there under waivers or a grandfather clause. You might be purchasing assets and there might not be a continuation of the prior license. You might have to get a new license, which means meeting new code standards—not only life and safety codes or federal Medicare and Medicaid requirements, but also state licensing requirements.

Reimbursement considerations: It is also urgent that you know what you are buying from the standpoint of third-party reimbursement. In that area, obviously, you want to know whether the facility you are buying qualifies for Medicare or Medicaid, and if it does not, whether there is any other kind of state or federal program that will pay for the particular kind of services being rendered in that institution.

Other considerations: Certificate of need, Section 1122 (where that program is in effect for the state), rate-setting and even cost containment considerations are all wound up in the question of what kind of an institution it is you are buying. Those programs may or may not apply, depending upon what you are getting.

Structuring the Purchase or Sale of a Nursing Home

When considering a purchase, you have to look at how you are going to structure it. There are a wide variety of options open to you. The principal choices (although certainly not the only ones) are a purchase of stock of the corporate owner, a purchase of assets, a merger (and there is more than one type of merger and they vary in accordance with the state law), consolidations, leases or a lease-purchase. Management contracts are still another way of getting involved in the situation.

Of course, it is also important to consider whether or not you are going to own the assets in the same entity that is going to operate the assets. There's a significant difference in liability exposure between owning passive assets and leasing them to an operating corporation and having an individual operate the facility—notwithstanding the availability of liability insurance.

It is very important that you look at the pros and cons of all these subjects *before* you get into negotiations. A deal that could be made very handily if you started off negotiating in a specific way can blow apart because of accusations of bad faith. For example, if you start negotiating and then the client goes to the lawyer, or the lawyer who is not a specialist finds he is in an area that he is not wholly comfortable with and goes to a specialist and finds out that the proposed deal cannot be structured in the way you've started negotiating upon, there can be accusations that you are backing off and the deal will blow apart. So, get into these questions of structure and form of the transaction, first.

Also, don't lose sight of the fact that all of the normal business considerations, representations, warranties, etc. are involved here. At the same time, remember we are in one of the most highly regulated businesses in America, so not only do normal business considerations have to be entertained, but also the special ones relating to the health care field.

One additional point on structuring the transaction. Once you have made your sale or purchase, it is very important, from a post-acquisition standpoint, to bear in mind the way you structure it. Where you hold the assets, the kind of entity that you create, can make a great deal of difference if the company making the purchase is also in the hospital field.

For example, in some states if you buy it as a division of the hospital corporation or company, you could very well wind up having an asset subject to rate regulation, which would not be subject to rate regulation under an independent structure.

Principal Legal Concerns

With respect to the areas I am going to discuss with you, I urge you to think of all of them in terms of practicing preventive law.

Tax: First, consider a situation where both parties, buyer and seller, are proprietary entities. If it is going to be a taxable transaction, it will generally be a situation where money or other property is exchanged for stock or assets. In that case, the seller will recognize gain or loss. If the seller does not take more than 30% down in one year, he can, of course, get the benefit of an installment sale (under IRC §453) and defer recognition of a substantial amount of the capital gain. Installment reporting generally would not be available, however, if there is a sale of assets and the seller is a corporation. If the corporation then is liquidated and distributes the note, you wind up under most circumstances losing the installment sale. There are ways, of course, of avoiding this by doing a prior in-kind distribution or liquidation, and then making your sale of assets.

Every step along the way you have to be thinking of the tax consequences of your actions. If you sell assets, generally speaking, the basis of those assets for tax purposes will not carry over to the buyer. If, on the other hand, you sell stock, generally, the basis of the assets in the company will carry over.

You must be concerned with allocation of the purchase price in both reimbursement and tax. From the tax standpoint, it is very important because it gives you the basis for your depreciation as well as indicates whether you are going to have depreciation recapture or investment credit recapture. If you are involved in a sales situation and you have a true arm's-length sale, IRS will respect the allocation by the parties. If the parties do not allocate, however, you will find that IRS will do the allocating, and not to the advantage of the parties.

An alternative to a taxable transaction that is often used is the tax-free reorganization. Generally, in that circumstance, the seller's stock basis will carry over and there will be no gain or loss recognized by either the seller or the buyer.

Tax-exempt buyer, for-profit seller: Now, let's take another situation, where you have a tax-exempt buyer and a for-profit seller. This is not going to be too infrequent, especially with the pressures upon hospitals to diversify and with more and more nonprofit hospital groups developing into multi-hospital systems. I see them, down the road, becoming buyers for nursing homes.

With the tax-exempt buyer and for-profit seller, take a look now at the question of allocation of the purchase price. For the buyer, it is not an important tax consideration unless it is somehow a transaction that is going to generate unrelated business taxable income, but generally that isn't the problem. It is, however, important to the nonprofit buyer from the standpoint of Medicare and Medicaid basis allocation.

There is a danger in a nonprofit buyer's buying stock and then liquidating the acquired corporation, either into itself or into another subsidiary. In that situation, even though you have a nonprofit buyer, you will very often wind up with ordinary income on the part of the acquired corporation in the form of depreciation recapture and investment credit recapture which must be recognized upon the liquidation of the acquired corporation into the buyer.

You also have to be careful about inurement problems when you are representing or negotiating a deal on behalf of the nonprofit buyer. You may be picking up contracts that existed with a physician or someone else that called for a percentage of the net—which would be a violation of the IRC §501(c)(3) tax exemption if it were to continue in effect. Even in an asset purchase where contracts were taken on, if there were any of those contracts existing, you could run into an inurement problem, so you have to be very careful.

Again, watch out along the way for unrelated business taxable income. The consequences of a deal to a nonprofit buyer depend on the activities that the seller's entity was engaged in at the time of the transaction.

Leasing: Let's take a look at lease transactions now. Whether IRS will treat a lease as a sale is the primary consideration. If it is a true lease, the lessee gets to deduct a reasonable rent and a for-profit lessor will take the rent into gross income. A nonprofit lessor will get unrelated business taxable income to the extent that the property leased to the for-profit entity is debt-financed. In addition, the lessor will get deductions for depreciation and expenses.

If, on the other hand, IRS treats it as a sale, a for-profit seller has gain or loss, probably capital gain or loss. A nonprofit seller, again, has no gain unless it is unrelated business taxable income because the property is debt-financed. The seller may be able to get the installment sale benefit even though the transaction was characterized as a lease (so long as IRS treats it as a sale). The seller may also, incidentally, have imputed interest income. The buyer will get deductions for depreciation expenses and imputed interest.

How do you determine whether you are going to wind up in a lease or sale transaction? There aren't any IRS guidelines for real estate, but there are personal property guidelines published by IRS, spelling out six main points involved in ascertaining whether or not IRS will look at it as a sale. (See *Rev. Rul. 55-540,* 1955-2 CB 39.) First, do the rental payments apply to build up an equity interest? Second, is the lessee going to get title at the end of the deal? Third, are there relatively large rent payments early on, as measured against the total rental over the entire length of lease? Fourth, is the rent being paid materially over the fair rental value? Fifth, is there a small final payment in relation to the fair market value of the asset at the end of the lease at which time title is delivered? And sixth, is part of the payments called for labelled interest or characterized in such a manner that it appears to be interest?

It is possible to get advance rulings, and my advice to you, if you are into one of these tricky lease-purchases, is that you might very well want to seek an advance ruling, particularly if the lawyers are being called upon to give opinions in these matters.

Reimbursement: You have heard a great deal about property cost problems, and how you are going to be reimbursed in that regard. I would like to talk to you a little bit about the Medicare reimbursement rules, which may or may not parallel some of the Medicaid problems. In Medicare, of course, and possibly in Medicaid, depending upon how the state program operates, the buyer would probably want an asset purchase rather than a stock purchase in order to get the maximum step-up in basis for depreciation and to increase the return on equity capital.

There are a number of cases that have gone for the provider (all except one), holding that even in a stock transaction, there should be a step-up in basis and an increase in the return on equity. (See, for example, *PCME v. Califano,* 440 F. Supp. 296 (C.D. Cal. 1977); *Memorial, Inc. dba Memorial Hospital of Panorama City v. Califano* (C.D. Cal. 1978), CCH Medicare and Medicaid Guide 1978 Transfer Binder ¶28,932; and *Homan and Crimen, Inc. v. Califano* (W.D. Tex. 1978), CCH Medicare and Medicaid Guide 1978 Transfer Binder ¶29,213. These cases hold that an acquisition of stock of a provider is the equivalent of a purchase of assets for reimbursement purposes. Note: All of these cases have been appealed by the government. A contrary result was reached in *Monterey Nursing Inn, Inc. v. Nationwide Mutual Insurance Co.,* CCH Medicare and Medicaid Guide 1976-77 Transfer Binder ¶27,942.)

The famous doctrine of Medicare in this area is set forth in what is called the "Wolkstein letter," named after an administrator who was with the Medicare Bureau for many years and is now consulting. Medicare has just issued new regulations on stock purchases, mergers and consolidations which, relatively speaking, parallel the "Wolkstein letter." As I said, that letter had been struck down by all but one of the courts. So, if you are looking at a new transaction and you are looking to how Medicare will treat it, or how a state that parallels Medicare and Medicaid programs may treat it, you are now dealing with a regulation, as opposed to the earlier matter of program policy interpretation (which was not binding on the PRRB). The PRRB is, however, bound by regulations, and therefore will have to follow the Secretary's dictate even though, again, the courts have held that they disagree with the Secretary. To repeat, most courts have held that they don't see any reason to treat asset or stock purchases differently, particularly when there is a purchase of stock, followed immediately thereafter by a liquidation of the corporation, and the assets are in the hands of the new owner.

Related organizations: Under Medicare, if you have any significant ownership or control of a provider and you do business with the provider, the Medicare Bureau is going to disallow charges made to you by the other party, and instead will only allow you to pass through the costs. There is a very narrow exception that has been allowed relatively infrequently by the Medicare Bureau. In both *South Boston General Hospital v. Blue Cross,* 409 F. Supp. 1380 (W.D. Va. 1976), and the *Memorial Hospital of Panorama City* case, the court held that the related organization rules don't apply in a sale transaction. There is, however, another case to the contrary, *Hillside Community Hospital of Ukiah v. Mathews,* 423 F. Supp. 1168 (N.D. Cal. 1976), holding that they do apply, at least under the specific facts of that transaction.

Again, we have a new proposed Medicare regulation that has just come out which would conform the Medicare regulations to what the BCA and PRRB decisions have been right along—i.e., any interest of any kind, or common control of any kind, will create a related-organization situation and you will only be allowed to pass through costs. The BCA and the PRRB will look to the time the contract was entered into to determine when the relationship existed. And, even though it ceases after the contract was entered into, and a new unrelated party comes into the transaction, taking over one end of the contract, it doesn't necessarily matter. Until the contract expires or is renegotiated, it may continue to be treated as though the parties were related, even though one might argue the fact that an unrelated party's adopting the contract should be sufficient to cure the "taint." They also have some new rules about the exception to the related-organization rule. Medicare has established an 80% test. That again is pretty much what they had held in the past—if 80% of the business of the related entity is supplying services, facilities or equipment to the provider community, and the things you purchase are things that you would normally buy from an outside source and the price is reasonable, then they allow you the charges.

They do disallow interest between related organizations, and the buyer, under the circumstances I am describing to you here, will also most likely be held to have only the depreciated historical costs of the seller and no step-up.

Purchase vs. donation: There have been a number of decisions by the PRRB and some court decisions on purchase vs. donation. You get into the basis question. (I am talking about reimbursement, now.) Where there is a donation, the basis is, under a regulation revised in the 70's, the fair market value at the time of donation. In a purchase, however, the basis is generally the cost incurred by the present owner in acquiring the asset and in preparing it for use. In addition to purchase price, the basis would include architectural fees. In purchasing a facility as an ongoing operation, the cost basis of the depreciable assets purchased will not exceed the lower of the current reproduction cost adjusted for straight-line depreciation or the fair market value of the assets purchased.

A problem arises in some of these nominal sales deals, where people want to charge a nominal price for the assets for some reason and the nominal price is lower than fair market value. You may then wind up getting stuck with the lower nominal purchase price even though it was intended as a donation, and you may not be able to get the higher fair market value of the existing provider.

Valuation problems: When you are looking at the subject of reimbursement, you must look to the question of the valuation of the components of a facility. Under the Medicare and the Medicaid programs that would parallel this, that means looking at the cost basis of each depreciable asset acquired. It cannot exceed the lower of current reproduction cost or fair market value at the time of purchase. Even if you allocate among assets in the contract of sale, you have to have a supporting appraisal for each item and other information in order to reflect your version of fair market value. Otherwise, the Medicare Bureau will allocate for you and tell you what it is going to be.

The failure to allocate properly or failure to allocate at all can very significantly reduce your reimbursement. You can wind up, through improper allocation to depreciable assets or the land or to goodwill (depending upon whether you are representing the seller or the buyer, and this should be a hotly fought-over deal point), with recognition of gain, depreciation recapture, and you can reduce the amount to be depreciated in the future and reduce the amount to be included in the return on equity.

Another deal point to keep in mind is that Medicare disallows interest on loans used to pay for the acquisition of goodwill. Of course, newly acquired goodwill is no longer an element being allowed in the computation of equity capital. Yet, if you are representing a seller, it could very well be to your best interests to seek to have a major allocation to goodwill to avoid recapture of depreciation and gain on the sale of depreciable assets.

Costs related to patient care: Costs related to patient care are another important consideration. It is the only type of cost which is allowed as a reimbursable cost. Therefore, when you are allocating the purchase price, if there is something involved in the deal that isn't also related to patient care under reimbursement rules, be sure you don't get too much allocated to it or else you are not going to get any benefit for it.

Another illustration would be a prepayment penalty. If you are going to refinance an interim loan or some other loan because it makes good business sense and because you can get a lower interest rate at a given time, a prepayment penalty may be recognized as a reimbursable cost. On the other hand, if you are refinancing because you want to buy some deceased stockholder's interest out of the estate or something like that, then the prepayment penalty may very well be disallowed as not being related to patient care.

You also have to look at the question of capitalization of improvements vs. the expensing of repairs. There are tests spelled out in the regulations on those subjects.

When you are looking at interest expense as an allowable cost to a purchasing provider, you should remember that loans from one provider fund or bank account to another are generally disallowed for interest purposes, but loans from donor-restricted funds in a nonprofit institution would be allowed, as far as the interest is concerned, as reimbursable cost—as well as borrowing by any kind of provider from its own funded depreciation or funded pension funds.

The Medicare Bureau says you have to capitalize interest during construction. There is a court case to the contrary that says you can expense it.

I've indicated to you that Medicare takes a dim view of interest on loans where part of the use is not related to patient care. Again, they won't allow the interest on that portion of the loan not related to an asset involved in patient care.

"Virtual purchase": When you are looking at this lease-purchase transaction from the reimbursement standpoint, and the treatment of rent for reimbursement, you have to be careful Medicare doesn't treat it as what they call a "virtual purchase." Similar to the tax problem, the Medicare test to see if you have a "virtual purchase" is whether there is a higher rent than market, the term is close to the useful life of the asset, there is a cheap rent on renewal or a bargain purchase at the end of the lease. If Medicare treats it as a "virtual purchase," they will only allow the lessor's costs and not the rent.

Certificate of Need—Section 1122 review: Must you have a certificate of need (CON) for the purchase of a nursing home? The answer in California is no. My understanding is that's not true in Kansas, Wisconsin or New York. You need a CON there. Other states will vary, so you have to check state law.

Section 1122 review: These are reviews of proposed capital expenditures of skilled nursing facilities (among other entities) pursuant to an agreement between HEW and the state. (Thirteen states have not entered into such an agreement.) When the cost of acquiring a skilled nursing facility is greater than $100,000, an 1122 review may be required. While HEW regulations do not address this question—they do not say when an 1122 review will be required—at least one regional office (Region X) has taken the position that the direct acquisition of a skilled nursing facility's assets or the acquisition of a partnership interest in a facility at a cost of more than $100,000 requires a Section 1122 review. But this is only one region, so you have to consider the rule in your particular jurisdiction.

What happens if you buy a facility that has a CON or 1122 approval? Can you acquire that CON or 1122 approval when you buy the facility? In one of the regions, they say they will probably allow you to have the 1122 transferred if you didn't need the 1122 for the original transaction itself. Again, it varies all over the map, so just be aware that it is a trap to be avoided.

If you are buying something and it only makes economic sense if you can remodel it, bear in mind that if you are in an 1122 jurisdiction and the expenditure is over $100,000, you are going to need 1122 approval. (Most states have used a $150,000 certificate-of-need threshold for remodeling.) If you are going to want to add beds, the dollar amount doesn't matter—in many, if not all of the states, you will need a certificate of need.

Penalties: The penalties for violating certificate-of-need laws or proceeding without Section 1122 approval can be significant. You can lose your reimbursement for costs of unapproved construction or other unapproved covered expenditures under the federal programs (Titles V, XVIII and XIX) for not getting Section 1122 approval. Under the certificate-of-need laws, you can have suspended or lose your license or the state can bring an injunctive proceeding to stop you from building. There are civil penalties and criminal prosecutions (including fines) available under most state laws.

New provider agreement: Will a new provider contract be required when you acquire a facility? The general rule is if there is a change in the legal entity, you will need a new provider contract. What constitutes a change in the legal entity? To me, there is a lot of sophistry in the regulations, and you are going to have to look at them to make sure you fall within or without their requirements.

Following are some examples of when the acquisition of a nursing home may be considered a transfer of ownership (i.e., where there is a change in the legal entity):

(a) If the skilled nursing facility is a corporate body, a transfer of corporate stock would not, in itself, constitute a change of ownership.

(b) A merger of one or more corporations with the participating provider corporation surviving would not generally require a new certification or the execution of a new provider agreement of the surviving entity.

(c) A consolidation of two or more corporations resulting in the creation of a new corporate entity would constitute a change of ownership, however, requiring a certification by the state agency and the filing of a provider agreement with the Secretary by the new corporation.

(d) If the entire provider facility is leased, the provider agreement with a former operator of the facility terminates. If only part of the provider facility is leased, the provider agreement remains in effect with respect to the unleased portions, but a survey must be conducted to determine whether the unleased portion continues to be in compliance with the conditions for participation of the program.

The biggest problem here is delay in reimbursement. An asset purchase, for example, gets you into a situation where you are going to need a new provider agreement—which has to be approved. While Medicare has not been much of a problem, Medicaid has been a significant problem. Transfer of ownership, in the Medicaid situation, interrupts all payment. It only starts again on the signing of a new provider agreement, which could mean as much as a two- to two-and-a-half-month delay—if there aren't any problems. If there are problems, in a survey, for example (required if there hasn't been one for compliance within the prior three months), the delay could be quite extensive. You have to check this out very, very carefully because although reimbursement will be retroactive, if you sail through with no problem until the day of purchase (you will only have encountered a major cash-flow problem), unless the facility was in substantial compliance at the time of the transfer of ownership, you may very well be denied your reimbursement until such time as you get the new provider agreement. That whole interim period would then be at a loss.

Contrast this situation with Medicare, where payments will continue while you are going through this process and will only stop if there is a failure of compliance which surfaces in the transfer process. New proposed regulations have just come out which would make both Medicare and Medicaid identical. There would be no interruption of payment. There would be an automatic assignment of the agreement upon the sale, with no action required either by the state agency for Medicaid or by HEW for Medicare. There would be no re-survey involved. On the other hand, there would not be an end to the need to comply with the prior deficiency report; instead, the prior deficiencies will continue and the new owner will have an obligation to correct.

Rate regulation and cost containment: There have been tremendous pressures towards cost containment in health care within the past two years. The big focus has been on hospitals. There were five major cost containment bills introduced in 1978 at the federal level. None of them addressed nursing homes, but the Talmadge bill (which almost got through) did cover skilled nursing and intermediate care in the hospital setting. What 1979 will bring, I can't tell you, except that there will be another push for cost containment.

The states are toppling one by one, and those states which have rate regulation don't all have the same kind of rate regulation. Some are merely rate review, some of them are line item budget setting, item by item. Some states which have rate setting are broadening their programs to cover all payors and are becoming much more stringent. (About twenty-eight states have some form of rate review; at least four, Arizona, Connecticut, Massachusetts and Oregon, cover nursing homes).

Wage and price controls: Another consideration if you are a proposed purchaser is to remember that wage and price controls do apply to nursing homes. The pay standards are not more than a 7% increase in a year; you can't raise your prices over a base formula or 9.5%, whichever is less; and it is only a voluntary program so long as you are not a federal contractor. So far, only one of the three agencies involved with health facilities has ruled that they are not federal contractors and that's the Wage and Price Stability Counsel itself. OMB and HEW have not yet ruled, although they have been asked about that question.

Other Areas of Interest

Financing: The tax exemption for industrial development bonds has been increased from $5,000,000 to $10,000,000 for those of you who are going to be putting up additional facilities or getting involved in deals of that magnitude.

A 1978 California Supreme Court case, *Wellenkamp v. Bank of America,* 21 Cal. 3rd 943, held a due-on-sale clause, in connection with the sale of a home, to be illegal. There are many in the industry who think it will be extended to all types of commercial properties which may give buyers an opportunity to take over favorable financing, notwithstanding such language. It is a good case if you are looking for some precedent.

Transferee liability: Another California case, *Ray v. Alad Corporation,* 19 Cal. 3d 22 (1977), held that the purchaser of assets had a continuing products liability exposure to someone who bought a product from the prior corporate owner of the assets. That case demands you take a careful view of the malpractice coverage of your seller and also of the contract provisions.

Acquisition Checklist

The following is an "acquisition checklist"—those factors which should be examined and evaluated prior to any purchase of a health care facility.

A. Areas for Investigation/Negotiation.

    1. General Corporate Matters.

        (a) Articles of Incorporation, bylaws, all amendments thereto and minutes for several years. (The exact number will depend on facts and circumstances.)

        (b) Stock register books or membership records.

        (c) If the seller is publicly held, listing applications, SEC reports and registration statements as well as proxy statements and periodic reports filed under the Act.

        (d) Outstanding loan agreements, trust indentures and the like as well as long term leases and other material agreements.

Even where no assumption is contemplated this review should be made to determine what consents will be needed in order to avoid conflicts with third parties.

(e)   Opinion of seller's counsel—this is a key document which should be negotiated early on. Some of the assurances that a buyer should seek are the following:

      i.   That no authorization, approval, consent or withholding of objection by any regulatory body, federal, state or local is required in connection with the execution and delivery of the acquisition agreement; and

      ii.   That the purchase agreement is valid, binding and enforceable in accordance with its terms.

2.   <u>Tax Matters.</u>

(a)   Federal and state income tax returns. If the nursing home to be acquired is tax exempt, review Forms 990 and 990-T, if any.

(b)   Any determination letters relating to tax-exempt status.

(c)   Tax allocation—This is an important item. See model clause below.

(d)   Property tax filings or returns.

3.   <u>Litigation Matters.</u>

(a)   All pending and threatened litigation occurring within the prior three years should be reviewed—request copies of all auditors' letters collected by the nursing home's auditors.

(b)   Review insurance coverage, especially malpractice.

(c)   Request docket search.

4. <u>Real Estate Matters.</u>

(a) Order and review preliminary title reports.

(b) Review zoning classification and any outstanding conditional use permits. These may be changed on sale.

(c) Leases—watch especially for options and escalation clauses.

5. <u>Reimbursement.</u>

    (a) Contracts or certifications by Blue Cross, Medicare and Medicaid.

    (b) Cost reports filed with governmental agencies and Blue Cross for a period of several years (depending on facts and history).

    (c) All notices of program reimbursement or other communications between governmental agencies and the nursing homes.

    (d) Any pending appeals filed by the nursing home or any governmental agency concerning past reimbursement.

    (e) Allocation of purchase price—just as important here as in the tax area. See model clause below.

6. <u>Certificate of Need/Licensing.</u>

    (a) Certificates of need, Section 1122 approvals—make sure that all ongoing construction is covered.

    (b) Review applications filed in connection with projects constructed since the facility became subject to Certificate of Need or Section 1122 review. Check for violations.

7. <u>Clayton Act, Section 7A And FTC Premerger Notification Rules.</u>

8. Patient Funds—consult state laws and regulations for particular requirements in this area.

Drafting the Acquisition Agreement

When it comes to drafting the acquisition agreement, I urge you to consider the psychology of it very carefully. If you are the buyer, you are going to want much in the way of representations and warranties. You can bet that the seller's attorney is not going to put them in there for you. Therefore, being the buyer, you would like to get the first crack at drafting those representations and warranties. If you are the seller, of course, you want first crack at it. You want to make it as innocuous as you can from your standpoint and as restrictive as you can in terms of ongoing obligations of the buyer. When you (the seller) make it very narrow, the buyer must come back in the awkward position of having to ask you to keep amending your agreement—this puts him on the defensive. So, who deals the deal, who drafts the agreement, can be important in structuring the transaction.

As mentioned before, the structure of the transaction (purchase of assets, purchase of stock, etc.) is important for tax, reimbursement and other purposes. The agreement should be drafted with these factors in mind.

Representations and warranties: The buyer should obtain from the seller clear representations and warranties in these areas:

(a) Cost Reports—A sample contract clause might read:

> The Nursing Home has or by the Closing Date will have timely filed or caused to be timely filed all cost reports and other reports of every kind whatsoever required by law or by written or oral contract or otherwise to be made with respect to the purchase of services by third-party purchasers, including but not limited to Medicare, Medicaid, Blue Cross and insurance carriers and all such reports are complete and accurate; and the Nursing Home has paid, or by the Closing Date will have caused to be paid, all material adjustments which have become due, whether pursuant to said reports or otherwise, and there is no further material liability (whether or not disclosed in any report heretofore or hereafter made) for any such adjustment, and no interest or penalties occurring with respect thereto, except as may be disclosed in the Financial Statements.

In addition to this clause, the parties should also make provision for possible refunds from third-party payors—determine who is entitled to any amounts received.

(b) Certificate of Need/Section 1122 Approval—The seller should give a general warranty and representation that all governmental approvals have been obtained. He should also specifically represent and warrant matters covered by Certificate of Need or Section 1122 review.

(c) Licensing/Accreditation—The seller should warrant that the nursing home has been duly licensèd and accredited in accordance with the buyer's understanding.

There are still other representations and warranties that should be obtained. In all events, be sure that the party giving the warranties and representations is not merely a subsidiary that is going to be liquidated following the sale.

Allocation of purchase price: Again, as we've discussed, the allocation of the purchase price among depreciable and nondepreciable assets can have significant tax and reimbursement consequences. Negotiation over these numbers will be intense. An example of an allocation clause:

> The parties hereby agree that the respective values of the assets purchased under this Agreement are properly allocated below in this section 2.1.3 and the parties hereby agree to report this transaction in accordance with such allocation on all federal, state and local tax returns and in all cost reports filed with any third party payer, including, without limitation, Medicare, Medicaid and Blue Cross:

ACCOUNTS RECEIVABLE	$1,086,979.00
INVENTORY	104,519.00
PREPAID EXPENSES	69,404.00
LAND	1,178,624.00
LAND IMPROVEMENTS	19,713.00
BUILDING	1,717,913.00
FURNITURE AND EQUIPMENT	558,005.00

You might break down the "Furniture and Equipment" allocation even further, allocating among specific assets.

The buyer may wish to allocate as much value as possible to assets with short remaining useful lives. Of course, what can be achieved in the allocation area depends on the sophistication of the parties, together with their respective tax and reimbursement positions.

QUESTIONS AND ANSWERS

Audience: Did you ever have occasion to frame a purchase agreement where it was a sale of stock with a specific allocation of value to the assets that were included in the purchase price of the stock—thereby giving capital gains treatment to the seller and a good argument before the Tax Court as to the proper value of the assets supported by the required documentation?

Sherwin Memel: The answer to that question is yes, it has been attempted; not by me. I am not sure that you can have your cake and eat it, too. I think that's what was done originally in the *PCME* case. The sellers wanted to try to treat it as a tax-free exchange and the buyers actually did a Section 334(b)(2) liquidation. That's the case where the Secretary twice reversed the PRRB and BCA, which had held that there could be a step-up for Medicare purposes and an increase in return on equity. The Secretary said no to this but the courts have now said yes. The buyers were allowed Section 334(b)(2) treatment; it went through an audit and was approved.

Audience: Can you speak to the issue of a father selling his facility to his son and whether or not that is actually a related-party transaction as the guidelines are being interpreted presently?

Memel: Well, I can guarantee that you will have an administrative hearing or litigation. Maybe you can demonstrate an emancipated individual who has sued his father six times, never relied on him for support and never does what he tells him. But, if you have the typical kind of situation where Pop and Son are in the business for a long time and Pop is now getting out and selling it to the son, that's going to be a tough one to uphold. There need only be the potential towards control—some of the examples in the manual are husband and wife or an employee and employer— that kind of situation where you have the ability to influence. The father and son situation is going to be a tough one to prove is unrelated.

Audience: Weren't those regulations originally intended, however, to cover the transactions between two separate corporations or entities with respect to provision of services or products?

Memel: They go way beyond that. They take the position of governing everything, including facilities.

Audience: Could you elaborate on the determination of values when a nursing home is donated to a tax-free organization?

Memel: When a nursing home is donated, you get the lower of fair market value or the seller's historical cost—if it is characterized as a true donation. Where you get into the trouble is in the bargain sale area, where it's intended there be a donation but for some reason they say, "Well, we want you to pay us for a little bit." Then, they wind up getting stuck without getting the best basis because they characterize it as a sale.

Union Organization of a Long Term Care Provider

JEROME BROWN
and
STEPHEN RONAI

Editor's Note: This chapter deals with labor relations in the long term care field. Mr. Brown offers a union viewpoint while Mr. Ronai's presentation takes a management perspective. Questions and answers follow Mr. Ronai's remarks.

The fact that you have labor relations on your agenda, whether from a management viewpoint or a labor viewpoint, is a recognition on your part that unions are going to be a significant factor in the industry for a long time to come. We like to think that when we represent employees, we represent them in a responsible fashion. We also like to think that we have the ability to work with management to give proper patient care. We want the industry to be healthy, because our members' jobs and livelihoods depend on the health of the industry.

It is this nation's policy (expressed in the Wagner Act) to encourage employees to engage in collective bargaining with their employers. Though some people forget nowadays, that is the policy of the federal government—it has not been changed and I don't think it will be changed. We are in a very complex economy and nursing homes are moving more and more into the realm of big business; we have an industry of health care, and I think that you know, without my telling you, that labor unions in health care are here to stay.

Organizing Experience

Since becoming involved with District 1199 (National Union of Hospital and Health Care Employees, R.W.D.S.U.) in Connecticut I have been responsible for organizing approximately 9,000 employees, about 2,000 of them in convalescent homes. We represent, in Connecticut and Rhode Island (where I am particularly responsible), about 2,500 convalescent home employees in thirty-one institutions. These institutions include profit, non-profit, church-related, and also some in the public sector, long term care facilities run by the state of Connecticut. The national union has a little over 100,000 members—the bulk of them in voluntary hospitals and about 15,000 in convalescent homes.

Organizing Nursing Homes

The health care industry is really broken up into three groups—the public sector (hospitals run by state, county and so forth), voluntary hospitals and nursing homes. You can further subdivide nursing homes into those run by chains, nonprofit, and "mom and pop"-type operations.

Our approach in organizing workers in convalescent homes differs depending on what kind of organization is involved. The future for our union in convalescent homes is not with the "mom and pops." It may be with the nonprofits, although you know that in some places some of the profit homes are becoming nonprofits and people are making money in management. Then, of course, there are the chains, where we expect there will be the most significant growth in labor organization. In fact, we feel that it is really inevitable that a large portion of the chains will be organized.

The problems are severe for employees of convalescent homes, and if the union is willing to spend the money and sometimes long periods of time in organizing, we think we can do it. For the last few years we have only been taking calls, and organizing among those people who call us, because the problems for the union in organizing among convalescent homes are severe, too.

You can't organize anybody who doesn't want to be organized. Outside agitators do not have any credibility with employees. The only time that we can organize employees is after the management gives them a kick in the rear-end in some way—or, if management doesn't actually provide the kick, if there is a perception on the part of the employees that they have been kicked.

It's a low-wage industry, there is high turnover, there is no job status for the service and maintenance employees and not as much status for the professional employees as there is in hospitals or in working for the state or city. Nursing home employees generally do not have pride in where they work.

They do enjoy the work; they enjoy taking care of patients. Long term care is much different from the situation in a hospital. Employees in long term care develop relationships with patients and with patients' families. But there is no status attached to the job. And a major reason why people organize in our union is that they feel that they are not accorded proper dignity on the job. They have no say in what goes on. They may work for years and feel that they are not accorded proper dignity by management or by society in general—because the wages are low, the benefits are low, the turnover is high, etc.

Another reason why we expect that union organization will continue stems from the convergence of two movements apart from labor. One is the civil rights movement, which is still going on. The other is the women's movement, which has just begun, especially among working people. In an industry where 90% of the employees are women—who perceive that low wages are partly due to the fact they are women—it is going to have a major impact. There is an awareness on the part of working people that they have rights and that they can exercise their rights.

In many cases they are not being fulfilled. For example, in nursing homes in Connecticut, wages average about ten cents more than the minimum wage. Health benefits for nursing home employees very often just cover the employee—they do not cover their families. I know of only one home in the state of Connecticut with pension coverage for its employees.

There is also what people perceive as a lack of management concern for proper patient care. The people who give the care every day, on weekends, on holidays, on the 11-to-7 shift, who are in direct contact with the patients, are very concerned. They're concerned about the fact that they don't have linen or that the meals are served cold or that they can't get the proper staff in order to give the kind of personal contact that they wish to give to patients—baths or showers, changes, nourishment, etc. They raise these questions—they raise the question of their own dignity on the job more than they raise the question of money when they begin to organize. Once they organize the question of money becomes very apparent because then they realize that the union is also a way for them to raise their salaries and benefits. But a desire for improved patient care and dignity on the job are more often than not the spurs to organization.

Union benefits: Our members average about a dollar more an hour or $40 more a week than do employees in unorganized homes in the state of Connecticut. Ninety percent of our members have family health insurance paid for by the employer. They have disability insurance; they have more holidays and more sick days. They have access to union funds to send their children to camp in the summer and access to scholarship programs for their children. We don't yet have pensions for convalescent home employees, basically because of the reimbursement system, but that is something we are working toward. Generally, the wages and the conditions are much better in organized homes.

We have not been able to do as much as we, or our members, would like to do about staffing. It is very hard to write in a contract what a staffing level is, and it is even harder to get an employer to agree with it. With the problems of patient mix, even if you wrote it in, it would only be for a couple of months and then things would change. We try to handle that through grievance procedures and sometimes through publicity, if that is necessary.

Our members have rights on the job—the right to complain, the right to speak up. We feel, and our members feel, that the benefits of unionization are substantial. In the places where we have organized, after the first couple of years, we see a much more stable work force. In some of our places, there is no turnover at all.

We represent people in some homes that you would not want to go into, and certainly you would not want to put a relative in there. We also represent people in some homes where the care is excellent and the physical surroundings are very good. Unionization certainly does not hurt patient care, though it may not necessarily help it either. We say that it *can* help by cutting the turnover rate and by making people more committed to their jobs.

We feel that the employees very often are more committed to decent patient care than is management. I've dealt with situations where we've gone in to talk about patient care issues—staffing, for example—and have had management read to us from computer sheets about the number of personnel per patient per week or the number of dietary hours. This does not shock *me* so much, but to have management do that when employees are coming in to talk about human problems—I want you to know it shocks the hell out of *them*.

One of the anti-union arguments used by management is that the union will reduce employee dedication, thus harming patient care. That argument might have worked in a small nursing home where management and the owners were directly involved in giving patient care. It does not work anymore in chains; it does not work anymore where the employees perceive that the managers are in business.

We think the prospect for unionization in nursing homes, certainly in New England, and also nationally (judging from what our staff tells us from around the country) is very good. As the concentration continues, as the management is removed further and further from the work itself, employees will perceive that their interests lie in collective action, in organizing a union.

Tactics in an Organizing Campaign

As far as our tactics are concerned, they are really very simple. I'm not giving away any secrets. The best way to organize is when employees come to the union and say, "Hey, we're fed up, we want to organize." That's easy.

In nursing homes, our tactics depend on the size of the home. They also depend on the staff we have available. If a home has fewer than 100 employees, normally an organizer has to "live" with those workers for a period of months, meet them every day or every other day outside work, hand out leaflets, work with a core group. When there are more than 100 employees, we try to work with committees. We have to work with committees because the organizers cannot get to know everybody on every shift.

The level of sophistication of the employees is also important. Some people have experience in working in committees and exercising leadership, and some people do not. If they do not, we have to supply that for them.

Either way, to organize in a nursing home when management is taking an adversary position (which is about 98% of the time) takes a real commitment of staff and a lot of time. That is why our ability to organize in nursing homes is only limited by the amount of staff and time that we have put into it.

National Labor Relations Board election: Once we get a majority, once we get people to meetings, there are two ways we can proceed. We can go with a National Labor Relations Board election. There, we ask management to recognize the union; if management refuses, we then petition the NLRB to hold an election. They will hold a hearing and, supposedly in a fairly short period of time, you will have an election supervised by the NLRB. The election procedure, if it happens in an orderly and speedy fashion, is our preferred way to organize.

Recognition strike: The other organizing alternative is, of course, a recognition strike. The Wagner Act, modified by Taft-Hartley and further modified by the 1974 Health Care Amendments, tries to civilize the process of union representation elections—the way employees have their union recognized (whether by election or any other way).

The history of labor relations is that the most bitter strikes, the most bitter conflicts, have been not over whether we get a nickel more an hour, but over whether or not we have the right to have the union. The Wagner Act was passed to try to give some order to that process; to let unions and employees have access to the NLRB to try to resolve this problem without strikes. When that works, that is by far preferable to us and, I think, to management and certainly to the community at large. When we are talking about convalescent homes, that community also includes the infirm, the sick, and the elderly. So, that is the way we would like to go.

Obstacles to Organizing

However, very often we perceive an attempt on the part of management to frustrate that process with legal maneuvers, delays, unfair labor practices and illegal acts. Management tries to destroy the union's majority in ways that we would say are illegal. In that instance, our recourse is to engage in a recognition strike. We say, "Forget the NLRB, we are going out on strike, so either recognize the union or you won't have any employees."

We try not to do that. But on the other hand, we find it necessary on occasion to do that, not so much for the particular employer as for the

137

industry in general. We want them to know that it is an alternative that the union will sometimes exercise—if they fool around with the election process too much, if they delay too much.

This particular tactic is made more difficult by the 1974 Health Care Amendments, which require ten days' notice before any strike or picketing (or lockout on the part of management). A recognition strike is normally used when there is an attempt to destroy the majority and the union feels that either it acts now or by next week the employees will be intimidated and not able to act at all.

Reimbursement as an obstacle to organizing: Another obstacle to organization is the whole question of reimbursement. When employees begin to organize, whether they are making the minimum wage or the benefits are low, managements always hide behind the statement, "Listen, we are giving whatever we can. We are only getting so much from the state. They are setting our rate. We can't raise the private rate either because it is controlled or because of competition down the street. The Medicaid rate, which provides the bulk of the money, is controlled."

This is something that both labor and management have to confront. It is interesting that governments, whether at the state or federal level, do not address the question of employee wages when they make up the reimbursement regulations. If the amount of money spent on anti-poverty programs were given to the working poor to raise wages, whether through subsidies to management or as a pass-through of decent wages for employees, it would do an awful lot to alleviate the problems of the working poor and some of the other problems in our society. Government really doesn't address that question. They're concerned, especially in the present atmosphere, about keeping taxes down. Unless somebody comes to them in an organized political way and forces them to address that question, they're going to sweep it under the rug.

Problems with the NLRB: The other serious problem we have is with the National Labor Relations Board itself. We feel that labor law reform is necessary because of the delays in the process—the frustration of employee rights. When people are fired or discriminated against for union activity, the remedies come six months, a year, two years later. The remedies, when they do come, are not nearly punitive enough to discourage that kind of activity. The only remedy we find that actually discourges these practices is a management concern that government is going to look very closely over their shoulder. However, the major deterrent is not the government, but the fear of employee reprisal through a strike or job action.

We have come across a number of problems where we have filed for a representation election and management brings unfair labor practice charges they know have no substance, but which gives them a two-month delay. We have situations where the attorneys ask for a long period of time to prepare briefs, and then ask for extensions which the NLRB goes along with (on occasion). There is sometimes even collusion between management and what we refer to as "labor racketeers," who wish to make some sort of "sweetheart" deal. In that situation, the "other" union (in collusion with management) might file charges against management, delaying the election, and this is something that can take forever.

Labor Law Reform

We have won many cases before the NLRB. But even if we get an aggrieved employee back to the job six months later with back pay, if in the meantime employees have been frightened out of exercising their rights, that is a victory for that particular management and its particular view of its responsibility for labor relations. Therefore, we feel that the NLRB should be reformed; we feel that the National Labor Relations Act should be reformed.

Every time we file a petition, the attorneys want a hearing on the make-up of the unit. There is no way in the world that the basic make-up of the bargaining unit is going to change. The precedents are just about chiseled in stone. But, because of this process, you'll have a two-day hearing, you'll have three extra weeks for briefs, you'll have a decision and then a right of appeal. And every step of the way, the attorneys are looking for some sort of procedural fault on the part of the NLRB so they can throw it back into court and keep the whole question boiling.

Notice of job action: One other problem is the question of notice. We are required to give notice before we can call any strikes or job actions. That is a very good law. It allows for adequate provisions to be made for patients. You are not talking about a factory where you make machines; you are talking about a nursing home or a hospital which is taking care of sick people. But that law is frustrated because 98% of the time the ten-day period is not used for making alternative preparations to take care of patients or to transfer them. It is instead used to hire strike-breakers. This is a problem because it makes it even more difficult for employees to exercise their right to strike (which is guaranteed by the law).

Strikes: On the question of strikes, our union has more often than not— 85% to 90% of the time—offered binding arbitration rather than a strike. Our members have a very real concern for the patients because they are the ones who deal with them everyday. They deal with their families. They don't want to walk out. The union has a responsibility not to interrupt patient care. A strike is a last resort—we have the legal right to do it, the employees have the legal right to do it. We try not to strike. But if it is forced upon us and arbitration is turned down and then management uses the notice requirements to further prepare to defeat what we consider to be the legitimate aims and aspirations of the people, we feel the ten-day notice requirement is unfair.

I think that if managements wish to spend enough money and enough time and suffer enough aggravation, they can, more often than not, defeat the union. They can bend the laws, they can disobey the law, they can stall, they can force strikes, they can hire strikebreakers. If they are willing to pay that price in public esteem, in bad reputation, in horrible employee relations for years to come, if they wish to do that, they can do it—we've had that happen, also.

Shared Concerns

We share the concern of managements, especially those managements that are on-site, about the quality of patient care. We share concern about the stability of the work force, about proper training and service. We also share concern about reimbursement.

Reimbursement is something that I happen to know a little about because in Connecticut we were very effective in getting a law passed that says the Medicaid rate has to take into account the reasonable cost of collective bargaining contracts. They can't just apply a formula and say 7% for employee wages this year and if you paid ten, that is too bad for you—they just can't do that. They have to take into account the reasonable costs related to collective bargaining.

Our union and the AFL-CIO statewide had a lot to do with loosening up the reimbursement rate in Connecticut over the past few years. This law has affected the non-union homes as well. And it could not have been done had we not pushed it and had the state AFL-CIO not pushed it.

Conclusion

We are here to stay. The employees wish to be heard, they have a right to be heard, and it's national policy that they should be heard. Cooperation with management is possible 98% of the time. As this industry matures you will find that, as in other mature industries in this country, stable labor relations with unions are necessary and proper.

[Mr. Ronai's remarks follow.]

There is probably no area of the law in which it is more important to exercise the preventive approach than labor relations law representing management. In Connecticut, we try to institute programs of preventive labor relations by conducting in-service analyses of personnel practices. We encourage a so-called self-audit of each employer's personnel practices. We try to give the employees a perception that management does care about their future and is involved in a regular program of improvements in wages and benefits. We do this so that when the union's organizing activities commence, we can at that time maintain our "credibility." If you don't have any credibility when a union organizing drive commences, a union organizer who comes on the premises has an easy job.

You should look at the *Southport Manor* case. *Southport Manor* involved a fifteen-month strike for contract renewal by District 1199. It involved all kinds of violence, and all kinds of problems for the health care facility. The NLRB entered an unusually explicit cease and desist order which was enforced by the Second Circuit Court of Appeals. It was required to be posted in the 1199 offices in New Haven, New York—wherever. When I saw it for the first time, it was shocking to me. Portions of the order read as follows: "We will not threaten any employees of Southport Manor; we will not threaten to kill; we will not threaten to assault; we will not spit on cars; we will not do the following..." These were the orders entered as a result of a mass finding of 8(b) violations against District 1199. Nevertheless, 1199 is a professional union. You always know what to expect when they are involved in a campaign. They have been described as irresponsible, violent, rude, tough and unreasonable. But they have also been described as dedicated, committed and effective. It is impossible for me, in five to seven minutes, to summarize my eleven years' experience in labor organization activities, primarily with respect to District 1199, but some general observations may be helpful.

Termination of employees involved in union activities: Jerry habitually sees the termination of any employee involved in union organizational activity from his own point of view. He sees it as a Section 7 violation, or an 8(a)(1) violation, in that it restrains and coerces the employee. We view a termination differently. If there is restraint and coercion, that is merely an incidental side effect of the implementation of a well-documented personnel program, whereby the employer has instituted a discipline program, and well-documented employee records concerning absenteeism, service and evaluation of performance. That goes hand-in-hand with a personnel program evaluated on a regular basis to review the personnel benefits and implement them. So, if in December the union starts an organizational campaign and you have already announced in September that your governing body has authorized a wage increase on January 1 in accordance with the rise in FLSA minimum wage, the union can come in and debunk your program. It can claim that you are implementing the wage increase merely to undercut unionization. But the NLRB has not yet held a previously authorized and announced implementation of benefits to be an unfair labor practice and interference under 8(a)(1), despite its implementation during a union organizing campaign.

As far as terminations are concerned, if you have a poor employee, who has a poor work record, that employee may end up being your in-house organizer. But if you have not documented his work record and if during the union campaign you seek to terminate him, your activity will be viewed very suspiciously by the Board, because the timing of any discharge raises a presumption of anti-union animus and intent and it may well be the subject of an 8(a)(3) order requiring the employee's reinstatement with back pay.

I think it is necessary for Jerry to be heard here. His point of view cuts across almost all of the areas in this industry represented here today. Jerry's point of view—the point of view of District 1199—addresses itself to the administrative management, the ownership, the employees, patients and their families and ultimately addresses itself to the state licensing agencies. District 1199 will look to a confrontation at a health care institution as not only a means to achieve its economic goals, but as impacting on the ability of the institution to render care in accordance with its license and in accordance with the conditions of participation of Medicaid and Medicare. District 1199's appeal during an organizational drive may also involve some consumer-protection overtones and the attempt to establish, in some cases, a receivership where, because of the type of activity that took place in Southport Manor, the delivery of effective patient care is endangered.

Jerry Brown is here to remind everyone that we have to do our homework. We have to do our homework on all levels and that includes improvements in Section 249 reimbursement levels. Over the years, we have worked with the unions in trying to get our single state agency to make some amendments to our 249 regulations to increase Medicaid reimbursement to include the mandated costs of collective bargaining agreements.

I can say a lot of things about this union. To say the least, they are dedicated. Jerry has been arrested. He has suffered personal injury on the picket line. He has committed himself to the principles of the union. It is interesting that only in the latter part of his discussion did he mention the Taft-Hartley Act. About two or three times he mentioned the Wagner Act. As we all know, the Wagner Act was a 1938 statute that reflected the early intensity of the industrial conflict when management and unions were really going at each other in the most adversarial proletarian vs. capitalist sense. Jerry mentioned the Wagner Act because, I think, 1199 is a throwback to that early era. I am sorry that Jerry didn't bring his recruiting film today—the one that was referred to in the program. It's called, "Like a Beautiful Child," and is not rated PG. It is probably rated LA—you can't see it without your lawyer's approval. The film is a beautiful propaganda appeal to disadvantaged employees, foreign employees, and minority group employees concerning the advantages of joining District 1199. The film is a civil rights minority group appeal against the so-called white establishment—the health care industry.

The inequities that the union used to focus upon—the civil rights movement—has been somewhat ameliorated by the advances made by federal and state legislation, i.e., by Title VII considerations, EEOC involvement, fair employment practices, and I think the general sense of dignity that the black person, the black employee, has now acquired. So the bare racial appeal that they employed in '68 and '69 by the use of Martin Luther King in the film, which you would have seen, would really not be that topical today.

I do agree with Jerry Brown that the feminist movement is a crucial part of 1199's story and it is reflected not only by what Jerry says but by what he does. They have an organizing director who came up to New Haven and commenced to talk to nurses about the need for organization. You've heard recently that Albert Shanker of the American Federation of Teachers has formed a division to turn that union's attention to the organization of nurses. I say to you that the orgainization of professional employees is the next frontier, both in nursing homes and in acute care institutions and hospitals. Nurses feel that they have been imposed upon. Their feelings are a combination of their own feminist concerns and their own dignity plus the fact that they, in a nursing home and many times in a hospital context, are really responsible for the tasks delegated to them by physicians. That has made the nurses' dissatisfaction a fruitful source of organizational activity for 1199. I have not spoken to Jerry about how he feels about Shanker's involvement. I am sure he would not share it with me anyway.

I don't agree with Jerry's statement that the union will strike for recognition. I haven't seen it. They play pretty straight on the first go-round of organization. You can run your campaign against their organizational drive pretty well by-the-book.

All of that is really "by the boards" if you haven't involved yourself and done your homework with your employees in this industry—where it is very difficult to really please people economically because of the limitations imposed by Medicaid reimbursement on economics. The people working in long term care institutions who really render the care are the nurses' aides. Those are people generally holding second jobs. Predominately, at least in urban areas, they are the poor and minority groups who are extremely receptive to the type of emotional and racial appeal used in organizing which 1199 through good training is able to implement.

Jerry may operate differently in different areas. We ran a different anti-union campaign in Stamford, Connecticut then we did in Willimantic, Connecticut, and different again in the Hartford area. In all of them, we learned—maybe not as much as we should have, but we are learning every day.

QUESTIONS AND ANSWERS

Jerome Brown: Before taking questions, let me just respond to Steve's remarks. Whether it is 1199 or the service employees or the teachers' or the nurses' association or other groups who are active in this field, or employees themselves in their own associations (which is where unions started in the first place)—it is a reality. As this industry matures, you are going to have to come to grips with labor unions and you are going to have to come to grips with the legitimate concerns and gripes of your employees. And, you are going to have to deal with them in a mature way. You may forestall it, and you have forestalled it for a long time. But it's going to happen.

Audience: What are the old-line unions—the AFL-CIO, the Teamsters— doing about independent unions that are being formed?

Jerome Brown: There are two types of independent unions. Some are what I would call very legitimate employee associations, formed to meet specific needs. Some are racketeers. You can make a lot of money in this business by making sweetheart deals with nursing homes who feel threatened by us and want protection by having another union in. A lot of people do it. That is a serious problem for us, and in the long run I think it may be a serious problem for the industry.

With respect to the legitimate independents who organize to address the concerns of employees, many old-line unions are starting to affiliate with them. They are bringing them in to give them the national services, a little bit more of a base to operate from and more money towards organization. It is the same thing that is happening in the economy generally. There is more and more centralization and the independent unions are finding that they have to affiliate.

Audience: In the New York City strike a couple of years back, the newspapers reported that something like 200 patients died. Do you think that kind of situation is beneficial to the health care system?

Brown: The estimate of the *New York Daily News* was 17, not 200. Of course, if there is one death, it is too many. That strike took place after we had offered binding compulsory arbitration and the hospitals had turned us down. The employees had the alternatives of turning tail and going back and saying, "What do you want to give us?" or of striking. They voted to strike, something federal law gave them the right to do. I don't think it's ideal that health care employees have to strike. I dislike it, the employees dislike it, but until somebody comes up with something better, that is the type of society we are living in.

Stephen Ronai: I agree with Jerry. One patient dying is one too many. There was a Health Department report documenting how many people died from transfer trauma.

The union is reasonably violent. They say they would not like to strike but they have to. That is the ultimate weapon. They employ it, and while they do protest and Jerry is perfectly sincere about perhaps inculcating a more stable environment in a nursing home, many of the henchmen and many of the people that he employs in an organizing capacity do not have the control over the employees that he might have. Consequently, the situation deteriorates and you are faced with an unhappy alternative.

Audience: Are you using your considerable lobbying strength in any way to obtain legislative relief for the reimbursement ceilings under 249?

Brown: In Connecticut we knocked out ceilings. They imposed a ceiling and, in fact, the ceiling they imposed caused a strike at the Jewish Home for the Aged in New Haven. We settled the contract with some contingency money, which we don't normally do. Our members' getting the money was contingent on our getting the legislature to knock out that ceiling. So, we knocked it out.

Audience: Mr. Ronai, you made a comment previously about union activity leading to nursing homes being put into receivership.

Ronai: That is true, yes.

Audience: You don't know of any specific cases?

Ronai: I don't know of any case where receivership has been instituted for anything more than fiscal problems. I don't know of a state appointing receivers because of a violent strike. But I can foresee that happening under receivership bills.

Audience: Wouldn't that be preempted?

Ronai: If that's a labor dispute it could be preempted as Section 7 and Section 8(b) activity.

Audience: Mr. Ronai, I would like to know what you think the long term impact is on nursing homes that have been unionized. Mr. Brown gave us his opinion—increased wages, greater benefits, and more stable employees. How do you see that? We've heard what the short term effects are, but how does it affect nursing homes five or six years down the road?

Ronai: I disagree with Jerry. It's bad. Everytime there is a contract renewal, there are problems. It forces the third-party payors to look to the table. In some states, the third-party payors are not interested in looking to the table. I think it has a deleterious effect on employee morale and patient care.

Audience: I would be interested in hearing from Mr. Brown as to what the union's position is regarding the patient abuse law.

Brown: We are very much in favor. We are very much in favor of patients' bills of rights. We've agreed to them in some contracts where management thought we wouldn't agree.

Union Organizational Campaign; Supervisor's Checklist re Permitted and Prohibited Tactics During Union Organization Drive

What You Cannot Do During an Organizational Drive

- Ask employees for an expression of their views about a union or its officers, its tactics, etc.
- Prevent employees from soliciting union memberships during their free time on company premises so long as such solicitation does not interfere with work being performed by others.
- Threaten loss of jobs, reduction of income, discontinuance of any privileges or benefits presently enjoyed, or use any intimidating language which may be designed to interfere with the employee's free choice.
- Threaten or actually discharge, discipline or lay off an employee because of his permissible activities in behalf of the union.
- Ask employees whether they have signed or intend to sign a card.
- Discriminate against employees actively supporting the union by intentionally assigning undesirable work to the union employee.
- Conduct yourself in a way which would indicate to the employees that you are watching them to determine whether or not they are participating in union activities. (Of course you can and should keep your eyes and ears open for any improper conduct.)
- Promise employees a pay increase, promotion, betterment, benefit or special favor which had not been planned and announced prior to the commencement of union activity, if they stay out of the union or vote against it.
- Make statements to the employees to the effect that they will be discharged or disciplined if they are active in behalf of the union.
- Urge employees to try to persuade others to oppose the union or stay out of it.

What You Can Do During an Organizational Drive

- Tell employees of the disadvantages that may result from belonging to a union—such as loss of income because of strikes, requirement to serve on picket lines, expense of dues, fines and assessments.
- Tell employees that you or a member of management is always willing to discuss with them any subject of interest to them, and that the door is always open. They do not need an outsider to talk for them.

- Tell employees that you prefer to deal with them directly, rather than through an outside organization, regarding problems arising from day-to-day operations.
- Tell employees about the benefits they presently enjoy.
- Tell employees that they are free to join or not to join any organization without prejudice to their status with the company.
- Tell employees *your opinion* about union policies and union leaders, even though in uncomplimentary terms.
- Tell employees about any untrue or misleading statements made by an organizer, or by handbill, or through any medium of union propaganda.
- Tell employees that the international union probably will try to dominate the local union, or at least try to influence the thinking of local members.
- Lay off, discipline and discharge for cause so long as such action follows customary past practice and is done without regard to union membership or non-union membership. This is one of the most dangerous and difficult areas of judgment. Counsel should be consulted prior to making this as well as other decisions. Documentation of such action in the personnel file is essential.
- Tell employees that no union can make the company agree to anything it does not wish to, or pay more than it is willing or able to do. All such things are subject to negotiations, and the company can still be deemed to bargain in "good faith" when it says no.
- Tell employees about any experience you may have had with unions.
- Tell employees how their wages, benefits and working conditions compare with other companies, whether unionized or not.

Regulations Implementing the Anti-Fraud and Abuse Amendments

IRWIN COHEN
and
MARSHALL B. KAPP

Editor's Note: This area is the subject of a pair of presentations. First, Mr. Cohen provides an overview of P.L. 95-142, together with a discussion of the law's criminal provisions, disclosure provisions, sections governing suspension of practitioners and state Medicaid fraud control units. Mr. Kapp's presentation follows, focusing on the protection of patients' funds. Questions and comments directed at both speakers follow Mr. Kapp's remarks.

P.L. 95-142—What and Why

The topic before us is P.L. 95-142, otherwise known as H.R. 3. It was signed into law on October 25, 1977 and is in fact the largest single piece of legislation that Congress ever passed to fight fraud and abuse in the health care programs. The impetus for congressional action in this area was a number of concerns brought to Congress' attention, first by the Administration and then by various Congressmen who had received complaints about how the programs (Medicaid and Medicare) were being defrauded and abused.

As a result of this, they put together a package of twenty-three separate amendments spanning all of the programs—Medicare, Medicaid, Title V, Title XX, the PSRO program, and all the other small programs administered by HEW. The twenty-three separate provisions have various effective dates. Some of them were applicable upon the signing of the law, others were phased in. The only way to keep track of what's in effect and when is to get a copy of P.L. 95-142.

Criminal Statutes—Section 4

Of foremost concern for us in the Office of Program Integrity (in the Health Care Financing Administration) are the criminal statutes. Those criminal statutes are found in Section 4 of P.L. 95-142. The law made various changes in these statutes, including the upgrading to felonies of many acts which previously were misdemeanors. This was done to make cases more acceptable to U.S. Attorneys by giving them a felony to pursue. It was also hoped that certain practices would be discouraged by upgrading them from misdemeanors to felonies and upgrading the penalties accordingly from one year to five years and from $5,000 to $25,000.

Assignment violations: The statute also defined several new crimes. One of them was assignment violations. Prior to the passage of P.L. 95-142, if a practitioner was guilty of an assignment violation, the program could take away that assignment privilege—which may not have been much of a penalty. What they would do was to stick the beneficiary with the entire bill.

Now, under P.L. 95-142, assignment violations can be criminal if there are a number of them in a continuing pattern. There is another provision which makes some assignments improper so that providers cannot reassign claims to certain collection agencies where they actually sell the claim. This anti-assignment type of provision is a civil provision which, along with the criminal statute, can be used on the same type of violation.

The most obvious assignment violation, of course, is the one where the doctor charges the patient the amount that he doesn't receive from the Medicare program—the Medicare program only pays part of the fee, and he turns around and charges the rest to the beneficiary. Once he takes an assignment, the doctor is required to accept that as a full payment except for any deductible or co-insurance. This is a frequent violation. Also, the improper selling of the amount due him is an assignment violation and could qualify under this criminal section.

Kickbacks, bribes and rebates: The definitions of kickbacks, bribes and rebates were expanded to make them clearer and easier to prosecute.

Section 1909 (d)

One of the major provisions affecting long term care providers is Section 1909 (d). This provision prohibits the solicitation or giving of contributions in exchange for a promise of admission to a long term care facility or continued stay in a long term care facility.

This statute does *not* prohibit the solicitation of contributions. There is a prohibition of solicitation of contributions where it is *tied in* to admission or to continued stay.

But let's be practical about it. Where you (the administrator) are making a contribution solicitation that could be interpreted as influential with respect to a person's stay or admission, you are running a risk of coming under the statute. If you make a general solicitation to everyone and can show exactly what the solicitation was and how it was done—showing it was clearly outside the scope of the statute—you will be all right. A problem will arise where you make a direct solicitation on an individual basis to the patient or the patient's family. If the patient or the patient's family later becomes disenchanted with the facility, or with some of the services, it is going to be a question of what that conversation actually meant. Then you could be in some trouble.

We're not saying you can't do that because we don't know how the courts will rule on it—we have not had any cases on it. And we haven't had any criminal convictions on it, so we don't know how tough the courts are going to be. But we are telling you to make sure to advise your clients to be very careful with this. With respect to this provision as well as the rest of the criminal statutes in Section 4, there are not going to be any regulations and there will be little direction from the Administration as to what they mean because, again, they are criminal statutes. Most of them, however, are very clear and very plain in what they mean. If there is any interpretation to be done, we will leave that to the courts.

Disclosure Provisions—Sections 3,8,9 and 15

The next sections we looked at in the Office of Program Integrity were the disclosure provisions—Sections 3,8,9 and 15. Because they all had to do with disclosure, we packaged them together into a single issuance. This does not mean that there is really one regulation or one set of regulations; we just packaged them together for convenience and because they did interrelate with each other.

There are four separate and distinct provisions. Section 15 requires the provider to disclose the hiring of certain former employees of fiscal intermediaries. If a provider hired a former employee of a fiscal intermediary who was in either a management or an accounting capacity with that intermediary (that served the provider), the provider would have to report the hiring.

Note: As long as full disclosure is made, the Administration does not take any action. It is not grounds for noncertification or nonrenewal of certification. It isn't grounds for any type of action on the part of the Administration. It just makes the Administration aware that those employees have moved into the provider setting, and we would possibly be looking at the provider to see if there is a conflict of interest, if anything were done before the employee left.

The question has come up as to chain office employees—Are they really and truly the providers? We will, in the final version of the regulation, make it clear that this would also include employees of a chain office that serviced the provider. So if the home office hired a former employee of a fiscal intermediary, the providers that particular intermediary serviced would have to report under this. Because it carries no penalty, the provision is really not very controversial. There is a penalty for failure to disclose, and because it is a certification requirement, it is possible that some certification action could be taken.

Federal access to records: Section 9 involves federal access to records. It provides the same access to Medicaid medical and financial records as was previously enjoyed only by the state agencies. The regulation also clarifies that when we say "state agency" we also mean fraud control units set up under the same statute. They would have the same access. So we would not have to go through the state agency and they would not have to go through the state agency in order to get access to the records.

Disclosure of convictions: Section 8 requires the disclosure by providers of owners and certain other individuals who are convicted of crimes against the program. The notice of proposed rulemaking required that the providers disclose an owner convicted at any time of a crime against Medicare or Medicaid—whether before or after the passage of P.L. 95-142. Connected with this provision is the ability of the Secretary, based on this information, to refuse to certify the facility, or to refuse to renew certification the next time it comes up. It does not require that it be done—someone could have been convicted and the Secretary may continue to certify the facility. The person may have been convicted of a crime which is in no way related to the duties he now performs, and that may influence the Secretary not to deny certification of the provider.

The problem with this provision that has been raised under the notice of rulemaking concerns what the provider doesn't know about the employee—Is there an obligation to find out? We feel providers are under an obligation to try to find out. If, after a reasonable effort they do find out, it is then their obligation to inform the Secretary. I might note that while the statute gives the Secretary the option of either refusing to certify the facility or refusing to renew, a violation of this provision—a failure to disclose—could result in an immediate decertification of the facility even if it is in the middle of the year or they're not up for recertification at that time.

Disclosure of ownership: The proposed disclosure regulations were issued with a sixty-day comment period. That sixty-day comment period has run, and we are pretty well along the way in putting out these regulations. What's holding us up, of course, are the many comments that came in under Section 3. This is a big provision which requires providers to disclose the ownership and related information on their ownership and those who have financial ownership of their facility. It also gives the Secretary the authority to ask for information and receive information on an as-needed basis on the dealings between providers and their subcontractors. Providers are required to give information as to the ownership of the subcontractors with which they deal.

Many of the comments ask how the providers are supposed to get this information. How do they know who their subcontractors' owners are? We suggest that when you are making the contract—since you know you may be asked for this information—you secure the information at that time. It is easier to do this as part of the contract negotiation than it is six months later after the contractor has already been paid. If you then come back and say HEW wants to know who your owners are, they'll tell you where to go.

There are times when, although you may know who your owners are, you may not know some of the information about them—for example, what other facilities and interests they have in the health care industry that are also participating in the program. This is one of the pieces of information that is required by the statute to be submitted.

We are putting into the final regulations what one might call a "good-faith effort" requirement. There must be some type of effort which would show that you have tried to collect this information; you must disclose to the government that this information was not secured, not merely that it didn't apply. If you leave the space on the form blank, it indicates there is no such person with an ownership interest. But if you leave the space blank because you can't find out about a person with an ownership interest, you must show us that you tried to secure such information. We could then, if need be, go in and try to secure that information ourselves.

We suggest that a good-faith effort requires at least several pieces of writing. You should keep on record the communications you have had with the owners or other related parties so as to protect yourselves against any possible incrimination under this statute.

In the final regulation, we are putting in some examples showing how to compute a disclosable ownership interest. Everybody was confused about the 5% ownership, direct ownership, indirect ownership, ownership via financing, etc. The examples in the final regulation will give an indication of how to compute whether someone actually has a 5% ownership interest—a disclosable interest.

Suspension of Practitioners

Another provision which tangentially affects the long term care industry is the suspension of practitioners under Sections 7 and 13. Section 13 is just taking away the program review teams, set up under the 1972 amendments, that never really got started and were never operational. Congress felt that where there was a need for peer review, it could be handled by existing peer review organizations—PSROs or what have you. Any suspension that previously needed PRT review before it could take effect no longer requires peer review. In most cases, though, we get peer review anyway from PSRO or local peer review bodies.

The difference between Section 7, which is the suspension of practitioners, and what we had before (Section 229 of the 1972 amendments) is that this provision automatically suspends a practitioner from both the Medicare and the Medicaid programs upon a conviction under either program. If a practitioner is convicted under Medicare, he is automatically out of both programs. There is an appeal mechanism (as there was under Section 229), but it takes place after the suspension has taken effect.

The suspension is for a fixed period of time and after the expiration of that fixed period of time, the practitioner may ask to come back into the program. The Secretary would then hear that petition to find out whether there have been further acts against any of the programs or acts by any other administrative agency that deals with practitioners or any other insurance companies or any other court. If the Secretary is convinced that the party is able to come back into the program, he may readmit the practitioner. If the Secretary denies readmittance, there would again be an appeal from that denial.

We have a large number of practitioners who have been suspended under these provisions compared to a smaller number who were thrown out prior to P.L. 95-142. So it is actually working. You might note that this provision only applies to physicians and other practitioners. It does not replace Section 229 of the 1972 amendments. Section 229 still exists and can be used against practitioners (including physicians) where there are no convictions, but rather a finding of abusive practices. It can still be used against institutions that we are going to suspend for fraud and abusive activities. This provision, the old 229 provision, has with it the right to an appeal prior to suspension.

With respect to Section 7, we are proposing some changes in the definition of a "practitioner." There is some question about groups of practitioners—whether that's a clinic or a provider corporation. If you look at the language in the notice of proposed rulemaking, you find a very tight definition of "group of practitioners" into which most practitioners would not fall. They would therefore be subject to the suspension provision. It is the intention of Congress not to get involved with anyone here except doctors and other physicians.

State Medicaid Fraud Control Units

Section 17 of P.L. 95-142 gave the federal government funding ability for state Medicaid fraud control units under the Medicaid program. It gave us the ability to give them 90% funding to set up such units for a three-year period, beginning in October, 1977. Most of these units are set up in the state attorney general's office and they have both investigation and prosecution authority. Congress expects that after three years, these units will be self-sustaining and the 90% funding will no longer be needed. We will have to see what happens at the end of the three years.

To date, twenty-two states have qualified and set up operational units. (These twenty-two states represent two-thirds of the Medicaid money being expended.) We expect to have about thirty states. Most of the large states have set up units, and the ones that haven't are generally too small to warrant it. They are waiting to see if they get some longer-term financing.

Medicaid Administrative Sanctions Requirement

Finally, I'd like to discuss one set of regulations we are putting out that isn't exactly a result of P.L. 95-142, but is something that I think you will be interested in knowing about.

We will soon be putting out a notice of proposed rulemaking on the Medicaid administrative sanction requirement. These regulations will establish minimum requirements for a state with respect to sanctions that it can take. We were surprised to find out that some states, under the Medicaid program, had no sanctions in their statutes that they could take against providers who were involved in fraud or abusive activities.

This provision would require states to have as part of their state plan certain minimum administrative sanctions. One such sanction is to be able to collect overpayments. Another one is to be able to suspend practitioners. A third is to be able to withhold payment from practitioners who are subject to pending investigations. These, for the most part, will be similar to what the Medicare program has.

Most states welcome this. Many were having problems getting such legislation through their state legislatures. But as you know, wherever a federal regulation requires the state to have something in order to qualify for the Medicaid program, that automatically becomes part of the state provisions. Thus, when we issue this regulation, all states will be required to have this as part of their state plans.

Referring Cases to the Inspector General

I would also like to mention that the Office of Program Integrity in HCFA checks the operation of both Medicare and Medicaid fraud and abuse activity by overseeing the state agencies in the Medicaid program and the contractors under the Medicare program. Where we identify cases of potential criminal fraud, we are now turning these cases over to the Office of the Inspector General. They—sometimes with our help, sometimes with the help of the FBI and other organizations—are responsible for the criminal investigation and prosecution of the cases.

What we are doing in the Office of Program Integrity is reviewing all of the abuse activity, overseeing the activities for taking the administrative sanctions—the programmatic type of review—and, where there is a criminal violation and a need for criminal investigation, we then turn that over to the Office of Investigations.

[Mr. Kapp's remarks follow.]

Protection of Patients' Funds

Before I speak about the patients' funds regulations, it is necessary to say a little about the structure of the Health Care Financing Administration (HCFA). The responsibility for developing patients' funds regulations rests in the HCFA component known as the Health Standards and Quality Bureau. The Health Standards and Quality Bureau is further broken down and the responsibility for the development of these regulations rests with the Division of Long Term Care, which is part of the Office of Standards and Certifications.

The reason that the responsibility for patients' funds regulations was lodged with the Health Standards and Quality Bureau was that it was felt that these regulations relate directly to patients' rights, as opposed to other regulations which relate more to the financial aspects of the nursing home industry.

Regulations Governing Patients' Funds

Section 21 of P.L. 95-142, the section that authorizes and requires regulations on patients' funds, resulted from a background of many years of, to be very blunt, horror stories about misappropriation and misapplication of patients' funds in long term care facilities. There was a General Accounting Office report several years ago discussing the problem, a number of HEW audit agency reports addressed the problem, and Section 21 arose in response to a combination of these factors.

For those of you who are not familiar with the legislation itself, let me briefly paraphrase Section 21. It is composed of two sections, 21(a) and 21(b). Section 21(a) directs HEW to promulgate regulations which require facilities to establish and maintain a system that assures a full and complete accounting of patients' personal funds, with the use of separate accounts for such funds to preclude any commingling of these funds with facility funds or the funds of any other person besides another patient.

Section 21(b) essentially requires HEW to promulgate regulations that define those costs that may be charged to the personal funds of patients in skilled nursing facilities or intermediate care facilities and those costs that must be included in the basic per diem or monthly rate in SNFs or ICFs.

Development of the regulations: A notice of proposed rulemaking as to Section 21(a) was published on September 1, 1978. We received several hundred comments representing a broad spectrum of providers and consumers. We are now in the process of rewriting the rule into a final rule, taking into account the comments we received. Basically, the policy decisions have now been made, and we are in the process of what we like to think of as fine tuning. In other words, we are now in the process of making sure we can accomplish the policy objectives that have been decided upon without, on one hand, making them so cumbersome and burdensome on the facility that it either cannot be done, or cannot be done without tremendous expense or defeating the purpose of protecting the patients' rights. On the other hand, we want to make sure that it is not so chock full of loopholes as to be meaningless and unable to accomplish its purpose.

No proposed rule has yet been developed with regard to Section 21(b). It was not done originally because of an uncertainty within HCFA as to the congressional intent with regard to 21(b). In light of the comments that we received on 21(a) relating to 21(b) and other considerations and general rethinking and discussion, the issue has now been resolved in favor of developing 21(b) regulations. The responsibility for this is with the Health Standards and Quality Bureau. We are currently beginning development of a regulation that will do what the statute directs it to do—which is to differentiate those services that must be included in a facility's basic per diem or monthly charge from those services for which a facility can impose an extra charge upon an individual patient. Also, reasonable costs for those extra charges will be defined.

Let me turn my attention to a few specific areas that are included in the 21(a) regulations. A number of controversial and troublesome issues are included in these regulations.

Should regulations be mandatory? A number of comments raised the issue of whether these patients' funds regulations should be mandatory for all facilities participating in Titles XVIII and XIX. The current position is to require that these regulations be applicable to all facilities that participate in Titles XVIII and XIX. Our thinking is that if facilities are permitted to opt out, essentially to establish a policy of not handling any patients' funds, then patients' funds simply won't be protected and the purpose of the legislation would be defeated. In order to meaningfully protect patients' funds, we feel it is necessary and proper for the regulations to apply to all facilities.

Incompetent patients: A number of comments raised the issue of the incompetent patient—the patient incapable of handling his own funds. We realize that given the patient population in these types of facilities, this is a real concern. The proposed rule suggests a procedure requiring facilities to institute formal incompetency proceedings or permitting certification of incompetency by a physician. This is going to be changed. It became apparent to us that the proposal was not satisfactory, that to require the facility to initiate incompetency proceedings would impose a tremendous and truly unreasonable burden on the facility. It also had negative policy implications, in the sense that we are not anxious for patients we are supposed to be protecting through our regulations to be hauled into court en masse in formal incompetency proceedings.

To resolve this problem, it appears we are going to adopt a position leaving the law of incompetency as it currently exists. We would make clear that a patient in a facility is to be presumed competent to manage his own funds (a rebuttable presumption). We make clear that the rights that are contained in our regulations are to apply to all patients at all times—except where there has been a formal adjudication of incompetency. This would, as I said, leave the law in its current state, where a facility or a family could institute formal incompetency proceedings, or where a patient could work out, through an ad hoc arrangement with family, or through a representative payee or through a friend or whatever, an informal arrangement for the management of his funds. Our intent is to leave the law as it is, realizing that any change would be unsatisfactory in some respect.

Individual interest-bearing accounts: Some comments posed a question regarding the requirement in the proposed rule that individual interest-bearing accounts for each patient who turns over his funds to a facility be established. We were convinced by these comments that this would be unduly cumbersome, and current thinking is to permit the facility the option of either depositing individual patient funds in individual accounts or depositing individual patient funds in a combined patient account (keeping track, of course, of the contribution of each patient and prorating the interest). We feel this would accomplish the same purpose.

There was also a question raised as to the proposed requirement that funds be deposited only in bank accounts insured by the FDIC. Our thinking is to change that to permit deposits in any account insured under federal or state law.

Cost of administering the regulations: A big concern in the comments was, who is going to pay the costs of administering the patients' funds regulations. Contrary to popular opinion, we are aware of the inequities in imposing burdens on facilities that require the expenditure of great sums of money without reimbursing the facilities. It is going to be the Health Standards Quality Bureau's position that the cost of administering patient accounts should be an allowable cost and reimbursable. (I can't forsee any circumstance under which a facility would be allowed to charge a patient the costs of administering this account.)

Petty cash: There were a number of comments as to petty cash requirements. In the proposed rule, there is a requirement that any funds in excess of $50 be placed in an interest-bearing account, and that only $50 of an individual patient's funds be kept in a petty cash amount. That will most likely be raised to $150—a figure I think more realistic.

Notification of state agencies: There was a provision in the proposed rule regarding the facility's duties when a patient, because of interest accruing or because of unspent personal needs funds, was in jeopardy of becoming ineligible for Medicaid or supplemental security income benefits. There was a duty imposed on facilities to notify both patients and the applicable state agency. Comments pointed out to us, and I think have convinced us, that this is both unduly burdensome on the facilities and, in fact, infringes upon the trust relationship—the fiduciary relationship—that we are attempting to establish between the facility and the patient with regard to his funds.

Our current thinking is not to require the facility to notify any state agency when this occurs. We are thinking in terms of requiring the facility to notify the patient since, when a facility has a Medicaid-eligible patient, it is in the facility's best interest to keep that patient eligible for Medicaid because if the patient becomes ineligible, it will have an empty bed.

Accounting procedures: One last point I would like to cover refers to the accounting procedures that are going to be used to administer the requirements we set up. A number of comments asked whether we were going to specify a particular procedure to be used. We realize that the perfect procedure does not exist or at least we don't know of it and, therefore, current thinking is not to require a specific accounting procedure but rather to leave it to the facility to develop a procedure that comes out to the end that we want to achieve. We hope to append as guidelines accounting procedures—but these would not be mandatory; they would simply serve as guidelines.

QUESTIONS AND ANSWERS

Joel Hamme: The ownership disclosure statute and the provisions in the proposal would require providers to disclose direct or indirect ownership interests of 5% or more in the provider. From reading the legislative history, I gathered that the reason Congress did this was to enhance the detection of related organizations and to deter unnecessary cost increases.

HEW has now issued proposed regulations which indicate that they would make a finding of a related organization whenever there is any common ownership, and not just as it is now, substantial common ownership.

In view of this most recent proposal, is there any possibility that HEW will change the ownership disclosure regulations to require disclosure of all ownership interest? Or, is there any possibility that HEW intends to view the congressional benchmark of 5% as what Congress thought of as the minimal amount needed to establish a common ownership and therefore will go back and ask Congress to change the statute to redefine related organizations?

Irwin Cohen: It is important to note that there really is no tie-in between this statute of disclosure and the definition of what are related organizations. This statute is intended to give the Administration a tool that can be used, among other things, to detect possible situations of related organizations.

The 5% is just a figure that we felt could be used as a starting point. That does not mean that someone with a 5% ownership is necessarily related. And it does not mean that someone with less than a 5% ownership is not related. The two are not tied together in any manner.

If we find that the 5% ownership is giving us more information than we can handle or not enough information, we will go back to Congress and make the changes. But as far as tying-in to what is a related organization and what is not, the two rules are not supposed to be the same.

Its other purpose, forgetting the disclosure of ownership information and the related organization principle, is to determine what types of services are being rendered by what types of organizations, and how control is being changed throughout the country. Much of our general history and our concept of where we are going in the health care industry relate to the changes that have taken place in ownership and control. That gives us a lot to do with our planning. So, there are purposes other than just trying to find related organizations.

Hamme: I guess the question I should have asked first was, are you involved at all in the proposed rewrite which redefines what a related organization would be?

Cohen: That is being done in the Medicare Bureau's Division of Provider Reimbursement and Accounting Policy. As most components do when they are writing regulations, they send those regulations, before they even go out for notice of proposed rulemaking, to other components within the Health Care Financing Administration. It goes to the Inspector General's office, the General Counsel's office, to see if there is any input that they would have as it may affect their organizations. From that point of view, we are involved in the regulations since we are one of the components being consulted on it, and we are trying to make sure there is coordination.

Hamme: The proposed ownership disclosure regulations require providers to disclose ownership interests or certain positions of employment that are held by a person previously convicted of program-related crime. The current proposals seem to envision that HEW will only make a decision on sanctions after the fact—after the provider discloses that it has hired somebody who was previously convicted of a program-related crime, or after it discloses the fact that it now has a part-owner who has previously been convicted of a Medicare or Medicaid program crime.

Is HEW contemplating the possibility of permitting the provider to seek opinions on sanctions before it employs these people or before ownership interests are transferred? Has it considered the fact that without a procedure, very likely, people with program-related crimes simply won't be hired?

Cohen: This question was raised during the notice of proposed rulemaking. Our general counsel had a lot of difficulty with our taking a position where we would review a decision before it actually happened —reviewing a provider's proposal to hire someone and saying whether this would or would not affect the provider's acceptability.

In a situation where a provider has hired someone who has been convicted of a crime and it is the Secretary's determination that this person in such a position would cause the provider to be terminated or not to be certified, from a practical point of view, the provider will generally be given an opportunity to reorganize itself so that that person will not be there anymore. We are not going to throw a provider out of the program if they have the ability to rectify the situation. (Again, there are many legal problems without getting involved in these decisions prior to any hiring so we are not going to change that at this time.)

Hamme: My last question is for Marshall Kapp. I gather that it is your feeling that the patients' funds regulations should apply to all Medicare and Medicaid facilities. With all due respect, I don't think that really is an issue. Everybody agrees that if you are a Medicaid or Medicare facility and you handle patients' funds you therefore agree to abide by whatever regulations there are. The issue really is: Should a facility be required, as a condition of Medicare or Medicaid participation, to handle a patient's funds upon his request?

My reading of the fraud and abuse legislative history is that what Congress was concerned with was not that there was a dearth of facilities that were handling patient funds, but simply that many of the facilities that did handle funds, were—either through confusion or outright fraud or abuse—mishandling them.

Have you any sort of response to the fact that facilities should be required to handle a patient's funds upon his request? Have you conducted any sort of study that would indicate that if you allowed facilities *not* to handle patient funds, the patients could do without this service?

Marshall Kapp: I can't refer to any empirical studies that have been done. But going on the basis of the public comments that we received in response to the notice of proposed rulemaking, my answer would be in the affirmative. We are convinced that there would be a large number of patients who, either because of their mental capacity or just because they are nursing home patients (without family or friends), would not be able to handle their own funds or to make appropriate arrangements.

There is a need to have some responsible party to whom that patient can turn as a last resort to handle the funds. If we don't impose that obligation on the facilities there will be patients left in the lurch. As I say, this feeling is based on the comments we have received. There may well be a study on it, but I am not aware of one.

Hamme: Many providers are outraged that they are going to be required to do this because at least a number of them in the past have simply had a policy of not handling patient funds—it's too much of a headache. Some of the public interest groups, who have a very different position from that of provider organizations on most issues, seem to agree with us—but only to the extent that they feel facilities have an inherent conflict of interest and therefore should never be allowed to handle patient funds. Have you considered that as well?

Kapp: Hopefully, any inherent conflict of interest will be alleviated by the requirements contained in the regulations for separate accounting. I don't know how else to respond—we realize that this is controversial and there is no way to avoid that.

Audience: Is any consideration being given by HEW to the fact that the passing of all these regulations en masse is eventually going to put the small long term care facility out of business?

I represent large, medium and small facilities. The large can cope with the regulations because they have the staff. Right now the medium are struggling. But there is absolutely no way the small can handle these regulations—they don't have any staff. It is the administrator who must do all of this work. And you're putting more and more criminal sanctions into the regulations.

Who is going to want to run a small long term care facility under these conditions, especially when there is no money? Are you considering that eventually you are going to drive the small facility out of business?

Kapp: Can I ask you to be specific as to which regulations you are referring to?

Audience: The patients' funds regulation in the State of New York says the funds must be put into an interest-bearing account. You can just imagine a full term facility—a resident is going to want 50 cents one day, a dollar the next day, and a quarter the day after that; and by regulation, the controller must distribute the interest on their accounts to each of the residents. It is absolutely impossible for him to do that.

Kapp: You raise a point that I hope won't be lost on people. Our regulations define minimum requirements for facilities. States are free to, and often do, impose much more stringent requirements on the facilities. This is something that we don't oppose and we don't really have anything to do with that. So, it should not be lost on you that our requirements are minimums and the various states can and often do impose more stringent requirements.

We are not unmindful of the cost implications of our regulations. This is something that preys on our minds constantly, given the current climate. I wish I were, in my current position, developing regulations for quality standards, fifteen years ago, when money was free and we had the smorgasbord approach to social problems—where we just laid out all our resources and said take what you need and as much as you need.

That isn't the current climate. We realize that we exist in a climate of very limited resources and we try to do our best to tailor our requirements with that in mind. There are those who would argue that we don't succeed; but that is a different question. As far as whether this is something we are cognizant of, and that we try to address, I would emphatically say yes.

Audience: Since you are putting the providers in the banking business, are we going to be obligated to disclose the savings rate on the individual accounts?

Kapp: Obviously, I don't have an answer for you. I would argue with the basic premise that we are putting you in the banking business. I would submit that we are putting you in the business of acting as a fiduciary.

Audience: My second question is more serious, and it is in the patients' rights area. It seems to me that the next logical step to be taken by HEW is to tell us what level of care and what private rate we can charge.

Kapp: I understand there are a number of states that have indeed abolished the rate differential between private-pay patients and Medical Assistance patients. I don't want to comment on that, other than to note that it has been done. It is my understanding of current HEW thinking that this is not being given consideration in HEW now.

Let me digress for a minute. Some of you may not be aware that apart from the regulations we have talked about this morning, the Health Standards and Quality Bureau is currently developing a proposed rule that would be a comprehensive rewrite of the Medicare and Medicaid regulations for skilled nursing facilities and intermediate care facilities. There will be an extensive section defining the condition of participation for patients' rights.

It was suggested, by patients' advocates, that we prohibit facilities from discriminating against any patient in either admission or provision of services based on their source of payment. Our current position is not to include such a provision but rather to include a provision—and this is going to generate a lot of controversy—prohibiting discrimination, based on source of payment, in admissions policies. We've heard an awful lot about Medicaid patients who are discriminated against in admissions and who can't get into facilities, and at least at the notice of proposed rulemaking stage, we are going to come out with this provision.

Audience: Have there been any empirical studies made by HEW in its proposed rulemaking as to the cost of allocating interest in a commingled account? Also, in view of the requirement now for interest-bearing accounts, what do you see the responsibility of the homes to be with respect to the great panoply of available accounts giving different rates of interest? Will liability be imposed if one does not seek the maximum rate of interest at any given time?

Kapp: To answer the second question first, the regulation as it stands in its current state of development just requires deposit in an account that is insured under federal or state law. It does not require, and I am sure it will not require, facilities to go shopping around—so I don't see that requirement being placed on a facility.

Regarding the first question, about studies of costs implications, I can't refer to any empirical studies. When proposed regulations are circulated within HEW, we ask for that type of response from the other agencies and from everybody that has the opportunity to comment. We, of course, have hundreds of public comments on the notice of proposed rulemaking, and we are currently, in our fine-tuning process, speaking with experts in the accounting and auditing field. Hopefully, they are going to help us fine-tune so we can strike a balance between impossible, unduly burdensome regulations on one hand, and those which have no substance to them at all, on the other hand. My answer is, no, there have not been any empirical studies but we are open to that kind of input.

Audience: I have a partial problem with the 21(b) approach, especially the preliminary stuff the Medicaid Bureau was talking about in relation to the sequence of timing. While the aggregate dollar of each regulation does not really make a difference, the sum may.

We have uniform cost accounting and reporting coming in later this year. Would you see some wisdom in delaying putting out the 21(b)-type regulation until we had some idea of what is in the uniform cost reporting experience—even though it may take us two years to get enough experience?

If you look at what is covered in an ICF benefit, something like routine care or nursing services is a generic category. But we have a tremendous amount of problems in how states have, in fact, defined that. Some states cover laundry services in their Medicaid plans, others don't. By putting out a rule that says that would be an excluded category that is part of the exclusion list instead of the inclusion list, you create all sorts of havoc. Social activities, part of the original draft, may kill all social components of care within a long term care setting. It further relates back over to Section 1909(d), where we have been trying to define what it is that solicitation of funds can or cannot be used for. We are going to be creating total havoc and it is going to be just another disruption that is going to reflect negatively and have potential cost consequences.

Some of us are pleading with the Department. Let us get a period to evaluate what we have done, so we can find out whether it has any impact other than filling out a lot of papers, a lot of forms, and giving you a lot of information that nobody is taking any time to read anyway.

Kapp: There are a couple of comments I would make. In the legislation itself, Section 21(c)(2), there is a provision that the Secretary of HEW shall issue the regulations required for subsection (b) within 90 days after date of enactment.

Audience: That was March 1977, if I recall.

Kapp: We are a little overdue already, which I think may somewhat limit our leeway.

Audience: Can you not go back to Congress and ask for some sort of extension? If you look at Section 19, you are already in violation of the law on that section. You're talking about putting out your manual by October 25th of this year and we are talking about a two- to three-year lead-time period on the hospital plan. The chaos in long term care is ten times worse than in the hospitals. If the Department really would like to help clean up and improve and professionalize the field, you need to go back to Congress with us and say, give us two years, give us three years; we are taking these steps but we've hit these problems. Sometimes, we don't see the Department telling Congress that the problems are not only the problems of the providers, but the problems of government trying to do its job, too.

Kapp: I don't really have an answer, other than that the point is well taken.

Audience: Do providers have to seek out the highest available interest rates for patient funds? Would failure to do so result in some civil liability?

Kapp: I don't anticipate that happening. Our regulations, by specifying accounts insured by FDIC or under state law, would cover the obligation of the facility to deposit the fund.

Cohen: You might point out that this is, of course, the federal minimum requirement. That does not mean that there may not be other good reasons for providers to seek out higher interest rates. There may be state rules or the threat of civil recrimination. The federal minimum standards won't require it. That does not mean you shouldn't do it.

Audience: What I'm saying is that by setting up this special fiduciary relationship, you are putting the burden on providers to seek the highest rate. Has anyone made a calculation of how much money it would cost the taxpayers of the United States if you added, for example, 10% a day in administrative costs by these regulations?

Kapp: I can't refer to any such study.

Audience: If the facility is required to deposit the patient's funds in an interest-bearing account, will they also be required to report monthly to the local department of social services how much interest has been earned for that patient, and will that patient's participation change every month?

Kapp: I thought I had addressed that when I said that our current thinking was not to require the facility to report to the local service department on each patient account and to give the patient the option of having the funds deposited in a non-interest-bearing account so that it wouldn't threaten his eligibility. We don't intend to impose a requirement of reporting to the social service agency.

Audience: But the local department of social services requires that it be notified of any change in income.

Audience: Is there going to be any clarification of the disclosure-of-ownership requirement with respect to publicly traded corporations and large chain organizations?

Cohen: At this point in time, we are not making a special rule for the chain organizations, although we are working on one to determine whether we can make a single disclosure for the chain organizations. But even within many of the chain organizations, the provider periods are different. They have different providers. They have changes of ownership in the middle of the year. They have purchases and sales which will require the individual providers to give us that information. Once we get our system rolling, if we can accommodate single reporting by a chain organization, and then a reference to that by each provider, that may be sufficient. We are working toward that goal. At this time, though, we are going to require it all and later we will accommodate the chains.

Investigation and Prosecution of Program Fraud by Long Term Care Providers

LAWRENCE LIPPE

Editor's Note: Formerly HEW Assistant Inspector General for Investigations, Mr. Lippe is now with the Department of Justice.

It is often said that the finest children are those born of illicit activities.

The activities of the Inspector General's office and the activities of the Medicaid fraud control units in twenty-two different states attest to the accuracy of that saying. Indeed, more often than we perhaps expected, we are referred to by the colloquial name sometimes given to illegitimate children—but if that tells me anything, it assures me that we are probably doing our job correctly. But we are no longer in our infancy stage—we are off and running.

I am going to describe a number of our activities, present and planned, many of which impact upon the long term care area, and many of which are addressed to individual providers.

HEW Inspector General

The concept of the Inspector General's office was long overdue. The Inspector General is independent. He is appointed by the President and, importantly, can only be removed by the President—not by the Secretary of the Department in which he serves. In the event that the President seeks to remove the Inspector General, full justification must be submitted by the President to Congress.

There is a dual reporting requirement, in that we report to the Secretary (and nobody else in the Department) and to Congress. One might describe us as a "mini-GAO" in that regard, although we are not creatures of Congress as are the GAO people. Under the new Inspector General (IG) bill, which has set up Inspector General offices in 12 other departments and agencies, there won't be an annual report; instead, there will be two semi-annual reports.

The Inspector General in HEW carries out his function through three principal components. One is the HEW audit agency, which today employs about a thousand people, a little over 800 of whom are professionals. The next major component is the Office of Investigations, the office that I head. Our responsibility is principally the investigation of all allegations which, if true, would constitute a crime and which involve any of the Department's programs. A very substantial portion of our caseload in the Office of Investigations is in the health care field. A third component that plays a significant role in the proactive activities that we are engaged in, and that we fondly refer to as our "think-tank," is the Health Care and Systems Review Group.

Each of these groups is headed by an Assistant Inspector General. The Health Care System Review Group is not limited simply to health care matters. It gives us the necessary programmatic expertise without our having constantly to go to the program people themselves; this again gives us a certain desired measure of independence from the programs. A senior staff of people who have had extensive experience in the various programs—both at the state and federal level—assist the Inspector General in carrying out that part of his mandate that is not just fraud and abuse but that also gets into the economy and efficiency area.

It is with a blend of these three groups that we often come into contact with you and your clients. For example, when we get into a complex criminal investigation of a nursing home, one that perhaps started out as a routine programmatic-type audit, my criminal investigators will call upon the expertise of the audit people. At that time, they (the auditors) will be detailed to assist in what is now characterized as a criminal investigation. At any given time, we have about 100 of the 800 audit professionals on detail to us, engaging in what would best be characterized as investigative audits.

Interaction with Medicaid fraud control units: We play a very substantial role in the IG office (a role we share with the HCFA people) in dealing with the Medicaid fraud control units. We work very closely with them. We play a large role in providing the necessary training for those units which have staffs that are not very experienced but are learning and gathering that experience.

We are beginning to play an even larger role in working out relationships between these fraud control units and their federal counterparts. In almost any Medicaid investigation or activity, there is concomitant and concurrent federal, as well as state, jurisdiction.

You may ask yourselves, who makes the cut, in terms of when the state fraud control units will be dealing with your clients in an investigation, versus when, say, the local U.S. Attorney will? As evidenced by the congressional intent when they set up these fraud control units, and as evidenced by our philosophy, we believe that the bulk of the fraud and abuse activity, insofar as the Medicaid program is concerned, ought to be the responsibility of the fraud control units.

However, there are considerations that will bring federal jurisdiction into play. One of the principal considerations that often goes into a decision as to whether it will be handled federally or by the fraud control unit, or jointly, is the existence of a far more pervasive federal criminal statutory scheme than that present in most, if not all, of the states. As an example, mail fraud is a statute which has broad application and often is able to come into play when the state statutory scheme is quite weak.

Perhaps a more dramatic example is the innovative use to which the Department of Justice is putting the so-called RICO (Racketeer Influenced and Corrupt Organization) statute. Indeed, recently, in the state of Tennessee, we returned an all-encompassing 300-count indictment against a major medical provider, charging him not only with numerous substantive counts (false filing, false claims and fraud), but also with a RICO count. This is dramatic in that, upon conviction, there is a mandatory property seizure and forfeiture provision. In other words, we are claiming and intend to prove in that case (and I anticipate we will be doing this in other cases) that the clinic, the medical practice of which he was the sole entrepreneur, was financed with capital which was generated by his pervasive illegal activity. Upon conviction, that doctor not only is going to do some good, hard jail time but will also lose his practice.

I am citing some of these examples as the basis for the process by which decisions are made as to whether state versus federal emphasis will be put on a given investigation. Another instance where we, on the federal level, may have to take the case (often working jointly with the state) involves a situation in which the nursing home under scrutiny is part of a larger organization—where it is part of a chain operation with the home office in one state, records in another state, and there is multi-state (in some cases, multinational) activity. To have a fraud control unit deal with this matter may present a problem, for example, in terms of nationwide process—the state does not have it. If we convene a federal grand jury, we have nationwide process. That is often a very critical consideration. Of course, if the person involved in a particular scheme is a federal employee or official, that is an even more compelling reason why we will want to take jurisdiction of the matter at the federal level.

But I am citing the exceptions, because the bulk of the activities involving investigation of long term care providers and skilled facility providers is going to be handled more and more—and certainly in the twenty-two states in which these units have been certified—by those fraud control units. There will, however, always be a rather visible federal presence, not to the exclusion of, but in coordination with, the fraud control units. We are encouraging, in a number of states, the fraud control unit heads and the local U.S. Attorney to get together and work out an arrangement by which the fraud control unit's prosecutors can be sworn in as Special Assistant U.S. Attorneys—thereby not only bringing to the investigation the local expertise they have, but making available the tools that the federal criminal procedure system provides.

Project Integrity

One thing we learned early on when the Inspector General's office in HEW became operative in March 1977, was that for too many years the investigative and audit function had been in a reactive rather than a proactive mode. Instead of waiting for the information to come to us, one of the ways in which we felt we could go out and seek information was an effort known as Project Integrity I—which has spawned its progeny, Project Integrity II, and maybe even Project Integrity III.

We used computer screens, having first sat down with a number of medical experts to come up with what we hoped were reasonable parameters by which the norm could be measured. How many of certain kinds of procedures would be performed by a certain doctor of a certain discipline on x number of Medicaid patients? You come up with certain numbers of procedures and then you have a norm; if the norm were exceeded, the computer would let you know about it.

Exceeding the parameter or the norm that was devised didn't mean you were a crook—we never went into it thinking that. But at least it was the first step in identifying a provider or an activity which warranted a little further and harder look.

Through computer screens, we reviewed over 250 million transactions involving 270,000 providers. The first group of providers who came under this scrutiny were physicians and pharmacists. We got printouts which reflected aberrations with respect to 47,000 providers. We determined that in each of the fifty-one jurisdictions where we ran these screens, we would select fifty of the most aberrant—trying to split it, twenty-five pharmacists, twenty-five physicians. (These numbers were not always absolute, but we tried to keep the mix as close as we could.)

Again, we recognized that the mere fact that these providers showed up in a computer screen as having highly aberrant characteristics did not necessarily mean that they warranted full-field criminal investigation, or other kinds of administrative or civil sanctions. First, of course, we had to go through a validation process.

When we checked the computer screen with the hard copy records, there were errors in the computer system, duplicate billings which were not intentional—we found a number of errors and screened out a whole lot that way. We wound up with 2,500 good, hard, solid cases and after about a year's activity involving preliminary screens, preliminary contacts—including obtaining provider records—we have approximately 600 that are undergoing full-field criminal investigation, the bulk of which are at the state level. In those states having fraud control units, the FCUs are the ones handling them. We also have 650 to 700 undergoing administrative or other kinds of activity; we closed about 1,100 and about 100 are still awaiting classification and determination of what we ought to do with them.

We returned approximately thirty indictments as a result of the project, and about 180 other cases have progressed to the point where they are awaiting prosecutive decision. In terms of recommended recoveries, we have identified in the range of four million dollars of overpayments which we will, principally through state activity, seek to recover.

Patterns emerging from Project Integrity I: We've learned a number of lessons; we've seen a number of patterns arise from these kinds of screens. We find physicians billing at the highest applicable procedure code in an alarming ratio. When, for example, there are different levels of a physical examination that may be given, we find that where there is the slightest bit of latitude given to the physician, he is, of course, coming in with the highest procedure code. That is not always criminal, but it is something that clearly falls in the overutilization category and we're going to take a very hard look at it.

We found a number of instances of duplicate billings. An egregious example was the case of two practitioners in the same specialty who practiced together in the same clinic. We found 3,902 instances where they were shown to have been billing for the same procedure in the same treatment to the same patients on the same days. We were talking there in the range of $60,000 in fraud.

We find an alarming lack of documentation in connection with a number of these aberrant providers. We often find that they charged for full office visits when they were not warranted. For example, people will come in merely for injections, never see the doctor, and we are getting the full doctor's bill. They go in to fill a prescription and we are getting charged for a full physical examination. They go in and see a social worker, a midwife or a nurse and we are getting charged for a full doctor's visit.

171

In hospitals we are finding a relatively large number of instances where the provider bills for visits not made or bills for more than one service per visit. (For example, he will bill for special psychiatric care and for a visit.) We find—where there is a surgical fee that's all encompassing and is supposed to include follow-up visits—that we are then being billed individually for each follow-up visit. In the nursing home area, we see where a provider will go in and see a series of patients and then charge us the highest rate as if he had seen each patient individually.

On the pharmacy side, we saw a whole broad range of activity—billing for services not rendered, prescription splitting, and an alarming number of instances in which we were being billed for brand name drugs when indeed they were dispensing generic drugs. We found relatively large numbers of instances in which they would charge for drugs for which there was no indication or documentary proof that they were ever prescribed.

While not all of these instances have resulted in criminal investigations, indictments or convictions, they certainly have taught a very important lesson to the state agencies that administer the program. It has resulted in a number of front end audits in a number of jurisdictions where they never existed before. Quite frankly, we are not going to get the major over-charges, the major dollar recoveries we are entitled to, through criminal prosecutions. The deterrent effect, of course, must be there and we will vigorously go after selective criminal prosecutions. But the way to attack this problem is at the front end. Try to stop it before it goes out, and if we learn nothing else from our various Projects Intergrity, we are learning that.

Project Integrity II

Project Integrity II is a spin-off, or the progeny of I. What we are doing is simply refining these computer screening techniques and branching out into other areas where Medicaid providers practice. For example, we've got the hospital-inpatient-physician billing situation. What the computer will do is match the dates of service of the physician's billings with the dates of service shown on the hospital-inpatient billings. Again, that does not automatically mean you are a crook, but when we have a mismatch it will tell us to go and take a further in-depth look at the situation.

With respect to the pervasive practice of billing at the highest physician code, we are developing computer screens along certain parameters which have been devised to try to pick out the aberrant providers in that area. Out-patient hospital services are coming under scrutiny. We are going to identify those providers whose billing patterns indicate a high or abnormal utilization of services. We are going to identify all recipients who exceed the limits, as well as the number of visits within each group that are exceeded.

We are also developing computer screens that we hope will identify the so-called "ping-ponging of services" practice—possibly unnecessary referral practices among two or more facilities on the same day or one day apart.

We are going to take a hard look at medical suppliers and equipment providers. For example, we have developed computer screens that we believe will identify situations where there is the routine delivery of items on a route basis, but then either Medicare or Medicaid gets billed as if this were an individual, special kind of delivery. We will be matching death tapes against billings to determine which of these suppliers are billing us for people who are dead.(We wind up with an alarming number of hits there, by the way.) We have developed screens that will detect the billing for individual components rather than fully-assembled items when the assembled item is less costly than the sum of the individual components.

What we have learned is that the computer is probably the most effective tool to put us in a proactive rather than in a reactive mode. This does not mean to say that we are not continuing to initiate investigations as a result of the traditional sources of information with which I am sure you are all familiar.

Nursing Homes

In the nursing home area, we are going to expand our scrutinizing activities. We are beginning to take a very hard look at the proliferation of chain operations of nursing homes to see if it is creating situations in which there are less than arm's-length transactions which will result in the pyramiding of costs and profits from which some unreasonable payroll costs will perhaps flow. We see an alarming number of sale-leaseback arrangements. We want to take a hard look at nursing homes that are part of other entities that also are involved in real estate development companies, construction companies, lumber and supply companies, management companies, medical equipment, mortgage trust, supplies, pharmaceuticals, etc.

We are not suggesting that this is wrong per se; but it is clearly a situation that presents the potential for this pyramiding of costs and for kickbacks—all of which are ultimately passed on in higher costs to the Medicaid and Medicare programs. When we recognize that roughly 40% of the Medicaid expenditures are the result of nursing home operations throughout the country, we have to take a federal interest in those activities.

We are very much now in a research and review mode. Again, I have to repeat, we are not suggesting that any of this is per se illegal—not until we get in and find out what the effects of this proliferation of corporate structures are. Clearly, this proliferation will provide for a greater federal interest. In connection with some of these activities, where you have home offices and corporate structures in a variety of states, the ability of the federal government to use national process will be an important factor.

Access to Provider Records

With the kinds of dollars that are being expended when the provider chooses to engage in and become part of this federal program, there must be accountability. The statute that created the program and the Inspector General's bill, with its subpoena power, make it very clear that we have been given the tools—the vehicle—by which we can discharge our responsibility to make sure there is the necessary accountability.

H.R. 3 makes it clear there shall be access to records and the Inspector General's bill, in giving us a very unique subpoena power, makes it equally clear. Under the Inspector General's bill, the subpoena power is there to enable the IG to carry out his mandate. His mandate is about as broad as anybody could conceive—it is not only fraud and abuse, it is economy, efficiency and anything else that affects the operation of that Department and the programs it administers. Indeed, it gives us the use of a subpoena in the nature of an administrative subpoena in criminal investigations.

It is inconceivable to me that Congress, in evidencing its intent to beef up the fight against fraud and abuse in connection with the Medicaid program when it enacted the legislation and created these fraud control units, did not intend for them to have the ability (through access to provider records) to do what they were created to do in the first place. There is no way you can run the kind of investigation that is involved in Medicaid without books and records. I've heard some comments that perhaps Congress, by not saying specifically in Section 17 of the Act that they have access, intended for them not to have access. Quite frankly, I think that argument is ludicrous. If these fraud control units don't have the power to obtain records, they might as well close up shop. I am confident that is not the intent of Congress.

Legislative Proposals

Let me run through a couple of legislative ideas that we have, and that we are encouraging Congress to seriously consider. In virtually every state we found that if you, or an employee of an intermediary or carrier, or any nonfederal employee involved in making decisions with respect to the dispensing of dollars which are federal in character, were bribed, there was no bribery statute under which to bring charges. For example, if you were to bribe a Blue Cross/Blue Shield employee, there isn't a federal bribery statute which encompasses that act. We are encouraging Congress to bring those kinds of people in under the federal bribery statute.

We are very strongly urging the enactment of the so-called Civil Money Penalty bill which will provide substantial penalties for the filing of false claims in cases where there are compelling reasons to deal with the matter civilly, rather than in a criminal mode. It will avoid clogging up the courts by permitting the Secretary to do this in an administrative context (which will, of course, give the provider who is under scrutiny full rights of confrontation with witnesses, cross-examination and, upon an adverse determination, access to the U.S. circuit court in his district). We hope this will provide quick and efficient civil deterrence.

QUESTIONS AND ANSWERS

Thomas C. Fox: Does your office give opinions on transactions or practices?

Lippe: Typically, no. I would doubt that you are going to get opinions on whether what you are doing is right or wrong from an organization that has a criminal investigative responsibility as one of its major components. For those of you who have had dealings with state or federal prosecutors, you know when you ask them for pre-transactional advice as to whether or not your client, if he does this, is going to be commiting a crime, you will not get that advice. Well, a criminal investigative organization is in the same position. We just cannot give advice to prospectively assist your client.

Robert J. Gerst: You have to file a cost report and claim a cost in order to appeal it (if there is going to be a disallowance). Put another way, you can't get a cost reimbursement unless you put it in your cost report. But there is much uncertainty as to what costs are or are not allowable. So, if there is a gray area and if you can't get any interpretation as to whether it is going to be allowable, unless you put it in a cost report you don't have a chance of getting any reimbursement for it. You have to file a certification that says you have claimed costs in accordance with general instructions. You may disagree with those general instructions—you may think they are wrong, you may think that the rate is wrong—but unless you file a cost report including those costs you will never be able to test them.

The problem providers are facing all over the country is that if they file a cost report and include a cost which is ultimately adjusted out, they run the risk of your office or the U.S. Attorney's office saying that you filed a false certification. Under the false certification statute you run the risk of having an indictment. The problem is one of your attitude or your office's attitude, as to whether or not there is going to be an understanding of the reason why we claimed those costs.

Lippe: We are very conscious of the uncertainties in some of the provisions in the regulatory scheme under which the Medicare and Medicaid programs are administered. I would be less than candid if I tried to suggest to you that those regulations are all absolute and any person who has a fifth grade education can understand them—that is anything but the case.

However, I am unaware of any situation in which the U.S. Attorney's office has gone to an indictment when it is crystal clear to us that, while technically we may have a case, the argument of the prospective defendant is persuasive that what we are dealing with is not a willful intent situation but a very confusing regulation. If the particular cost item is well known to us to be in a very fuzzy, hazy area, I am unaware of any situations in which the U.S. Attorneys—who are very conscious of the jury appeal factor and are very aware of the argument that the provider's counsel is going to make about the fuzziness of the particular regulation which led to the investigation in the first place—are going to pursue the matter. We just aren't going to return an indictment in that case.

Role of the Accountant in a Criminal Investigation of a Long Term Care Provider

ALAN SCHACHTER

My talk is addressed primarily to those of you in the audience who are members of the health bar to help you develop an understanding of the role of the Certified Public Accountant during a criminal investigation: what his professional responsibilities are, and how he views those responsibilities. This becomes very important to a health lawyer representing providers. The financial area is complex because you must deal with capital costs, reimbursement, theory, and a whole slew of items relating to dollars. When we talk about dollars, we talk about accounting and accounting principles. And, unfortunately, when we talk about white-collar crime, we talk about the wave of white-collar prosecutions in the health care field of late. Particularly in New York State, these issues have come to the forefront.

White-Collar Crime

White-collar crime is defined as "an illegal act or series of illegal acts committed by nonphysical means and by concealment or guile to obtain money or property or to avoid payment or loss of money or property or to obtain business or personal advantage." White-collar crime includes misrepresentations to government agencies by omission or otherwise—and this includes the area, of course, of Medicare and Medicaid fraud.

A white-collar crime has several basic components. Perhaps the most important component is that of intent. There must be an intent to commit a wrongful act or to achieve a purpose inconsistent with law or public policy. Intent can sometimes be determined by comparing the suspect's activity to normal business practice. Very often the government will bring in an expert witness to indicate that a particular practice is not a normal or customary practice in order to pinpoint intent.

In a white-collar crime, disguise of purpose is paramount. False reports or false documents are used to disguise the suspect's purpose with respect to what he is intending to do. (Contrast this with a violent crime where somebody walks into the room and shoots somebody.) The white-collar criminal disguises his or her intent to commit the crime.

The white-collar criminal relies on the ignorance or carelessness of the victim. Particularly in New York State, where, in 1969, there were six auditors (one assigned to the New York City area) to audit hundreds of nursing homes. It can be said in that case that the white collar criminal relied on ignorance or carelessness on the part of the victim—the New York State Department of Health.

The victim voluntarily acts to assist the offender in a white-collar crime. That act in a Medicaid or Medicare fraud is perhaps the act of payment or the act of accepting a false report. The intermediaries, in a sense, assist the white-collar criminal.

Along with the disguise of an ongoing white-collar crime, you have the factor of concealment—the white-collar criminal seeks to conceal his attempt at committing a particular crime, sometimes by lulling the public into thinking that he's an upstanding member of the community. It's just that type of person who does, in fact, commit white-collar crimes. There aren't too many nursing home owners who are not upstanding people to the community; they usually are community-oriented or religious people. That type of defense just doesn't seem to work, because that, essentially, is an attribute of a white-collar criminal.

Prosecution of white-collar crime: There's no question that in dealing with prosecutorial bodies you must be realistic. Prosecution is a business. Prosecutorial agencies are in the business of making cases; make no bones about it. But different agencies have different goals. Some prosecutorial agencies investigate the maximum number of cases. Some are concerned with crimes of maximum impact on the public. Some are concerned with maximizing citizen satisfaction with the agency. Some are concerned solely with convictions, and some will bring cases to deter others from committing crime. Some agencies will have multiple goals—maybe all of these.

If you are dealing with white-collar crime you might find the Law Enforcement Assistance Administration (LEAA) publication called "The Investigation of White Collar Crime" interesting. It's an excellent, basic document indicating investigative techniques, and it specifically lays out how a prosecutorial agency should conduct itself and what its goals should be. When you read this, it has a very sobering impact. Most people consider crime in terms of threats of violence or overt acts. Prior to the "Nixonian era" a great deal of attention was paid to violent crime because the offender was dangerous, the victim knew the harm he suffered, the investigation of these crimes was relatively simple and conviction was usually followed by incarceration. Today, in the "post-Nixonian era," white-collar crime is real crime.

Perhaps the feeling of the general community in dealing with the white-collar criminal was summed up in *U.S. v. Benjamin,* where the judge said, "In our complex society, the accountant's certificate and the lawyer's opinion can be instruments for inflicting pecuniary loss more potent than the chisel and crowbar. If that's the way the judiciary views the accountant's certificate and the lawyer's opinion, I think we have to be concerned with white-collar crime, and I know we should be particularly concerned with it as it relates to Medicare or Medicaid because we practice in that area.

Until recently, local district attorneys were not enthusiastic about prosecuting white-collar criminals because there were alternative civil remedies. It was difficult for the local D.A. to even determine if there was a crime because of the vast amount of documents and papers that had to be reviewed and examined. Their organizations were simply not geared for that.

In many cases in the white-collar area the victim is not overly cooperative (as he usually is in the case of violent crime). We may look at the victim in New York State as being perhaps the New York State Department of Health or the Social Services Department. Yet, I know for a fact that the Office of the Special Prosecutor for Health in New York State has an ongoing investigation of that agency. In fact, he's very anxious to prosecute people within that agency and has filed a civil suit against at least one past employee to recover a substantial sum of money.

Sharp business practice vs. criminal act: The LEAA publication I mentioned before states that "white collar thieves are not just legitimate businessmen who have crossed into the gray area of sharp business practice." That is our biggest problem today in terms of dealing with Medicare and Medicaid (or any white-collar) crime. Six years after the fact, what was once deemed sharp business practice and good business acumen is now perhaps deemed to be a criminal act. That fine line of sharp business practice versus criminal act is not so clear. After the first few glaring cases in New York were prosecuted, there was a whole host of other cases that could have gone either way, but which, due to the publicity and the outcry, were handled in a criminal context.

Getting back to the goals of the prosecutorial agency, the LEAA manual also talks about motivation of investigators: "If prosecutions are the goal, then investigators need to see some of their cases being taken to court, even if some of them do not result in convictions. Able prosecutors know there is a right to be in court where conviction possibilities are marginal, but where the wrong cries out for public attention and deterrence to others."

I don't know if any of you have ever experienced the suffering to an individual that can result from an investigation and indictment. It's a real shame where the chances for conviction are slight but nevertheless the case is made to motivate the investigators. It just doesn't seem right to me that a prosecutorial agency should bring a case to motivate its own investigators, and have the particular defendant incur hundreds of thousands of dollars in legal fees and other expenses defending himself, his reputation and his family's reputation.

Accountant's Dual Role

What's important to you as lawyers is that you understand the role of the accountant-CPA. He has really a dual role in dealing with these situations. First, you have your independent outside CPA who comes in, annually in most cases, to do an audit, and perhaps prepare certified financial statements and cost reports.

On the other hand, you have the role of the accountant as the investigator. I'd like you to understand both roles. It's important, in dealing with prosecutorial bodies, that the legal accounting team be utilized because that's the very team that you are going to be facing on the other side of the fence.

CPA-client privilege: In terms of the regular CPA—the person your client sees regularly—you must realize that in many states the CPA does not have a privileged communication with his client. That's an important fact, particularly in the long term care area, because where you've got individual proprietors and smaller organizations, most parties have more interaction with their CPA than with, perhaps, even their lawyer. The accountant is more visible, getting involved with day-to-day managerial problems. In the normal course of events accountants hear more and know a lot more about the client than the lawyer does. And when that provider becomes your client, he has to know that CPAs do not have privileged communications in most jurisdictions. That trusted CPA—that trusted business advisor—someday may be called to testify before a grand jury or an inquest. Information that he gathered during his routine work is not privileged, and can be used against your client.

The task of the independent accountant is not primarily the detection of fraud. His job is to render an opinion on the financial statements (the balance sheet, the income statement, the statement of changes in financial position). When he states his opinion he really says the statements are fairly presented in accordance with Generally Accepted Accounting Principles (GAAP).

Generally Accepted Accounting Principles are essentially a body of knowledge encompassing procedures, practices and promulgations by various professional organizations. The two that you should be most familiar with are the American Institute of Certified Public Accountants

(AICPA) and the Financial Accounting Standards Board (FASB). In New York State, we are also concerned with the New York State Department of Health because it has issued a nursing home accounting and reporting manual in which it attempts to take these accounting pronouncements and integrate them into its own manual. Also, there's an excellent service put out by the AICPA called *Professional Standards,* which is a periodically up-dated compilation of all the pertinent accounting principles and theoretical material on all subjects. I'm not suggesting to you that you know everything in there, but it is certainly a valuable reference tool when you start getting into·some of these cases, be they civil or criminal.

Accountant's responsibility: What is the independent accountant's responsibility for detecting fraud? There are two pronouncements which I suggest you look at—Statement on Auditing Standards #16 and #17. They deal with the accountant's responsibility for the detection of errors and irregularities and illegal acts and how they must be disclosed.

Errors are defined as unintentional mistakes such as calculation errors. Irregularities are intentional distortions of financial statements. They're broken down into two areas: (1) management fraud, which is deliberate misrepresentations by management, and (2) misappropriations of assets, also known as defalcations. Irregularities result from the misrepresentation or omission of the effects of certain transactions—a provider may indicate that a loan was for business purposes when in fact the funds were used for personal purposes. Irregularities result from the manipulation or alteration of records or documents (phony invoices for supplies not delivered, or any number of other record-manipulating techniques). Omission of significant information from the records or documents might be an irregularity in a particular nursing home. Recording transactions without substance (recording of bills from a related company when in fact the supplies were never delivered or where the company really doesn't render any services) is an irregularity. The intentional misapplication of accounting principles— the failure to capitalize a lease, treating it as rental payments resulting in an over-or-under-reimbursement—is an irregularity.

What Is an Audit?

The independent auditor accountant has the responsibility, within the inherent limitations of the auditing process, to plan his examination to search for errors and irregularities that would have a material effect on the financial statements, and to exercise due care and skill in the conduct of his audit. But what is an audit and how does an auditor operate?

First, you must understand what internal control is, and how we evaluate internal control. Internal control is defined as a plan of organization, procedures and records that is concerned with safeguarding assets and the reliability of financial records. It is that plan of organization in the particular hospital or nursing home which is set up to protect the assets, i.e., to protect against unauthorized defalcations. The components of a system of internal control can be specific records requiring approval, computer checks, a whole host of items making up that competent system of internal control whose sole purpose is to assure that the assets are going to be safeguarded and that the financial statements are going to be prepared in accordance with GAAP to properly reflect operations, financial position, reimbursable costs, etc.

We view the system of internal control as management's responsibility. However, the auditor—the accountant—must evaluate the system to establish a basis for reliance. The internal control system can vary in any organization. It can encompass dual signatures on checks, proper approval of purchase orders, and authorized receiving reports. The whole host of built-in checks within the accounting system is reviewed by the independent accountant in order to determine whether the system of internal control is satisfactory to detect the errors and irregularities that might occur in the particular long term care provider or hospital.

When we talk of errors and irregularities in the health care field, and we talk about illegal acts, we are talking about the same thing. In other businesses, it's not that way. I can be a controller or chief financial officer in a textile house, and I can tell my accountant that everything is O.K. and make certain representations about the financial condition of the enterprise, and my accountant may rely on that. Well, I've made a misrepresentation, but I don't think it is necessarily illegal. I don't think it's a criminal act. In the nursing home or hospital context, when your accountant relies on that and you make that kind of statement and it becomes a basis for reimbursement, you start to get into the criminal area. So, while errors and irregularities and illegal acts are dealt with separately by the AICPA statements, in the health care field, they are inseparable. You can't audit a nursing home or a hospital today without any background in the health care field. You have to understand what reimbursement is and what the cost report is. If you are going to function as an accountant in this particular industry, it's incumbent upon you professionally to be familiar with the rules and regulations of the particular governmental agencies involved. In addition to that, once you have that background, you must be able to determine, based on your review of the system of internal control, what errors and irregularities could occur and the required control procedures necessary to prevent those errors and irregularities.

Once you know the errors and irregularities that could occur, once you know what the system is, you want to test the system. You want to make sure that there is compliance with that system. After you test the system by vouching various transactions, you then can evaluate the weaknesses and make recommendations to management.

The final step in the auditing process, once you have evaluated the system of internal control, once you've tested it for compliance and determined that it is adequate, is to develop substantive auditing procedures so as to properly verify account balances. You expand or contract those procedures based on your review of the system of internal control. You document your work. All accountants should have internal control questionnaires indicating that they have gone through this procedure and they should include them in their accounting work papers.

Certainly, the accountant has to be concerned with errors or discrepancies that he finds. One of his audit procedures will be to confirm independently with outside third parties—debtors and creditors of the business. If there are too few responses to these confirmation requests, if the outside confirmation doesn't agree with the books and records or there's internal inconsistency within the books and records, there's going to be concern and follow-up procedures performed.

Management's integrity is crucial, and in the normal course of events, we, as auditors, accept the representations made by management unless we find evidence to the contrary. You know that management can certainly override the entire system of internal control. The biggest hospital case in New York State—the alleged fraudulent items amounted to two or three million dollars—resulted from the fact that the corruption in that particular organization went from the bookkeepers right up to the chief operating officer.

That brings me to the inherent weakness in the auditing process. First of all, we don't check 100%. We don't verify every transaction. We're not required to do that. We use sampling techniques. Management can always override the system and collusion is very difficult to detect in the normal auditing process. We don't have subpoena power, and we must rely on management's representations. Subsequent discovery of errors and irregularities does not in itself indicate inadequate performance of the accountant. The auditor is not an insurer nor is he a guarantor. Our opinion says "fairly presented," it doesn't say "100% correct."

The Investigator's Role

Client-prosecutor-lawyer squeeze: Beware of the client-prosecutor-lawyer squeeze—the eternal triangle. The accountant is paid by the client. He doesn't have privileged communication but he's got custody of the work papers. The prosecutor wants the client. The prosecutor is going to call the accountant into his office. And the prosecutor will say: "Mr. Accountant, we're not interested in you. But if you don't cooperate with us, well, I don't have to tell you that you're licensed in the State of New York." There's a tremendous squeeze put on the accountant to give up the client. And, if he doesn't have that privileged communication, it's difficult for him to resist. At the same time, the client says, "Hey, wait a second, Mr. Prosecutor, I don't know anything. I don't know from financial statements, from numbers— my accountant did it all." Finally, you've got your lawyer, defense counsel for the client, saying, "What do you have to worry about, Mr. Accountant? Turn your work papers over to me."

There's a tremendous squeeze on an independent accountant, and it's a real problem. And you've got to be sensitized to it.

Perhaps the best thing to do is to tell that accountant that he should retain counsel, and there should be a working relationship between the independent accountant's lawyer and the client's lawyer. If there are motions to be made to quash subpoenas, there should be some type of coordination in that area.

Selecting the Investigative Accountant: Your client, the owner-operator or perhaps administrator of a 200-bed nursing home in a large metropolitan area, has just informed you that he's been told by various suppliers and employees that they have been subpoenaed to appear before the special prosecutor on matters relating to operation of the client's facility. Your client is well respected in the community, he's never had any scrapes with the law other than a traffic violation, and he can't understand why anybody would consider investigating him.

Remember that in program fraud, intent is of paramount importan·e. More often than not your client's intent in submitting what may have been an inflated cost report will be buried in a complex series of financial transactions, recorded in the books and records and further transcribed into cost reports and reimbursement formulae. Because most program frauds, particularly Medicare and Medicaid, involve books and records and complex analysis, the new role of the investigative accountant becomes very important to you as lawyers. He—the investigative accountant—becomes your interpreter and assists you in the defense.

Once you have been retained and have ascertained that it is a books and records case, you then want to start looking for an investigative accountant. What do you look for? You want someone who understands GAAP as well as current accounting theory. You want a man capable of making a creative extension of the logic behind these principles. Normally they would be applied to a regular commerical enterprise and you want him to extend them, for your benefit, to the health care situation. You need someone that's going to take the eyeshade off, and who's going to get into some creative defense work.

You need somebody with a competent staff that's trained to focus on issues. The investigative accountant does not have time to audit all the transactions. He's got to zero-in on specific problems.

His organization has got to be sensitive to security. Believe me when I tell you body recorders and phone taps are common practices of prosecutorial agencies. The investigative accountant's staff must know not to talk to anybody about the case, other than perhaps the particular senior investigator on the job. Idle chatter spreads like wildfire and rumors can be tremendously detrimental to your case.

You need somebody with impeccable qualifications both in business and scholastically, and you need somebody who can address a jury and deal with very complex issues on a simple, layman's level. In addition to that, you want to hire a firm of investigative accountants that has more than one person who can serve as your expert witness, because you may want a different personality, depending on where the case comes before a jury. (New York is different from Kansas City.)

Retainer agreement: Once you find your accountant, you have to set up a retainer agreement, which protects the accountant by cloaking him with the attorney-client privilege. That retainer agreement should specify the date of the agreement, that the accountant is working under the direction of the lawyer and is an adjunct to producing legal services, that all communications are confidential between the lawyer and the accountant, and that written permission is required before any information is turned over by the accountant.

Dealing with the Investigation

Your next step after retaining the accountant is a debriefing session with the client. Your client is probably going to have to be convinced that retaining an attorney is not synonymous with an admission of guilt. Like most businessmen he's never been under investigation. You have to explain to him that he is going to be a target. You must let him know that he can't discuss this matter with anyone. He can't talk on the telephone because his phone may be tapped. He can't talk to his suppliers or to his closest employees about this particular matter because any one of them may be a witness who's been pressured by the special prosecutor to become an informant.

Having talked with your client, you then must determine what stage the investigation is at. You may want to call up the agency and indicate you represent X Nursing Home and memorialize that call with a letter to the agency. Indicate to the agency that any communications now come through you, the client's attorney. You may get some valuable information discussing these matters with the special prosecutor.

There are many different approaches to the special prosecutor. You as lawyers will have to determine what is the best approach. The best approach is not necessarily the path of least resistance. The best approach sometimes may be to vigorously attack the subpoenas—making repeated motions to quash them. The best approach might not necessarily be to turn over the books and records, but only you can determine that after talking with the client to determine what the problems are.

You may want to consider interviewing potential witnesses (e.g., controllers, accountants) to determine what they know. You can gain valuable information that may tell you what you are up against. Once you retain an investigative accountant, you are then working together as a team, sizing up what the problems are—inflated invoices, kick-backs, phantom employees, etc. You want to know what your worst case is, so you can be prepared to defend against it.

Avoiding the Indictment

The next question is, can that indictment be avoided? Your task, with the assistance of the investigative accountant, is to convince the prosecutor that he hasn't got a case against your client. In this regard, I have found that prosecutorial bodies do not understand GAAP. That allows you to interpose some accounting defenses. You can try to show that your client did not have the required intent by coming up with understated expenditures to offset overstated expenditures which the prosecutor found. You might assert as a defense that the client has bad records or sloppy bookkeeping methods. There are other fruitful areas. Many times the provider fails to accrue sick and vacation pay, which can be a legitimate and sizable expense in the particular period.

You might show the prosecutor that your client would be entitled to x dollars if he had used accelerated depreciation or component depreciation (instead of straight-line). Amortization of pre-opening expenditures, accounting for leases and pensions, related party questions—these are all gray areas with which to work in trying to show the prosecutor that his case is not iron-clad.

There are any number of creative logical extensions to accounting principles to be used at that stage where you try to talk the prosecutor out of the indictment. You are going to have to convince him, without turning all your cards over, that you have good authoritative support for your position. Your client did not have intent and may, in fact, be owed substantial unclaimed sums from the program.

Challenging the indictment: If, in fact, you cannot convince the prosecutor not to indict, you still can challenge and maybe defeat the indictment. Perhaps the client is charged with grand larceny but there is no larceny because he didn't reap the benefits. Maybe the indictment is incorrect. There have been cases which have been dismissed for a faulty indictment or faulty conduct on the part of the grand jury.

Investigative accountant at trial: If the defenses raised by the accountant do not succeed in avoiding the indictment, you must be prepared to go to trial. There, the investigative accountant is going to serve as your expert and right-hand man. He should be at the defense table with you while the government expert is being cross-examined. He can assist you in the development of proper questions and answers for cross-examination.

I was on one case where, on clever cross-examination, the expert for the prosecution broke down in tears. It can be done, and you need help from the investigative accountant to make the government's witness (who is usually not a CPA) look foolish and unprepared.

Referrals to Other Agencies

Finally, if and when you talk them out of the indictment, are you finished with the case? I don't know of any investigation that has ever ended—until the prosecutorial agency terminates. You have got to warn your client to keep his mouth shut because they (the prosecutors) will never stop looking; they've got to justify their budget.

Also, you have to be concerned with referrals to other agencies. Many cases that have not been made on the basis of Medicare and Medicaid have been made on the basis of income tax invasion. You need to be sensitive to criminal referrals to state and federal income tax agencies because various prosecutorial agencies do cooperate with each other.

In addition to that, you have to be concerned with civil lawsuits. In New York State, once the criminal case is over, it is routinely turned over to the civil division. The civil division will then bring a lawsuit against the provider for treble damages and interest. Though certainly your prime concern is to keep your client out of jail, you have to pay attention to civil matters, civil penalties, civil lawsuits, and, perhaps most importantly, licensure procedures. In New York, when a man is convicted of a felony in the nursing home or hospital area, it means there will automatically be a hearing to revoke his operator's certificate.

Prosecution of nursing home representatives: As representatives of nursing homes, you've got to be concerned because there is no question that a vigorous prosecutor is going to look at *you* as a potential target—perhaps on a conspiracy theme. In addition to rendering good advice to your clients and assisting them in a defense, as representatives of health care institutions, you too must be careful. A vigorous prosecutor may consider taking a pot-shot at you as well, because you are juicy targets. Whether you like to conceive of yourselves as that or not, you are, and I think you have some cause to be concerned in the way you conduct yourselves in relation to governmental agencies as well as with your clients.

QUESTIONS AND ANSWERS

Audience: For the benefit of some of the attorneys general in the audience, what do you perceive as the state's responsibility to provide qualified auditors in the auditing function itself?

Alan Schachter: That is really a double question, because you have auditors who are doing civil audits for the state Medicaid agency and, in New York, we have auditors who are working directly with the Special Prosecutor or Attorney General in the preparation of criminal cases. There is a responsibility and there should be a concern on the part of state agencies to adequately train their personnel. In fact, one of the generally accepted standards of auditing indicates that you have to have personnel at the proper level doing a particular job.

I do know that competent accounting graduates are at a premium today. State salaries are such that they are not the most attractive in terms of attracting qualified people, so the state is at somewhat of a disadvantage because those positions are not necessarily highly paid and that they are not usually stepping stones toward career goals.

Certainly, it is incumbent upon them, even if they do not get the superstar accountants or the high draft choices, to adequately train their people. In terms of my role as an investigative accountant, I am not going to encourage them. But at the civil level, with Medicaid, it is a real problem. It is so frustrating to have an audit, and the auditor disallows an item obviously related to patient care.

I feel that it is incumbent upon the state to have people who are objective. The problem is that with the Special Prosecutor around, realistically speaking, they are scared out of their shoes. The Special Prosecutor has a unit investigating the Health Department. Why should the Health Department rule favorably in a gray area when they are going to have a prosecutor come in and say, "You know, John Jones, we are not interested in you, you make $12,000 a year, *but* if you don't give us XYZ provider..." It is a terrible problem compounded by these criminal investigations. You and I know that what we need are good qualified people, well schooled, with the ability and authority to negotiate.

Audience: In New York, you have probably one of the most vigorous special prosecutors in this country. Could you give us an idea of about how many indictments he has been successful in, and make an educated guess of what percentage would have been overturned if the procedure you outlined had been followed?

Schachter: I have here a copy of a report by Charles J. Hynes, Deputy Attorney General of the State of New York. He's the Special Prosecutor and he does have some interesting statistics. He has had many indictments and has been very successful as a prosecutor. In due respect to him, if you would measure him against, perhaps, a Maurice Nadjari special prosecutor-type, Joe Hynes has been very successful, and is a capable prosecutor.

Most cases have been disposed of on a plea bargaining basis. In cases that have gone to trial, I only know of four acquittals.

Access to Nursing Home Care for Medicaid Recipients

TOBY EDELMAN

Editor's Note: This presentation by Toby Edelman, and the presentation by Sally Kelly which follows, highlights issues of current concern to health care consumer advocates. Questions and comments directed to both speakers follow Ms. Kelly's remarks.

Discrimination against poor people (i.e., Medicaid recipients) by nursing homes is a common and widespread problem. There have been several reports recently which begin to document this problem with statistics and hard information. One is the report of the Ohio General Assembly Nursing Home Commission (interim report issued June 1978) and another is the report from the Pennsylvania Nursing Home Ombudsman Project (issued January 1979). These reports are documenting what has long been recognized by families trying to find beds for Medicaid recipients and by other advocates involved with long term care.

The discrimination problem takes basically two forms—one in the admissions (initial placement) area, and the other in what is called conversion situations. The admissions problem itself has two aspects. First, a number of nursing homes choose not to participate in Medicaid at all. A facility has this right under present law. A home does not participate in Medicaid unless it chooses to do so. The second aspect of the admissions problem focuses on nursing homes that do voluntarily participate in Medicaid, but which, nevertheless, refuse to accept individual Medicaid recipients who apply for admission. Nursing homes are generally not required to accept any particular number or percentage of Medicaid recipients even if they participate in the program. The nursing homes see themselves as being free to decide on whatever basis they choose whether or not they are going to accept an individual applicant who is a Medicaid recipient. There have been, as far as I know, few challenges to this practice—the denial of admission because of Medicaid status.

The second discrimination problem is conversion. Conversion occurs when a person who entered a nursing home as a private-pay resident exhausts his or her personal resources paying for nursing home care and then turns to the Medical Assistance Program.

The conversion situation can be illustrated by the case of a New Jersey woman who spent $90,000 of her own money on nursing home care and then became a Medicaid recipient. She had to be hospitalized for a short period of time but, when it came time for her release, the nursing home refused to accept her back. Another case with which I was connected involved a client who had spent $16,000 in fifteen months. That was all the money she had and when she used it up, the nursing home explicitly said, "You have not been a private-pay person for two years and you have to leave."

In New Jersey, figures from the industry indicate the private rate in the state is $48-$63 a day. When you work that out on an annual basis, you find that it is between $17,885 and $22,995. While some people can afford to pay in the tens of thousands of dollars a year for nursing care for awhile, it's quite obvious that most people cannot keep that up indefinitely. And these are not isolated instances, the cases I have mentioned. In 1977, the Congressional Budget Office (using 1974 figures) estimated that almost half of the Medicaid recipients in nursing homes entered the facilities as private-pay residents, exhausted their money, and then turned to Medicaid; i.e., they "converted." In this country there are somewhere between a million and a million and a half nursing home residents. The nationwide figure for Medicaid payment is about 50%. (At least that's the old statistic—I assume, at this point, it is somewhat higher. But it is safe to say it is between 50% and 60%.) Try to figure out how many people have converted and you come up with at least a quarter of a million people (assuming there are a million people in nursing homes and half of the 50% on Medicaid converted). A low estimate then would be about a quarter of a million people, who, after becoming impoverished paying for their nursing home care, turned to Medicaid. And I think a more realistic estimate is that half a million people are presently in nursing homes who spent all their money and had to go on Medicaid.

The seriousness of this problem stems from the fact that, frequently, people who convert or try to convert to Medical Assistance are told that they have to leave and are then transferred to other facilities. I am sure that many of you, if not all of you, know that transfer trauma is a very serious problem for elderly nursing home residents—particularly for those people transferred without adequate advance preparation. (I should mention that an attorney who got a $500,000 punitive damage judgment for misappropriation of residents' funds also filed what was the first wrongful death action in a transfer trauma situation. It was not a discriminatory transfer situation, but it was a wrongful death case, which he settled for more than $30,000.)

State Remedies

Massachusetts has a state law prohibiting discrimination against public assistance recipients, including people who receive Medical Assistance. The statute says it is an awful practice for any person furnishing services to discriminate against any individual who is a recipient of federal, state or local public assistance, including Medical Assistance, solely because the individual is such a recipient.

Using this statutory base and pursuant to its authority to make rules and regulations in the area of public welfare, and also as the single state agency with responsibility for carrying out the Medical Assistance Program, the Massachusetts Department of Public Welfare promulgated an antidiscrimination provision in the Medical Assistance Manual covering both the admissions and conversion situations. Providers may not refuse to accept an eligible Medical Assistance recipient if a bed is available at the level of care required by the patient. Providers may not transfer or discharge a nursing home resident against the resident's wishes, solely because that resident has been determined eligible for Medical Assistance. This provision in the Medical Assistance Manual was upheld following a challenge by the industry. (See *Massachusetts Federation of Nursing Home and Related Facilities, Inc. v. Sharp,* C.A. No. 18915 (Superior Court).) The court said not only is the "antidiscrimination regulation suitable or necessary to carry out the provisions of the Medical Assistance Program" but also it "is required by federal and state law to prohibit discrimination in the provision of medical care and services against Medicaid recipients."

The Massachusetts State Attorney General (in the person of Sally Kelly) has brought three separate actions against nursing homes allegedly in violation of these provisions (and a couple of other state laws). (See *Bellotti v. Kimwell Nursing Home,* C.A. No. 124-745 (Superior Court, Norfolk County, filed and settled by consent judgment June 23, 1978); *Commonwealth of Massachusetts v. Twin Pines Corporation dba Western Manor Nursing and Retirement Home,* C.A. No. 78-2768 (Superior Court, Middlesex County, filed May 24, 1978 and settled by consent judgment May 28, 1978); and *Commonwealth of Massachusetts v. Berkshire Nursing Home, Inc.,* No. 28894 (Superior Court, Suffolk County, filed and settled by consent judgment June 2, 1978).)

In each of the cases, the Attorney General alleged that the nursing homes had participated in a number of unlawful acts of discrimination against both Medicaid recipients applying for admission and private-pay residents who sought to convert to Medicaid after they had exhausted their personal financial resources. Among the specific allegations were charges that the facilities falsely represented to consumers that they had a limited number of beds available for Medicaid recipients; that they refused to accept Medicaid recipients as residents for certain periods of time or until transferred; that they threatened to transfer private-pay residents who exhausted their personal resources and sought to convert to Medicaid; and they attempted to collect charges from residents for services covered by Medical Assistance.

All three cases ended in a consent judgment. Each facility denied that it had engaged in any unlawful conduct. At the same time, each was permanently enjoined from engaging in the acts alleged in the complaint. In addition, the defendants agreed to write corrective letters to residents and their sponsors who had signed contracts agreeing to pay the private rate for a certain period of time. The letter had to advise the resident and sponsor that residents have the right to apply for Medical Assistance; that residents will not be transferred or discharged because of eligibility for or receipt of application for payment by the Medical Assistance Program; and that residents applying and found eligible for Medical Assistance and their sponsors are not liable for services covered by Medical Assistance. Finally, the defendants agreed to pay "restitution" in an amount up to ninety times the daily private rate for residents of the facility who had been victims of the unlawful practices.

Minnesota rate equalization: Minnesota has also enacted a law directed at nursing homes that voluntarily choose to participate in Medicaid. As a condition of participation, nursing homes must agree that they will not charge their private residents more than the Medicaid rate, (See Minnesota Statutes Section 256 B. 48, as amended.) That law was phased in gradually and for a time a 10% differential was permitted. However, as of July 1, 1978, any nursing home that participates in Medicaid cannot charge any private resident anything above the Medicaid rate.

In part, the law was designed to help private-pay people, because there was not really too much that could be said in favor of having private-pay nursing home residents subsidize the state and federal governments for the care of Medical Assistance recipients. A second motivation for the law, I believe, was a desire to help Medicaid recipients and prevent discrimination. If the financial incentive for facilities to prefer private-pay residents is removed (as this statute certainly does), then there may be less discrimination against Medicaid beneficiaries—either those applying as Medicaid recipients or those who are converting.

A lawsuit challenging the Minnesota law was filed in federal district court in October 1977. (See *Minnesota Association of Health Care Facilities v. Perpich,* C.A. No. 377-467 (D. Minn., filed October 26, 1977).) The plaintiffs contend the state statute violates the Medicaid statute because it imposes an illegal condition for future participation in Medicaid; that it violates the Medicaid regulations because the state did not obtain prior federal approval of what the plaintiffs are calling an amendment to the state plan; and that the statute is unconstitutional under the due process clause and the contract clause of both the state and federal constitutions. There is an intervenor in this case—the Nursing Home Residents' Advisory Council, an independent nonprofit organization of nursing home and board-and-care residents. (Some of the residents in this organization are private-pay and some are Medicaid recipients.) The Residents' Advisory Council maintains that the statute is constitutional and should be upheld.

On September 11, 1978 the judge in this case denied all motions for summary judgment (including motions made in the companion case, *Minnesota Hospital Association v. Minnesota Department of Public Health,* C.A. No. 3-78-88 (D. Minn, filed February 17, 1978). The plaintiffs then filed a motion for a preliminary injunction—which was also denied. The Eighth Circuit heard argument on the denial of the preliminary injunction in February 1979.

New Jersey licensing regulations: New Jersey, the third state I would like to talk about has taken quite a different approach. While Massachusetts and Minnesota are both dealing with providers that voluntarily participate in the Medicaid program, New Jersey is attempting to deal with *all* providers in the state. The Department of Health promulgated regulations which require the acceptance of indigents (which the state defines as Medicaid-eligibles or Medicaid recipients) as a condition of state licensure. Since facilities can't do business at all without a state license, the effect of these regulations is to require that every facility accept some Medicaid recipients.

The facilities have two ways of satisfying their obligation under the regulations. Either they can accept indigent persons as new admissions, or they can keep residents regardless of any change in their economic status. Thus, residents who convert would have to be retained in the facility. Charitable and nonprofit facilities which can show to the satisfaction of the Department that they already have a policy of keeping people who exhaust their money and convert to Medicaid are excluded from the regulations entirely.

The regulations have been challenged in *New Jersey Association of Health Care Facilities v. Finley,* Docket Numbers A-1950-77 through A-1954-77; A-2207-77 (Superior Court of New Jersey, Appellate Division). Supporting the state in this litigation are the New Jersey Public Advocate, intervening as a party defendant, and the Gray Panthers, as *amicus.* The appellants, the New Jersey Association of Health Care Facilities and some individual nursing homes, argue that the regulations involve a taking of property without due process; that they are *ultra vires* and exceed the authority the legislature delegated to the Health Department; and that they are unconstitutionally vague and ambiguous. The state argues that the Department has authority to issue the regulations; that they are a reasonable exercise of state police power; and that they do not result in an unconstitutional taking.

The Gray Panthers have taken the position that the regulations recognize the special status of nursing homes in the health care field as quasi-public institutions. This is a fairly strong principle which is presently applied to hospitals in New Jersey. In *Griesman v. Newcomb Hospital,* 40 N.J. 389 (1963), the Supreme Court of New Jersey stated:

> Hospital officials are properly vested with large measures of managing discretion and to the extent they exert their effort towards the elevation of hospital standards and high medical care, they will receive broad judicial support. But they must never lose sight of the fact that the hospitals are operated, not for private end, but for the benefit of the public, and that their assistance is for the purpose of faithfully furnishing facilities to the members of the medical profession in aid of their service to the public.

In a second case, *Doe v. Bridgeton Hospital Association, Inc.,* 71 N.J. 478 (1976), the court said:

> The properties of these hospitals are devoted to a use in which the public has an interest and are subject to control for the common good. As quasi-public institutions, their actions must not contravene the public interest. They must serve the public without discrimination. Their board of directors or trustees are managing quasi-public trust and each has a fiduciary relationship with the public.

The Panthers are trying to establish this same principle in nursing homes: that nursing homes are also quasi-public institutions and have an obligation to serve members of the public without discrimination.

Federal Remedies

Last year, Senator Gaylord Nelson introduced an amendment to a bill then pending, Senator Talmadge's Medicare-Medicaid Reimbursement and Administrative Reform Act (H.R. 5285), which would have required facilities participating in Medicare or Medicaid to participate in both. The amendment would require dual certification for Medicare and Medicaid (something which I understand some states already have). The amendment was not enacted last year and it is not entirely clear whether Senator Nelson will introduce it again this year. But it is a strategy that some people are considering at the federal level.

Another possible federal remedy relates to the Medicare-Medicaid Anti-Fraud and Abuse Amendments of 1977. Section 4 makes it a felony for a hospital or a long term care provider to charge a recipient any amount in addition to the sum that the state pays, or to charge, solicit, accept or receive "any gift, money, donation of other consideration" either as a condition of admitting the Medicaid recipient or as a condition of the recipient's continued stay.

It is my position (as well as the position of others I have discussed this issue with) that the fairly common provider practice of requiring people to be private-pay for a specified amount of time is "other consideration," and therefore a felony in violation of the law. I've seen several contracts which facilities have people sign, saying, "I will be private-pay for two years and then I can be a Medicaid recipient," and though, as far as I know, no U.S. Attorney has yet prosecuted anybody for this practice, I think it constitutes "other consideration" as a condition for being admitted as a Medicaid recipient.

Recent Litigation

I would like to talk about cases where legal services attorneys are representing people who are being evicted due to their Medicaid status.

In situations where facilities have sought to transfer residents because of their Medicaid status (either because they had not been private-pay for a specified period of time or because the facility simply wanted to reduce its Medicaid population), residents have brought suit to enjoin their transfers, relying in large part on the federal transfer regulations. Other legal theories have been asserted, including state action on the part of the facility; implied private right of action; contract; and third-party beneficiary of the provider agreement between the state and the facility.

In *Fuzie v. Manor Care, Inc.*, C.A. No. C77-265 (N.D. Ohio, filed April 21, 1977), we challenged what we alleged was a practice of the nursing home of evicting all people who were Medicaid recipients who had not been private-pay residents for a period of at least two years before they converted to Medicaid. It was also our position that they were trying to transfer those people who had entered the facility as Medicaid recipients, as well. The plaintiffs in that case survived a motion to dismiss, but the judge did not certify the class. In February 1978 the case was settled, with the stipulation that Mrs. Fuzie could stay in the nursing home as long as she was a Medicaid recipient and as long as the facility participated in the program.

Three months later the facility entered a new provider agreement with the state. The previous provider agreement had been open-ended, and authorized payment for whatever number of Medicaid recipients the facility had. The new (May 1978) provider agreement, however, said that the nursing home would have 15 Medicaid recipients. At the time the May provider agreement was signed, there were 30 Medicaid recipients residing in the facility. The facility began transferring Medicaid recipients. When there were 16 left, a suit was filed—*Stitt v. Manor Care of Willoughby, Inc.*, C.A. No. C-78-630 (N.D. Ohio, filed June 8, 1978).

On October 24, 1978 the judge issued findings of fact and conclusions of law based on the facts the parties had stipulated. The facility's practice (which I understand is quite common) of using Medicaid when operations begin in a new facility in order to fill beds and develop a reputation was finally recognized by the court. The judge said that "Medicaid allows corporations such as Manor Care to commence operations, because it provides nursing homes with patients who have a controlled source of income. When the facility later determines it is economically feasible, it can then decrease its Medicaid population and convert those beds to more profitable private patients. In effect, the nursing home reaps the benefits of the Medicaid program, but sheds the responsibility of continuing to provide for Medicaid patients when it is able to make a profit elsewhere.'' The court continued, ''the court is mindful that private nursing facilities operate in a free enterprise system and that Congress and the respective states have determined that in the long run, it is more efficient to encourage the private facilities to participate in the Medicaid program than to have all facilities run by the government.''

The court then found that the practice of transferring a person in order to convert his or her bed to private-pay was in clear violation of the transfer regulation in the Patients' Bill of Rights. The court also observed that state action is implicated when the provider voluntarily reduces its Medicaid commitment by signing a new provider agreement the way it did in this situation. Persuasive to the court in finding state action were the heavy regulation and dependency on government funding and the fact that the services provided by the facility are so much in the public interest. These factors were sufficient to create the close nexus necessary to find state action.

In finding state action, the judge in *Stitt* explicitly rejected the *Fuzie* analysis—which refused to find state action. The *Stitt* court says that *Fuzie* did not draw a crucial distinction between the nursing facility's operation in a purely private capacity as to private patients and its function as the state's partner and agent with respect to its Medicaid patients. The realities of the Medicaid program compel a finding of state action.

The court then looked to see whether the nursing home residents—the Medicaid recipients--had any interests which were protected by the due process clause. The court ruled for plaintiff on this issue as well, saying that since Medicaid recipients have the right under the Medicaid statute to select the providers they want, the plaintiff has a legitimate legal expectancy in continued occupancy at the nursing home that is finally selected. A second protectable interest, according to the court, was maintaining the current level of Medicaid benefits to which the Medicaid recipient is entitled. The court took judicial notice of the phenomenon of transfer trauma, observing that at a minimum, transfer trauma works a grievous loss and presents serious psychological danger and that, at a maximum, the trauma suffered during transfer may ultimately take the life of the patient.

The court ruled that only a pre-transfer hearing would satisfy these due process rights. And here the decision gets a little strange, at least from our point of view. The court said that what would have to happen is that all 16 Medicaid recipients would have to get notice of the proposed transfer. Anybody who did not object to being transferred would go. If there were disagreement—if people did not want to move—then everybody would have a hearing. It is not clear if the hearing is to be a joint hearing or individual hearings. But people would have hearings with the right to say why they shouldn't have to go and why they would be harmed by transfer trauma. According to the court, the hearing officer would then decide who would be least likely to suffer from transfer trauma, and that person would be transferred. In essence, what the court is saying is that the people have to compete and the one who loses has to leave, even though the court also says that forcing a person to move because of Medicaid status is illegal. The case is on appeal (by all parties) to the Sixth Circuit.

Roberson case: In *Roberson v. Wood,* C.A. No. 78-4 321 (E.D. Ill., filed August 30, 1978), an Illinois nursing home sent letters to the families of residents saying, "We are trying to move out the Medical Assistance recipients so you have to move your mother." On January 7, 1979, the court denied the defendant's motion to dismiss.

The court found the plaintiff has a protectable property interest in staying in the same nursing home. The court concluded that residents have an implied private right of action to enforce the Medicaid statutes and regulations, including the Patients' Bill of Rights. (This is in line with the Supreme Court's analysis in *Cort v. Ash,* 422 U.S. 66 (1975).)

The court also ruled that nursing home residents were third-party beneficiaries of the provider agreement and also could enforce their private individual contract—the admissions contract between residents and the nursing home. The court went on to say that it would exercise its pendent jurisdiction and hear the contract claim.

Conclusion

The problem of discrimination against Medicaid recipients is a very significant one. It affects a lot of people—there are a half-million people who are converting, and another large group of people trying to get into nursing homes as Medicaid recipients. I think the states, and now, finally, the federal government, are beginning to address this problem in some creative ways.

Appointment of a Medical Receiver to Run a Nursing Home as a Remedy in Patient Abuse Cases

SALLY A. KELLY

I would like to read to you from an affidavit filed by the attorney general in state and federal court in Massachusetts. The person who submitted the affidavit is a registered nurse and a nurse-surveyor for the Massachusetts Department of Public Health.

> I was at the facility on September 5th, 6th and 7th from 8:00 A.M. until at least 4:00 P.M. The facility was odorous, noisy, crowded and dirty. Patients were slumped in wheelchairs or poorly positioned and aligned in bed. Some patients were lying in urine and feces. Some decubi dressings were wet with urine. Patients were poorly groomed and many lacked undergarments. Many lacked shoes and socks. No between-meal nourishments were observed being served. Some patients were served breakfast while lying in their own urine and feces. Unsupervised patients ate with their hands. In many instances breakfast was served cold to the majority of incontinent patients. No diet restrictions, ordered by the physicians, appeared to be followed. Cockroaches were plentiful. I also observed cockroaches and ants in the bathrooms. The jar of betadine ointment used on patients' dressings was left uncovered and flies were observed walking around the edge of the open jar. When I entered Room 126 I experienced a wave of nausea because of the overwhelming odor of urine and feces emanating from the body and the room of the patient. Flies were observed upon and about both of the patients.

This is one paragraph from a series of approximately 20 affidavits filed in the Massachusetts receivership case, *Bellotti v. Hill* (Middlesex Superior Court, Civil Action No. 78-4855 (filed September 14, 1978)). I am sure that all of you were as shocked as we were on hearing the material contained in the affidavit I just read to you. The problem we face is how does a state, particularly a state attorney general, respond to this type of nursing home problem.

In Massachusetts, the Attorney General has two mechanisms for responding to nursing home problems. We have the Medicaid fraud control unit, which consists of approximately 70 people. They are charged with combating fraud and patient abuse. In some patient abuse situations, our Medicaid fraud control unit has indicted people, and that is one avenue we can pursue.

The other is the Public Protection Bureau of the attorney general's office. We attempt to use civil remedies to protect patients in nursing homes. We work closely with the Medicaid fraud control unit and decide, on a case-by-case basis, whether a civil or criminal remedy is the most appropriate response to patient abuse.

Traditional Remedies for Patient Abuse

In the patient abuse situation, the first avenues of relief are the traditional remedies, with which I am sure many of you are familiar. The first, of course, is to consult with the nursing home, something that is typically done by the state's survey agency. The second alternative is to deny, cancel or revoke the facility's Medicaid certification for failure to meet conditions or standards of participation. The problem with this remedy is that the revocation of certification results in a termination of Medicaid payments to the facility. That, in our opinion, typically helps no one and most certainly injures the Medicaid patients in the home, who are left without any money being paid for their care.

The third traditional remedy would be termination of the provider agreement by the Department of Public Welfare or HEW. Again, this remedy is not much good in a severe patient abuse situation because it results in the same sort of economic abandonment of the patients by the state.

The fourth traditional remedy is to deny or revoke the state license. This, of course, in many situations, would result in eliminating services altogether to the patients—and for that reason it is not attractive.

A related remedy is to move the patients out of the nursing home. This remedy often becomes necessary if the Medicaid certification is revoked or the license is cancelled. As you are all aware, the problem of transfer trauma must be faced when the state (or anybody) decides to move a patient. In a patient abuse situation, where you are talking about 130 to 200 patients, transferring them out of the home is just not feasible in many instances because state certificate-of-need laws have limited the supply of beds in any one area of the state.

The next traditional remedy, and perhaps the best one, is an injunction. If the state is successful in obtaining a temporary restraining order or a preliminary injunction, and if the provider abides by the injunction, I would say that is definitely the best remedy. Patients do not have to be moved and the provider does not lose the home. Typically, if it is a civil action, the provider does not lose a tremendous amount of money, either. Unfortunately, in many instances, injunctions are obtained but, for a number of reasons, are not obeyed by the providers.

The last and most serious sanction for patient abuse is criminal action.

In the Massachusetts cases and in the other receivership cases I am familiar with throughout the country, when patient advocates have attempted to use these traditional remedies they have become acutely aware that they do not always work. We are then faced with a terribly difficult situation. A relatively new remedy that has been suggested and used effectively is the medical receivership.

Medical Receivership

The medical receivership was first suggested by Professor Frank P. Grad in a 1971 law review article. (See "Upgrading Health Facilities: Medical Receiverships as an Alternative to License Revocation," 42 *University of Colorado Law Review* 419.) Professor Grad stated: "The remedy here proposed would be a new species of receivership, less concerned than existing models with the preservation of property interests, and more directly concerned with the protection of human life, health and safety... To differentiate it from other forms of receivership, it is referred to as a *medical* receivership. The traditional purpose of receivership is to maintain property interests and to prevent valuable assets from being lost. In the hospital and health facility situation, the problem is a different one, because a hospital which is being soundly run from the economic point of view may well be wholly inadequate, from the point of view of patient welfare....''

Professor Grad's article has encouraged many people throughout the country to seek medical receiverships. Some states have also taken Professor Grad's suggestion and enacted state receivership statutes. Wisconsin, New York, Minnesota, Connecticut, New Jersey, Kansas and Kentucky all have such statutes.

Of course, if you are in a state that has a medical receivership statute, the likelihood of that remedy being available or applied is much greater. Typically, these statutes empower the receiver to operate the facility, and to receive and spend all incoming funds to protect the health and safety of the residents. Generally, the receiver is authorized to take this action until all the residents are safely transferred to another facility, or until other provisions are made for the residents' safety—including returning the nursing home to the original owner once the patient problems have been remedied.

The Wisconsin statute and a proposed Massachusetts statute also provide that, in certain situations, the receiver is empowered to refuse to honor preexisting contracts, leases and mortgages if the person seeking payment under the contract was an owner, operator or controlling person, or if the rent, price or rate of interest sought is substantially in excess of a reasonable rental, price or interest rate.

New Jersey enacted its medical receivership statute in 1977, and the first case brought under it was filed by the New Jersey public advocate. In that case (*Van Ness v. Hinson and Clifford Brookbend Convalescent Home and Mountain View Nursing Home,* C.A. No. Superior Court, Chancery Division, Passaic Co., Filed August 14, 1978), the public advocate alleged that two homes were in habitual violation of minimum standards of health, safety and patient care. The complaint also alleged a long history of violations of federal and state regulations. One interesting aspect of the New Jersey complaint is the public advocate's statement that both nursing homes were "threatened with closure or full loss of Medicaid funding to cajole compliance with minimum standards required by law but such measures failed to achieve that result." (The complaint is also interesting because it contains allegations of abuse of the Medicaid patients' personal needs accounts.)

Some state receivership statutes allow for two kinds of receivers. One is the involuntary receiver, where the state or another entity puts the nursing home into receivership. The other is the voluntary receivership. In New York, Minnesota and Connecticut, nursing homes may request that they be placed in receivership.

Monitors: Some of these statutes also provide for a lesser form of receivership by providing that "monitors" may be placed in nursing homes. These monitors typically act as the eyes and ears of the court or the state licensing agency and also act to keep the nursing home from full receivership by suggesting or directing corrective measures.

Texas has placed monitors in nursing homes even without any specific provision for it in its statute—a move which, it has been suggested, could be undertaken in many other states. Wisconsin, on the other hand, specifically authorizes the use of monitors by statute, as does the proposed Massachusetts legislation.

Money is always a problem in a receivership action. Wisconsin establishes, by statute, a contingency fund to which the receiver may apply.. Many of the other statutes, however, are silent on this point.

Common law receivers: It is also possible to obtain a receiver through the use of common law remedies. In Massachusetts, where we are without a medical receivership statute, the equitable power of the court was invoked to fashion a remedy to protect the patients in the nursing homes. We filed the action in state court originally and I believe the court would have issued the medical receivership. But, several days after the court granted a temporary restraining order, the facility filed for Chapter 11 reorganization in the bankruptcy court. Thereafter, we sued the facility in bankruptcy court, and asked the judge to immediately appoint a receiver, thus requesting essentially the same relief we asked for in the state court. The bankruptcy court appointed what we might call a medical receiver, but what is in effect a true bankruptcy receiver. The receiver is charged with preserving the assets of the creditors as well as with protecting the patients.

The common law receiver is fairly widespread now. They have been appointed to run prisons, to run schools in the midst of desegregation cases, and to improve mental health facilities in various states. See, e.g., *Inmates of Attica Correctional Facility v. Rockefeller,* 453 F.2d 12, 25 (2nd Cir. 1971); *Morgan v. McDonough,* 540 F.2d 527, 533 (1976); *Turner v. Goodsby,* 255 F. Supp. 724 (S.D. Ga. 1966).

Plaintiffs in Texas have also been successful in obtaining a medical receiver absent a statute by appealing to the equity power of the court to appoint a receiver ex parte. (See *State v. Forest Manor Nursing Home, et al.,* Cause No. 77-8555-H, 160th Judicial District Court, Dallas County, Texas. See also, "Injunctions and Receivership in Patient Abuse and Neglect," Attorney General of Texas Nursing Home Task Force, March, 1978.) Ohio also has a receivership case even though it doesn't have a receivership statute. A very interesting aspect of that case, for patient advocates, is that it appears to be the first class action where the class was certified based on the aged and disabled condition of the nursing home residents. For advocates that is an important helping hand in protecting the rights of nursing home patients.

Bankruptcy receiver: The other type of receiver I have touched on briefly is the bankruptcy receiver. I urge anyone who seeks a receiver to make sure that you are aware of the bankruptcy laws. Oftentimes, as you know, a nursing home that is experiencing severe patient problems also has severe financial problems. If the nursing home applies to the bankruptcy court, the Massachusetts experience shows that that court can act as a protector of both the patient and the owner. But, one must be aware of the bankruptcy law and familiar with its powers and its limitations before seeking such a remedy.

Defenses to a request for receivership: I am sure some of you have been accused of abusing patients. If you can show that simply is not true, then, of course, that is a good defense.

Some of the states set out defenses in their statutes. Connecticut, for instance, supplies two defenses. One is that the owner can avoid a receivership by proving that he or she did not have any knowledge of the conditions which prompted the request for the receiver or could not reasonably have known that the conditions existed. The owner can also claim that he or she did not have the time to correct the violations. Of course, the owner can also claim the violations did not exist at all.

The New Jersey statute provides that the owner can defeat a petition for a receiver by showing that the conditions have been remedied or removed. He can also defend by establishing that the conditions did not exist as a pattern or practice, but instead were isolated incidents not sufficient to push the home into receivership.

Consumer Protection Principles

Through the use of the consumer protection statute, Chapter 93A, the Attorney General in Massachusetts is empowered to enforce numerous other laws and regulations to protect the public. Consumer protection is sort of a heart-and-soul body of law. If you read the cases, you will be amazed at how broad they are. There are cases, on both the state and federal level, holding that it is a violation of consumer protection statutes to treat people unfairly or to withhold information from them, where the withholding of the information causes them to do something that they would not otherwise have done. This is a very broad standard, and though many times I've had people suggest that it would not hold up in court, in Massachusetts and throughout the country it has held up.

Right now, consumer protection principles are being applied to health care. In Massachusetts, we have applied these principles to the problem of access to health care for Medicaid recipients, both through the discrimination cases and in another case where a nursing home refused to allow legal services lawyers, paralegals and community groups to come into the home and meet with patients. We successfully sued that nursing home and obtained an order from the state trial court, upheld on appeal, prohibiting the nursing home owner from excluding these community groups. The court also altered visiting hours—extending hours that had been in effect for 15 years.

We also have been successful in protecting patients' personal-needs accounts under the consumer protection statute. Last year we recovered, from one owner, $25,000 which was restored to patients whose money had not been given them. That owner is also under permanent injunction, pursuant to the consumer protection statute, not to tamper with the patient-needs accounts again.

Patient abuse is also covered by the consumer protection statute. *Bellotti v. Hill* (cited above) was filed in state court under the consumer protection statute.

One direction that Massachusetts has taken which is unique in this area is the promulgation, by the Attorney General, of nursing home regulations pursuant to the consumer protection statute. The Attorney General enforces the regulations. In fact, the personal-needs account case I mentioned was predicated on those regulations. They serve as great protection for both private patients and Medicaid patients.

The wave of the future for health care advocates, legal services lawyers, and attorneys general is the utilization of consumer protection principles to protect health care consumers. There is a wealth of case law in this area. In fact, most state statutes, including Massachusetts', specifically direct the state court to use federal decisions as precedent in interpreting the state statutes. This should result in even further protection for the rights of health care consumers.

QUESTIONS AND ANSWERS

Robert J. Gerst: Consider the case of a profitable facility providing quality services to private patients who come into that facility as private patients because they want to receive that quality of care. To the extent that you have acknowledged that there is some correlation between profitability and quality in a facility, do you think it is unreasonable for the facility, as a condition for permitting someone to come in as a private patient, to say that at such period of time that you become a Medicaid patient, we want you to agree to leave voluntarily—so we will be able to continue to provide that quality of care to other private patients who want to come into the facility in the same way that you did when you presented yourself at the front door?

Toby Edelman: In that situation, if the facility chooses not to participate in Medicaid the facility has the right to do that—in all states. My question to you in response is, if the facility wants the right to say to people, O.K., you come in as a private patient and when you use up your money you have to voluntarily agree to leave, why is that facility participating in Medicaid? (I also want to make clear that I do not agree with your initial premise that there is a correlation between profitability and quality.)

Gerst: The answer many of them have is that as a convenience to patients who have been there for a long enough period of time so that the concept of transfer trauma, the concept of the place being their home, is a real one, they will permit them to stay in the facility as Medicaid patients.

Edelman: I disagree with that position—where you participate in Medicaid, but you want the total discretion to decide whether or not any particular person can stay as a Medicaid recipient.

Gerst: Should there be such a differential between what private patients are willing to pay and what states are willing to pay that would cause people to make this distinction in who they would permit to come in and stay in?

To carry it one step further, to the extent that Congress has passed a law that permits the states to participate and has not required facilities that participate in the Medicaid program to admit or keep a given number of Medicaid patients, it would seem that Congress, in its wisdom, has made a decision that the private enterprise system can do as good or better a job of taking care of the patients and has not required that they must take care of all the Medicaid patients who present themselves.

Sally A. Kelly: My answer to your first question is if a provider feels the rate it is receiving is inadequate, it has a remedy at law which we encourage and urge it to pursue. I don't believe that providers should be economically punished for taking Medicaid recipients. I will not say that across the board I think they are, but I certainly believe that in certain instances rates received by providers are inadequate.

In Massachusetts we have a rate setting commission which is charged by statute with setting fair, reasonable and just rates. There is a method of challenging those rates. In our discrimination cases, we urge providers to challenge those rates, aware, and more aware after attending this conference, of what a process that involves—and how hard it is to challenge a rate. But it comes down to who is going to suffer from an inadequate rate—my position is that is shouldn't be the Medicaid patient.

Gerst: I think there would be a great deal of relief in the industry if the consumer groups would more actively support efforts at getting a better reimbursement rate. Perhaps the carrot-and-stick approach might work. That is going to take more cooperation because I think the legislatures find it easier to resist the efforts of the facilities but would not be able to resist advocates who would be presenting their positions so well.

Edelman: In New York, a legal services program worked to get the reimbursement rate raised. In New York, the reimbursement rate was being cut by cost centers, and the cost center of "nursing" was one of the areas that the state wanted to cut. For that the legal services people were very happy to go in and say, "No. Do not cut nursing services. We must have nursing services." But I don't think we want to be in a position of running in to every state legislature and saying, "Yes, give more money and then, of course, that care will improve," because I don't think we have too much evidence of that.

My other point about reimbursement is that I think facilities make different arguments in different contexts. When they are trying to get the rate increased, their constant complaint is that they can't make it on the Medicaid rates. But if nursing homes are talking to their shareholders they're talking about how well they're doing. This was really brought home to me when I was working on one of the involuntary transfer cases, and the nursing home said, "we can't make it on the Medicaid rate, we're losing money, we just can't do it." A few weeks later, I was reading an article and the nursing home corporation was going on the New York Stock Exchange, proudly announcing that profits had gone up over 300% in the previous year. I could not be sympathetic that they were not making money—they were obviously doing very, very well.

There are situations where the rate is inadequate, but I don't agree generally with "give more money and everything will be better."

Kelly: There are a number of proposals kicking around in Massachusetts and in other states to link reimbursement to quality-of-care incentives. I think providers would find support from liberals, legal services and other such people in that there are definitely areas where our interests are the same. Unfortunately, I don't think any of us have enough time to represent our clients and your clients as well.

Gerst: I think that unless you get involved and see things from the side of the providers, we're going to have an inevitable conflict and a real crisis. You're going to end up, if you're successful, as in some areas you have been, forcing facilities to keep private patients who become Medicaid patients, to accept Medicaid patients, and to have the same rate for Medicaid and private and make that the lower rate. Inevitably, you're going to take what is a private enterprise system and turn it into a state-operated one. That is not something that you really want because I don't think I've ever heard anybody argue, whether a patient advocate or someone who has been a patient, that they would rather be in a state-run or a Veteran's Administration-run facility than in a private enterprise facility. Inevitably, you're going to have to face up to the fact that you have to have responsible conduct or else you are going to create a problem.

I would like to turn to the issue of receivers. I don't think anybody here would have real difficulty in the concept of receivers being appointed if there were an adequate standard, if there were fair and reasonable due process for the facilities that are involved—if they had a right to a hearing and notice and had an opportunity to present evidence and defend themselves, and if the receiver had the responsibility to meet all of the existing financial obligations. That means that any state that is going to permit a receiver to be appointed is going to have to put its bank account behind the receiver for questions of liability if the receiver doesn't run it right, for questions of meeting existing obligations, for new obligations that have to be incurred, and a system for getting someone else to take over the facility. I have not seen any of the existing laws or proposed laws that really set out all of those provisions for receivership, and for that reason I think the industry is really concerned about it and doesn't really favor it.

Edelman: The receivership laws I have seen do set out those protections— prompt hearings, notice to the owner before the receiver would go into effect, etc.

Audience: Yesterday I heard all sorts of conversation about reimbursement—where they are talking about Medicaid reimbursement at a 50th percentile and a 60th percentile. I'd like to ask our consumer advocate how you achieve adequate care in nursing home facilities when the Medicaid rate is really only the 50th or 60th percentile of costs within these facilities. If every facility were paid at the 50th or 60th percentile cost, half of your facilities in every state in the Union would go bankrupt because there aren't enough dollars to pay for the staffs and the buildings. If everyone becomes a Medicaid patient, and they're only paying at the 50th or 60th percentile, where are the dollars available to pay for the care and the facility?

Kelly: I have a couple of answers to that. One, I have yet to see a nursing home that I have sued, say, for discrimination, go into bankruptcy and have severe financial problems. Two, I am not yet the Secretary of HEW and I don't control the reimbursement system. I think consumer advocates are aware of the problems that nursing homes have with the system, and again, I'll restate that I think there are areas where the two groups—providers and advocates—could perhaps work together. But with the larger issue of can you have quality care for Medicaid patients?—I think the answer has got to be yes.

I've seen homes, and I'm sure many of you have seen homes, with 90 to 95 percent Medicaid patients, that were run in a quality way. Again, the solution for providers when the rates are, in their opinion, unjust, is to pursue their own legal remedies.

The Federal Trade Commission's Investigation of the Nursing Home Industry

ELIZABETH A. TAYLOR

You and I, and, in fact, almost everybody in this country, have something in common: We are all consumers. For the past seven years, I have been an investigator of consumer problems for the Federal Trade Commission. For the last two of these years, I have concentrated on the consumer problems of elderly people in nursing homes. Last summer, I was named director of a nationwide investigation to determine the need to issue a trade regulation rule for the nursing home industry.

The FTC's interest in nursing homes is significantly different from the way other government agencies, the media, the public and maybe even you view them. Typically, one thinks of and hears about nursing homes in terms of quality-of-care issues—the headline-making stories about inadequate food, staffing, and sanitary conditions. But the FTC is interested in the business relationship between nursing homes and their residents. While HEW is concerned whether there are enough aides on a floor, the FTC is looking to protect the resident's pocketbook, and that of the taxpayers, too, from unfair and deceptive business practices. We are concerned, for example, about whether prospective residents receive adequate information prior to admission about nursing home costs and policies. We are interested in whether residents and their families are able to keep track of how their money is spent to determine if they are getting the best buy.

In this sense, the FTC's investigation of nursing home practices is no different from its investigation of any industry's practices. What is surprising, however, is the lack of attention that such issues have received in this particular industry until now. We appear to be asking questions that have seldom been asked before. We're receiving complaints about practices that have not existed in other parts of the marketplace for years. Some of these problems are not the result of fraud, but of industry practices that have perhaps grown up without scrutiny. Others seem to be symptomatic of small businesses that lack sophisticated market know-how. Other practices, however, appear to be nothing short of purposeful rip-offs, and the skill with which they are perpetrated make them all the more difficult to detect.

On the basis of my investigation to date, I believe the nursing home industry presents considerable and serious problems for consumers. These may not be isolated incidents, or merely the creation of a few rotten apples, for they appear to be widespread. Further, evidence suggests they are lucrative, and that they are increasing the cost of nursing home care unnecessarily.

I am going to discuss in detail the FTC's investigation of the nursing home industry. I'm going to tell you what we're looking for, what we've found, and what we propose to do about it.

The Nursing Home Market

Let me begin by briefly describing several characteristics of the nursing home market. There are a little over 18,000 nursing homes in the United States today, three quarters of which are owned and operated by proprietary companies. Annual revenues in 1960 were just $500 million but rose to $14 *billion* in 1978—a 3,000% increase in just under two decades. Of course, much of this growth, if not many of the industry's headaches, has resulted from the massive presence of the federal government in nursing home affairs. Between HEW and the states, government today pays for the care of approximately 70% of all nursing home residents.

As in many industries, the trend in the nursing home market is toward larger companies. The mom-and-pop facilities are becoming scarce. Because of government restrictions against new construction, however, much of the industry's growth is now a consequence of mergers and acquisitions. Revenues for the largest independent chain alone rose from $47.5 million five years ago to $200 million today, primarily as a result of mergers.

But these statistics are pretty dry stuff compared to the day-to-day realities of the nursing home business. As a part of this investigation, my staff and I have visited nursing homes in various parts of the country. Some were small operations, while others were part of major chains. I know from this experience that there are excellent facilities on the market, run by good and caring people. I also believe that operating a good facility is a tough business with many difficult problems, not the least of which are the sometimes conflicting government regulations that often seem more oriented to paper than to people.

To the nursing home operators in this audience, I can assure you that the FTC does not want to add unnecessarily to your regulation burdens. If we appear to do otherwise someday, however, it will be because of a demonstrated need to provide greater protection for your customers.

It would be difficult to find a more vulnerable and easily exploitable class of consumers than nursing home residents. While you and I can blame our own gullibility for making unwise purchases, we are generally able to protect ourselves in the market. But the very factors that bring people to nursing homes place them at a severe disadvantage as consumers. The average age of nursing home residents is 80, most are poor, each has at least two chronic diseases, and half of them have been diagnosed as senile. Many have outlived their closest friends and family, and consequently have few visitors. Yet the average resident lives in a nursing home for over two years, and it is often her last home before she dies. Two other characteristics are important. Most nursing home residents are women—many of whom grew up to be far more dependent and submissive than today's younger women. Further, their generation had no anti-war or civil rights movement to teach them the techniques of protest, and they have no tradition of complaining to authority when things go wrong. This combination of age, illness and submissiveness makes nursing home residents exceedingly vulnerable.

The Nursing Home Transaction

Attributes of the nursing home transaction itself make it different from most other purchasing decisions in the American marketplace. First, for most elderly people, entering a nursing home is viewed as a prelude to death. Even under the best of circumstances, it is an extremely traumatizing, highly emotional experience, made worse by the depression and lack of control that accompany illness.

Second, prospective residents and their families engage in very little comparison shopping when selecting nursing homes. Time is short, and the need is immediate. Worse, most people are ignorant about what to look for, what questions to ask, how to judge their needs in comparison to what they see.

Third, there is a serious shortage of nursing home beds in many parts of the country. When selecting a particular facility, most people base their choice on simply finding an available bed. Unlike most consumer purchases, cost and quality are often not considered until after the resident has moved in.

Fourth, the consumer in this instance—the prospective resident herself—is seldom consulted in the selection process. Physicians and hospital staff make the majority of placement recommendations.

Finally, another factor that makes the transaction unique between nursing homes and consumers is its irrevocability. Because the elderly find movement from one setting to another to be very traumatic, there is a great reluctance on the part of nursing home residents to move to another facility once the initial decision has been made.

As a result of these factors, nursing homes hold the balance of power in their transactions with residents—not for any malevolent or sinister reason, but because it is inherent to the circumstances. The FTC's concern is to examine the way this power is being used, and to determine whether the elements of the transaction between consumer and facility are fair.

Nursing Home Practices

We have been looking to see whether the market itself is providing consumers and their relatives with the kinds of information needed to make an appropriate placement decision. We have been looking for full disclosures of costs and policies, easy-to-understand contracts, complete descriptions of what may be in store for residents should their finances, level of care or other circumstances change. We have been looking for adequate accounting procedures for the handling of resident funds. Here are the highlights of some of the practices that we have found.

When any of us buys something, particularly if it is expensive and we must pay for it over a long period of time, we expect to be told its price. In fact, we *need* to know its price in order to determine whether we can afford it.

The same thing is true for consumers entering a nursing home. The Patients' Bill of Rights requires Medicaid and Medicare facilities to inform prospective residents in writing about the costs of their daily and extra charges. While most nursing homes disclose their daily rates, however, few appear to list their extra charges in a meaningful way. This is no small omission. For a private resident who may pay $1,000 for basic care, extra charges can amount to an additional $100 or $300 a month, depending on her needs and the facility's policy.

What is a consumer to think when she reads the fine print in her contract that says "extra charges will be made for ancillaries"? Does this mean her kleenex, aspirin, and wheelchair? Will she be charged extra for hand-feeding, incontinent care, or something called "unruly behavior"? If so, how much? Consumers need to know. They not only need to know prior to admission, when they are selecting a facility; they also need to know during their stay, so that they or their families can keep track of charges or question a bill.

For private residents, cost disclosures are even more important. What they pay for their care often determines how long their resources will last. Since some nursing homes will not keep private residents after they have run out of money, the initial selection should be calculated on the basis of total cost versus their assets.

This absence of written price information, and the absence of advance notices of price changes, opens up nursing homes to charges of capriciousness and fraud. One complaint in my files is from the son of a nursing home resident in the East. When his mother's condition seemed to deteriorate rapidly, the son complained to management. The mother's basic rate was immediately increased by $4.50 a day without explanation. The son viewed this rate increase as the nursing home's way of punishing him for complaining. Another explanation might be that the mother's condition was deteriorating despite the nursing home's best attempts to care for her. Because her condition worsened, she needed a more expensive level of care, forcing the nursing home to increase its rate. The nursing home's failure to set out this information clearly and in advance, however, led the son to believe the charge was increased arbitrarily and for revenge.

In another incident that has been brought to my attention, the resident of one facility was charged $30 for use of a wheelchair. When the administrator was told that the man owned the wheelchair, the charge was changed to $30 for *cleaning* the wheelchair.

Reasonable business practices would appear to dictate that consumers receive full cost disclosures and advance notice of price changes by industry members. Indeed, the absence of such information exacerbates many of the problems that I am about to describe.

Refunds: Refunds can be a source of problems for nursing home residents, especially private residents who pay for their care on a month-to-month basis in advance of services. If a resident is discharged or dies before the month's end, is she or her guardian entitled to a refund of the unused portion? This is an ill-defined aspect of most nursing home contractual arrangements. One large chain, for example, states in its admission agreement that it provides refunds within 30 days of discharge. Another refers merely to a "reasonable time." Many make no reference at all to when a refund might be forthcoming. But more importantly, most nursing homes appear not even to have a stated policy concerning the basis upon which refunds are determined. As a result, residents and their relatives must rely on the good graces of the facility's administrator to determine their refunds fairly.

Resident trust funds: Resident trust funds represent a considerable sum of money and a considerable headache for many nursing homes. These, of course, are the $25-a-month allotments provided by the states for the personal needs of Medicaid recipients. The term also includes, in my mind, the assets of private residents who may have no one to help look after their funds. Several nursing home administrators have told me they want nothing to do with this money, that it is pure trouble to them in terms of added bookkeeping and, in the hands of unscrupulous operators, it can be a temptation to steal. I sympathize with their problem. Regulations in many states have been extremely lax in articulating proper trust fund accounting procedures. Consequently, a number of criminal actions have been brought against nursing home administrators around the country for embezzling their residents' funds. One TV news team in Chicago found an 80-year-old woman who had been bilked out of $42,000 by an unscrupulous nursing home administrator. In less dramatic fashion, we have received complaints that trust funds are used as interest-free loans by nursing home administrators, and that they are often dissipated by numerous and inflated charges.

As a result of the Medicaid/Medicare Anti-Fraud and Abuse Amendments, HEW is currently rewriting its regulations for the handling of resident trust funds. We will be looking at the remedies they devise. Although there are complicated issues involved here, HEW's current proposals indicate that certain accounting procedures and mandatory disclosures will be minimum new requirements.

Itemized bills: The failure of nursing homes to itemize their residents' bills each month also appears to be a problem for consumers. Although we all expect to know exactly what we're paying for in most business dealings, many nursing homes bill their residents in lump sums under such general categories as "Prescriptions," "Laundry," "Therapy," and "Miscellaneous." Consequently, neither residents nor their families are able to determine exactly what items they are paying for or to challenge a facility's charges for goods and services that it claims to have rendered. Because of the absence of refund policies and price information generally, lump-sum billing seems to intensify the resident's powerlessness as a consumer.

A nursing home ombudsman has provided me with information about one nursing home in a large metropolitan area. Of the 41 complaints that her office has received about this facility, over half have been for billing practices, including arbitrary refunds, overcharging, double charging, outrageously inflated charges, and "erroneous" charges—where, time after time, the facility has "guessed" it made a mistake. One of the difficulties in determining whether this company has violated any consumer protection standards is that it bills residents in lump sums.

Several of the nation's largest chains follow a similar practice, however. One company has assured us that if residents are interested in receiving a more specific breakdown of their charges, additional information may be sought directly from company headquarters. While this may be appropriate in some businesses, it may not be here. Having to ask for substantiation of a bill each month brings attention to the individual resident, identifying her as a likely troublemaker. Yet most nursing home residents are afraid to ask questions or appear to complain. Perhaps nursing homes should go further than current practice to satisfy residents and their families of the legitimacy of their bills.

Transfers: Once placed in a nursing home, it is very important that a resident not be transferred involuntarily and arbitrarily to another institution. Studies show that such moves, when poorly prepared, can actually precipitate a person's death. For a nursing home to force a resident to leave without good cause is thus a life-threatening situation. Unfortunately, most nursing home admission contracts are silent in regard to the conditions that would allow them to transfer a resident. When they refer at all to termination practices, it is usually only in connection with delinquent bills. Otherwise, many contracts are worded so that a resident can be evicted solely upon the judgment or whim of the administrator. Perhaps most nursing home operators do not abuse their ability to move residents. Nevertheless, the opportunity is there to use the threat of sudden transfer as punishment for residents who complain.

Another transfer issue that I know is important to you concerns the right of nursing homes to transfer private residents to other institutions when they run out of money. Some states and courts have determined that Medicaid-certified facilities have an obligation to keep on those who have exhausted their funds and must be supported by Medicaid. The staff of the FTC does not have an answer for this problem yet, for the issues are extremely complicated. It is nevertheless an important policy issue for which we are seeking comments.

Ancillary Charges

Nursing home residents often need goods and services that the facilities themselves do not provide, such as medicines, therapy, and laboratory work. Since residents are seldom able to shop for these things on their own, nursing homes usually arrange with vendors to supply them from the outside. The sales from these transactions can represent a substantial volume of business to the merchants or professionals involved. Because these goods must be paid for over and above the nursing home's regular charges, however, they can also impact significantly on the total cost of care for consumers. How wisely and carefully nursing homes select the vendors that do business with them is thus important. But market incentives in this relationship appear not to be in the consumer's favor.

Residents are not likely to engage in comparison shopping when they need drugs, wheelchairs, or other ancillaries, as you and I might. Some have families who bring in various goods from the outside, but many do not. The consumer is thus the epitome of a "captive audience" and almost routinely relies on the nursing home's choice of drug store, laboratory or therapist to supply her needs. On its face, there is nothing wrong with this situation. Upon examining specific situations, however, we have found that there is little to protect the consumer against unreasonable and inflated costs.

For example, there are no regulations governing the cost of ancillary goods and services for private nursing home residents. The rule of thumb in most industries is to charge customers whatever the competitive market will bear. In this instance, the so-called "market" may be a 90-year-old, bed-ridden woman who is mentally incapacitated and has no one to oversee her interests. Who is to complain if she's charged $1.00 for a small box of kleenex or a quarter for an aspirin? Even if she realizes that she is paying too much, there is little she can do about it. She is an easy target for merchants who overcharge.

The government attempts through various reimbursement schemes to control ancillary costs for publicly supported nursing home residents. Nevertheless, all costs for public residents are not borne by the government alone. Because there are a number of goods and services for which Medicaid will not reimburse, public residents must pay for them from their own trust accounts. These funds are considered their own personal property, however, and the government has little interest in monitoring how they are used.

Certain laws may also inadvertently increase the price of ancillary goods. For example, some states require all prescription drugs to be delivered to nursing homes only by a pharmacy. This prevents families from shopping for a relative's medicine at a discount drug store and delivering the medicines themselves. Other states have especially strict labeling requirements for nursing home medicines which make it unlikely that the average drug store will even want the business of an occasional nursing home resident. While beneficial in some respects, these laws and others appear to inhibit competition among potential ancillary providers and increase the costs of goods for nursing home residents.

Finally, and perhaps most importantly, nursing homes themselves appear to have little incentive to select ancillary providers that offer the lowest prices. On the contrary, certain schemes involving high-priced vendors actually benefit the unscrupulous operator. Kickbacks are the most obvious of these, where, in order to get a nursing home's business, a retailer must kick-in a little extra for the operator. This "little extra" is then passed on to the residents in the form of higher prices. I will not dwell on this practice, for the FTC, as a civil enforcement agency, has no jurisdiction over such criminal activities. However, various prosecutions of nursing home vendors, as well as testimony before Congress, suggest that kickbacks have been fairly prevalent in the nursing home market.

Related-party transactions: There is a second means to increase ancillary charges for residents that has only recently begun to receive public attention. These are related-party transactions, where nursing homes own the companies that sell the ancillary goods and services to their residents. Now, nothing is inherently wrong with self-dealing transactions. It occurs in many industries, enabling them to gain efficiencies in the manufacturing and distribution of products and to keep prices down. While this could be true for nursing homes, my files reflect another story. Even with cost-related reimbursement systems, there appear to be numerous ways that nursing home corporations can benefit unduly from related-party transactions. One chain that I know about recently purchased its own pharmacy. It has been reported to me that the prices for its drugs immediately shot up by 40%, and its service declined. Some unit dose systems for pharmaceuticals may be used to excuse unwarranted increases in drug prices by nursing home chains that own an interest in the companies that manufacture the unit dose equipment.

These are serious matters. They call into question a basic tenet of the free enterprise system, where, if a company can afford to become vertically integrated, both company and consumer should benefit. But in the nursing home industry, normal market forces such as a mobile and alert consumer, a free flow of information, and ample competition do not exist. Here, vertical integration may present an inherent conflict of interest that has negative side effects. Certainly, when nursing homes are in the business of supplying medicine, eyeglasses, wheelchairs and physical therapists, and their prices are extraordinarily high, one must question whether the purpose of such relationships is to benefit the nursing home resident or the corporation and its officers and stockholders.

We know there are nursing homes that contract with pharmacies charging as much as 20% below retail prices for their drugs. We have talked with pharmacists who tell us that their volume of business with most nursing homes allows them to reduce their prices to residents. There are nursing homes that obtain competitive bids from ancillary providers, selecting the outlet that offers the lowest price and the highest quality. Obviously this can be done. The FTC's interest in this aspect of the nursing home industry is its impact upon the cost of care to consumers.

Unnecessary Charges

This brings me to a related topic: The amount of unnecessary and non-care-related costs that may be hidden in today's nursing home charges.

The government's reimbursement formulae for nursing home care have varied over the years as both HEW and some states have sought to reduce costs and root out fraud. Before we had the cost-related systems now in use, we saw flat rate, cost-plus, prospective, retrospective, and points systems take effect, later to be replaced by another. Three things have remained constant over this time, however. First, by law, private residents could not be charged less than their government-subsidized counterparts, Medicaid and Medicare residents. The government's rates thus set the floor for the private.

Second, the nursing home industry has consistently claimed that the government's reimbursement level was too low.

Third, while reimbursement levels may indeed have been held to a minimum for such care-related categories as staff salaries and food, other categories like administration and real estate have been allowed to rise, reflecting the government's assumption that nursing homes had little control over these costs. I think this assumption may be incorrect. In fact, there is evidence to suggest that real estate and administration may have been used by some parts of the industry to falsely inflate costs for purposes of reimbursement.

For example, an 86-bed facility was sold last year for $1,200,000. However, the state's health department calculated the nursing home's book value, including land, building, and equipment, at $300,000—less than one-third of the agreed-to sale price. Officials estimated that the sale increased the nursing home's cost to taxpayers by $54,000 a year in additional Medicaid reimbursement. The new owners, however, "added not a single backrub, or aspirin or new service," according to a newspaper account.

Elsewhere, an investigation has revealed that a group of nursing home investors stand to recover nearly $1.7 million over costs by leasing several nursing homes to others. Each lease has renewal clauses doubling the terms. This same group of investors sold equipment to its nursing home lessees at prices that were more than twice book value and about 86% in excess of cost, even though the equipment had been purchased as used.

We have received information from other sources that some nursing homes have entered into phony management contracts, either with themselves or with outsiders, which offer little in the way of services in return for a showing of high costs for reimbursement purposes.

Some experts blame these situations upon the government's reimbursement system, which, in one author's opinion, "has largely eliminated risk from the health industry." In a game of making profit off cost, nursing homes are able to enter into inflated operating and real estate transactions and make disguised profits from their mortgage and lease expenses, amortization and depreciation, interest and excise tax rates, as well as contracts for management, computer, consulting, and even housekeeping services. Since the government's rates are used as the floor for private resident rates, however, both taxpayers and private residents may be paying more than is necessary for nursing home care.

Arguments Against FTC Involvement

The FTC's involvement in nursing home problems has been attacked for two basic reasons. The first is regulatory overkill—a charge that on the surface may appear to have merit. Certainly, there are few industries in this country with as many government regulations and strings attached as nursing homes. Insofar as protecting the consumer, however, I believe the FTC's authority is unique. No agency other than the FTC, for example, has jurisdiction over the transactions of private residents in noncertified facilities. Approximately one-quarter of the industry's nursing homes, according to HEW figures, are noncertified.

Nevertheless, the majority of private residents live in Medicaid or Medicare-certified facilities. While HEW and the states concern themselves with the well-being of government-reimbursed residents, however, little attention is given to those who pay for their own care. Although private nursing home residents are estimated to fill only about a third of the industry's beds, they contribute nearly half of their revenues—paying considerably more than their proportionate share. Further, more people enter nursing homes as private pay residents than remain there in this status. In other words, as the expense of a nursing home exhausts their resources, many are forced to turn to Medicaid. Thus, the private market is an important, but little-examined segment of the industry today. The FTC may be needed to fill this gap and ensure a measure of protection that has not existed before.

The second argument against the FTC's involvement is money—who's going to pay for the newly mandated requirements if a trade regulation rule is issued? My answer is that we all will, both taxpayers and private residents alike. The FTC is not a reimbursement agency, like HEW, and does not provide funds for the implementation of a rule. We assume in any of our enforcement actions that the market itself will absorb the extra costs, and we strive to bring actions where the benefits will far outweigh those costs. Clearly, nursing homes may incur increased expenses by providing adequate cost disclosures, advance notices, refunds, itemized bills, and the various other measures that my talk today has suggested. But market pressures have forced other industries to provide such information for years, and we have all been paying for and benefiting from them. On the other hand, if Commission action can reduce false costs in the industry, the price of nursing home care may go down or at least be stabilized.

Meeting the needs of the elderly in this country is expensive. In a society dedicated to youth, we are uncomfortable with the certainty of our own aging, let alone the need to spend money on the care of those who are old. Nevertheless, our median age is getting older; as more and more of us age, or see our parents become old, we may begin to place more emphasis and resources on their care. I hope that when we do, we will also make sure that we are getting our money's worth.

FTC Strategies

The Federal Trade Commission has two alternatives when it contemplates bringing an enforcement action in any industry. The first is to identify particular companies that may be engaged in unfair or deceptive business practices, charging them with violations of Section 5 of the Federal Trade Commission Act. This action can result in consent orders or litigated orders with individual companies.

Trade regulation: The second is to issue a trade regulation rule for the entire industry, defining with specificity what practices have been determined by the Commission to be unfair or deceptive and containing appropriate remedies. The advantage of this latter action, when certain abuses appear to be widespread, is that it saves the government the expense of bringing numerous lawsuits on the same issues. Rulemaking offers advantages to industry members, too, for it establishes a standard for everyone to follow. Violators no longer have an edge over their more law-abiding competitors.

FTC rulemaking is inherently an open process. Industry, as well as state and consumer representatives and academicians, are all given ample opportunity to make their views known. Written comments are solicited. Public hearings are held, conducted by a presiding official, and individual members of the public are asked to offer testimony.

The FTC staff and the presiding official then prepare independent reports and both are subject to additional comment. The Commissioners themselves then review the record. If they agree that a rule would be in the public interest, they can issue a final rule in a form that is determined to be supported by the rulemaking record.

Once in place, a final trade regulation rule has the force of law, and violations can result in civil penalties of up to $10,000 per violation. Commission enforcement actions are chain-wide, and they can hold the parent corporation responsible for the acts of all employees, agents and subsidiaries when the parent controls and directs their activities.

Our investigation of the nursing home industry is a long, long way from this final rulemaking stage. Indeed, we are only now at the point of determining the need for proposing a rule. I have told you several of the issues that interest us. As a means to obtain concrete responses to these issues from industry, government, and consumers, the FTC staff prepared a draft proposed rule several months ago which contains some of the remedies that we have considered. I'm sure most of you have seen at least one or two of these drafts, for there are a number of copies in existence. In fact, we have received such a variety of comments that we don't even have a "latest" version anymore. We've stopped tinkering with it and are now evaluating the data that we have gathered in preparation for presenting our preliminary findings to the Commission. Some of the issues are so complex that it will take a great deal more research before we can come up with definitive conclusions.

I want to emphasize the "first draft" quality of our rulemaking investigation. More work must be done and more comments received before the Commission makes its decision whether or not to initiate a rulemaking proceeding. If, on the basis of the staff's recommendations, the Commission determines that it would be in the public interest to proceed with rule-making, this conference will probably be the first of many opportunities for you to hear my views, and for me to hear yours.

QUESTIONS AND ANSWERS

William Hermelin: Granted that an elderly prospective resident has numerous vulnerabilities as a consumer, let me pose the question as to whether it's not the same vulnerability (i.e., the resident's physical condition) that has him or her in a nursing home and under the supervision of medical and other specialized staff? You and others on the Commission have stated on a number of previous occasions that the Commission will not be like HEW is authorized to be—i.e., involved in determining the quality of care. Yet, is it not essential that in promulgating a rule (and those of us that have seen the earlier drafts recognize that it would potentially be a rule which would govern in many ways, many practices, many policies and many procedures in the nursing home) the FTC balance and consider the resident's rights—his right to receive and the facility's obligation to provide quality medical and other appropriate care? I found that lacking in your analysis of who this person is. You've dealt with him solely as a consumer, but I'd like you to address if you would, his place as a resident of a nursing home and the role and responsibility of the facility, together with the professionals it employs, to provide him with care.

Elizabeth Taylor: That's a very interesting statement. I really haven't been challenged on this point before. Are you suggesting the FTC get more deeply involved in the quality-of-care issue?

Hermelin: No. I'm suggesting that when and if the FTC begins to consider specific provisions, evidence as to whether or not a particular procedure, practice, requirement or prohibition must be evaluated in terms of its impact medically or psychologically, on the resident. To cite one example, consider the freedom-of-choice concept in terms of drugs and biologicals—the ability, which you made reference to, of a family member to go out and secure drugs and biologicals. I'm just wondering at what point the mandated responsibility of a facility to provide quality of care—and that specifically is applicable to drugs and biologicals as well as other matters—must come into play?

Taylor: In terms of anything we're going to do—if we do anything—we will be considering the impact upon the resident. Earlier, I thought you meant that we should be somehow getting into evaluating the quality of care in a nursing home. You were right in suggesting that our rule doesn't go to that at all. We don't evaluate the quality of supermarket goods when we say that certain prices have to be displayed. We're trying to stay away from HEW's and the states' quality of care bailiwick. We're addressing things that, according to the complaints I've received, have not been addressed before. But, in putting together any proposed rule or anything that's going to be final, impact upon the resident is, I'm sure, going to be given a lot of consideration.

The whole freedom of choice issue is one of those things that I find mind-boggling and we're going to have to put a lot more attention into it. We haven't had the time at this point, and I can't even say what we would be coming out with ultimately—because we just have not done the kind of homework that we need to do.

Thomas E. Hermann: I'd like to find out a little bit more about how you view the jurisdiction of the FTC over various entities. Section 4 of the Federal Trade Commission Act defines "corporation" as an organization which carries on business for its own profit or that of its members. The word corporation is found in Sections 5 and 19 of the FTC Act, which describe the Commission's remedial powers. Therefore, the definition would appear to exclude nonprofit corporations or organizations from the purview of the Act and FTC jurisdiction. Furthermore, at least one circuit has ruled that the Commission does not have unrestricted jurisdiction over nonprofit entities. Considering the fact that you mentioned that approximately 25% of the beds of facilities are nonprofit, do you anticipate the Commission or any proposed rule covering nonprofit facilities and those facilities under nonprofit auspices?

Taylor: I anticipate that the Commission and the people who are working with me will give that a lot of research. I'm not prepared at this time to give a definitive answer on whether our proposed rule would affect the nonprofit facilities. I know from just this conference that the proprietary part of the industry and the nonprofit part of the industry both think that it would be unjust, for various reasons, for the nonprofits to be excluded or included—depending on the source of the comment. I can't tell you—if I gave you any kind of a definitive answer, it would be wrong of me at this point. I think we're going to be getting as good an answer as we can achieve before the report that I'm preparing goes to the Commission. I think it's an important issue and I don't mean to delay it until we feel like figuring out an answer, but at this point, we don't have it.

Hermann: So, the way you see it right now, it's unclear. Let me just quote from a September 1976 FTC News Bulletin which says the Commission has authorized the investigation of the *proprietary* nursing home industry to determine whether there are violations of the FTC Act. Is anything to be drawn from this '76 statement?

Taylor: You're right, it does talk about proprietary nursing homes there. Traditionally the Commission views itself as having jurisdiction over anything proprietary. But, it would be wrong of us in doing anything that would affect an entire industry not to test to see whether a fairly significant segment would be automatically excluded. I do think that, if we don't have a legitimate authority over nonprofits, this part of the industry would nevertheless want to keep its eyes and ears open and see what we're doing. I would like to have comments from the nonprofits throughout our investigation.

Jack MacDonald: You made reference to the fact that some states have on the books laws that would appear to dictate how a facility would be purchasing its services, ancillary services, drugs, etc. How would you visualize, or who would you see coordinating, any possible conflicts that might arise between HEW's rules, state laws and a proposed trade rule by the FTC?

Taylor: That's one of those $64,000 questions on which we have to do much more research. We're just not at the point of giving a good answer. I know that is probably extremely frustrating to all of you but your conference is too early. I will know more later, if we get off the ground.

A nursing home rule would not be the first time that these issues have been important. The issue of the FTC's authority to supersede state law is going to the Supreme Court on another rule matter. I'm sure that's going to have an impact on rules throughout the Commission, as well as this one. Some of our greatest opposition to this rule is from state governments that really are angry that we're putting our nose in their business. We're going to have to hear from the states, as well as the providers who get stuck with those conflicts, before we are going to be able to say too much. It's not something that we are going to be able to answer very soon.

MacDonald: Do you see this being answered before you make your report to the Commission or following your initial report?

Taylor: I really don't know the schedule of the issue that is coming before the Supreme Court on this other rule matter, and I think that's probably going to be the first big piece of information that we are going to get on it. I would hope to have a pretty good idea of what state regulations are and how they conflict with us before we get too far down the road, but we're probably not going to have a definitive answer for awhile.

MacDonald: I'd like to make one distinction in terms of your reference to the case before the Supreme Court. I believe that case relates to purely a state authority and state action in a given industry. In the health industry, you are dealing, or have the potential of dealing, with several state agencies as well as several federal agencies. For example, in the area of related-party transactions, where HEW is evaluating a new definition for what a related party is, one agency is doing that within HEW while another agency is defining what the effect will be and how that will be related to the reimbursement. Those two do not appear to be coordinating their activities that closely. Then, of course, we have a third entity known as the SEC, which controls the multiple-facility publicly held companies, where you have a 5% definition. I think we have the potential here for about five federal agencies as well as some state agencies interjecting themselves into this one issue. (That's just a passing thought.)

Turning to the issue of related parties, what type of evaluation are you doing of the individual examples that you cited for us as to their factual basis?

Taylor: You mean what am I doing to check up on their accuracy?

MacDonald: Yes, on their accuracy. Also, take property costs, for example. Everyone knows that in many markets around the country prices of land and buildings are increasing at a rate far exceeding the consumer price index. It's a little myopic for the Commission to view the nursing home industry and the cost to pay for a building or charge for the use of that building only on the basis of what the historical book value may be for that building. My question, then, is about the examination or the evaluation of the examples that you've given as well as the examination/evaluation of the economic theories that you are really going to be dealing with here.

Taylor: I'm not an economist, and I know very little about the reimbursement system, except as kind of an overview. The degree of information I have has been drawn mainly from other people whom I have talked to who have more knowledge than me. Oftentimes, I've relied upon the public record because I cannot march into nursing homes and obtain all the information. In fact, I have tried to get the information from nursing homes and have been stonewalled.

To get back for a moment to the whole issue of HEW, the SEC and the FTC all worrying about this related-party area and what beneficial interest means and so forth—we are at an early enough stage of the investigation where you can legitimately feel angry that I can't give you great pronouncements of what is going to eventually happen. But, it should make you feel a little better to know that we are working with HEW to develop regulations that are consistent with the Patients' Bill of Rights revisions. I want to be very careful, to the extent that I'm going to have any power over whatever happens, to try to make sure absolutely that we don't have conflicting regulations between the FTC and HEW. I would assume that's going to be the same kind of situation with related-party transactions, except to the extent that HEW really doesn't get into the whole competitive dealings between companies. They're more interested in the reimbursement effect. The FTC, of course, has some history with the impact of various practices on costs. To the extent that we're going to be developing definitions, I would say at this point that we're going to try to be consistent.

Hermelin: Will the FTC be initiating any cost benefit studies, feasibility studies in the areas where regulations are contemplated? Is the FTC obligated to conduct such kinds of analyses and, if so, at what stage will they occur? What I'm also asking is where the burden lies. You've made reference to a number of specific examples that I assume have come to you either through your own investigations or from what other people have told you. Who has the burden of demonstrating the extent of the problem, the validity of the remedy that you are going to be proposing?

Taylor: I like that question better than, who is going to pay for all this? I think we have the burden of proof, and obviously we're going to need industry input on it. I haven't operated a nursing home, and we're going to have to get together with people who do operate nursing homes of different sizes and types, with different needs and problems, and we're going to have to figure out those questions.

I've received letters from industry people who criticize the fact that no extra money is going to be sent their way because of us, and all I can say is that, in addition to that criticism, I would like to have some factual information. There are nursing homes that today do a lot of the things we are asking—so that when we call for better cost disclosures, it's not going to be a very big deal to them. I need to know what extra cost disclosures, refunds or all that kind of paper stuff is going to cost you. If you are not doing it now, perhaps there's a good reason. But, in terms of the timing, I don't think we're going to initiate any studies before we find out whether we're going to be on a rulemaking road.

Hermelin: How would you characterize your evidence—the evidence that there are prior costs and false costs, as you refer to them, in a number of areas? Would you say that evidence demonstrates widespread abuse or are you uncertain, and to what extent is there any plan for an effort to be undertaken to find out just how widespread the abuse may be?

Taylor: We're going to develop a lot more information. First of all, I said—and I don't know whether you really take this seriously—nursing home consumers are not prolific complainers. They, and their relatives, have never thought about coming to the FTC. We have complaints, however, from geographic areas throughout the country, we have complaints about problems that are in nursing homes, large and small. It's very difficult for anybody to say how widespread it is, and as you and I have said, we all need to dig up more information. I don't know how we do it in a consistent manner. That's always a problem when you're dealing with consumers. People write letters for some very strange reasons and it is not always the people with the worst problems who write the letters.

Hermann: Has consideration been given to the fact that when you're dealing with nursing home residents and nursing homes, you're talking about a unique kind of situation where you have Medicaid reimbursement being the majority or primary payor? Where you have the facility which has

85% to 95% Medicaid cost-related reimbursement, how do you anticipate these added costs being covered? Can you talk to HEW and make them consider that in their reimbursement plan? Or do you foresee that either facilities are not going to participate in Medicare or Medicaid, or that there's going to be a decrease in the quality of care?

Taylor: The issue whether facilities are going to drop out of Medicaid/Medicare participation is very interesting and I'm not sure it's going to be a result of our doing, but I think that there are going to be some big conflicts coming up. I don't know what to say about the costs. Our rule would be directed, for the most part, to the private nursing home resident. Some studies have shown that half the people entering nursing homes are private at the point of entrance.

To say that we're not concerned about costs is not true at all. Costs are going to be a very serious part of this whole investigation. But, for us to use cost as the one criteria for determining whether we're going to go ahead or not is unlikely. Because of the complaints I've gotten, and I have to tell you they exist, we're getting information that perhaps nursing home costs are higher than they need to be—because of the fact that people are not getting several hundred dollars worth of refunds when they leave or they're not finding out that a relative has a trust account. There are a number of things that we're talking about in terms of the nursing home situation which I have not seen come up through normal Medicaid/Medicare questions. Our rule is going to be directed predominantly to the private resident who will, I'm sure, end up paying for it. Now, if those costs turn out to be $30 a month extra, we're certainly going to have to give them a lot of scrutiny.

Hermann: You mentioned that your rule will be directed to the private pay patient. We've heard about Minnesota and other states where they're anxious that the payment source should not result in a different type of treatment for patients. Are you indicating that your recommendation will be to deal just with private pay patients rather than all nursing home patients? In Minnesota, where you do have a law dealing with rates for private pay versus Medicaid patients, a recent study concluded "...that nursing homes are forced to exceed their maximum ceilings as a result of complying with governmental orders and mandates." So, I question how you're going to structure your rule just at the private pay.

Taylor: One of the ways was suggested by one of the trade associations that looked at our rule. When we talk about cost disclosures and refunds or any of that stuff, it's really directed to the people who are paying those costs out of their own pockets. Medicaid pays a certain amount of money per patient day. The person who is in the nursing home being supported by Medicaid does not have money coming out of her pocket, except for a certain kind of charges. The Medicaid resident, as far as I'm concerned, will not be given cost disclosures for expenses that she is not going to be paying for herself. So, whether Minnesota has a rule that talks about not regarding the payment system, common sense would say that the person who is going to be paying for something out of her own pocket is going to be getting the disclosures.

Hermelin: You are not suggesting, then, that you're going to recommend limiting the scope of the rule to private pay patients only?

Taylor: I don't think so. The effect of it is going to be narrow, but as I said there are certain costs that public patients are charged, and to the extent that they have to pay for certain things out of their own pockets, the rule will cover it.

MacDonald: If there is a state law or a federal regulation on the books which is resulting in what you would characterize as false cost, or unnecessarily increasing the cost, are you or will the Commission be prepared to deal with that federal agency or that state agency vis-a-vis that particular law?

Taylor: I can't speak for the Commission, but I am going to be very interested in pursuing some of these things. I would, at least, hope that we would be on the record as expressing our concern about those issues. But I don't think the FTC is going to be in a position to tell HEW to disregard the system, or to go to the states and claim that their regulations for the delivery of pharmaceuticals should be outlawed. If we do, it would be on a case-by-case basis, each situation handled separately, one at a time. We would have to develop more information than I have now on the subject. And it probably would be dealt with through the legislature. Anybody who has dealt with all fifty state legislatures knows that it takes a long time to make much impact.

Hermelin: What unfair or deceptive practices are the sections that are now in the proposed regulation dealing with inventory of personal belongings, lockers, visiting hours, telephones, opening of residents' mail, designated to curb?

Taylor: What we have proposed to do has to do with the personal property of residents, allowing them to be provided some safeguards for protecting their own personal possessions. At one point, we were thinking that lockers would be a great way to help people keep track of their possessions. We've modified these things and some are so modified that they've become big question marks. We are concerned about complaints from people whose relatives in nursing homes have lost all of their personal possessions. When I talk to nursing home administrators about it, I know that this is probably as much a concern to them as it is to the residents. If we had come up with some wonderful solution, you probably would have heard about it in my speech today.

We are concerned about it because people can spend money on their personal possessions, and I know I would like to think that I could go into a nursing home and keep my personal things around. An inventory is associated with the whole idea of being able to keep track of at least what you have. There are some definite flaws in some of the suggestions so far.

As a non-lawyer, I could suggest that we could perhaps say it is an unfair practice for nursing homes not to take better care of residents' possessions and not provide lockers or whatever safeguards are needed. In terms of the uncensored mail and the telephones and the visiting hours, we view these kinds of things as helpful to our enforcement—in fact, necessary to our enforcement. We have complaints about nursing homes that won't let anybody inside. Nursing home residents have enough trouble just getting people to come inside and visit them, let alone for a nursing home to keep people out. We need more information to flow from nursing homes to the outside and vice versa. In terms of an unfair act or practice, I am not really sure.

Hermelin: Are you required to so state what that unfair practice might be?

Taylor: I'm sure we will be.

Hermann: You mentioned "regulatory overkill" and the desire to try to avoid that if possible. You also mentioned patient trust accounts. How do you see trying to reconcile the FTC, which is one type of rulemaking agency, with HEW regulations on a specific point like that?

Taylor: It depends on timing—HEW is going to work faster than the FTC does (if we do continue with our rulemaking). So, by the time we would be out there changing anything around, HEW would have promulgated its regulations. We might be in a position earlier of encouraging HEW to do certain things because we perceive that we would like to do it, too. But, I suppose you are asking who is going to come first.

Hermann: No, not so much as perhaps the potential for two somewhat inconsistent rules being proposed by different agencies dealing with one particular area such as patient trust accounts, and the different flexibilities in terms of the response or the reaction of these agencies.

Taylor: Responding to what—complaints?

Hermann: Responding to conforming their rules.

Taylor: In this kind of regulatory climate, the FTC isn't going to make it very far if we have conflicting regulations on specific instances like that. But, whatever comes out is going to be HEW's baby, first. I can't tell you how we're going to deal with the inconsistencies because we are just not at that point yet. I am quite sure, knowing how the FTC operates and knowing the regulatory climate right now, it behooves us a great deal to be consistent.

MacDonald: You mentioned the potential penalties that can be applied once the rule is in effect. What do you perceive as being the modus operandi in terms of the enforcement of that rule? Is the FTC going to be hiring surveyors to come into the facilities?

Taylor: The FTC's rulemaking power is so new that we are going to have to address this issue Commission-wide. I personally see us not having any surveyors. The Commission operates differently from HEW in a number of respects—one being that we tend to look for big profile operators of any industry. We can ask questions and develop our own theories as to what may be going on in different parts of the industry and pursue it that way. But, because the issue is undetermined as far as general enforcement is concerned—it is just unclear.

The FTC, however, is an extremely small agency—one statistic I heard was that we operate on an annual budget that keeps HEW operating for fifteen minutes—and we don't have the time or the resources to be going into all nursing homes.

Audience: What would be the enforcement mechanism for FTC if a rule were issued and then a nursing home signed a nonconforming contract? What would be the sanction imposed?

Taylor: We would ask the nursing home to tell us about it. We are not an agency that claims to be saving all people from all injustices. If one nursing home had one bad contract, the FTC would not get involved. We look for patterns of alleged misbehavior rather than one or two instances.

Audience: What I'm interested in, though, is the enforcement mechanism. Are there civil suits, might there be criminal prosecutions? Assume the most terrible egregious violation of this trade rule you put out. What would happen?

Taylor: We would go to federal court. We would seek civil (never criminal) penalties. We would develop our evidence, go to court and prove the case. Significantly, it would not be the FTC looking at our information, but a federal court.

Audience: Could you give us some idea of how long it might be before you come out with the final trade rule? Are we months away from the final trade rule, or years or decades?

Taylor: There are somehting like 18 rules in proposal stage now—and how many are final? Two? And this has been going on since 1974. One of the problems is that rulemaking does get bogged down in public comments. The Commission is looking to tighten up the way it has been operating. In fact, I have very little control over the events that are likely to occur. I'm past due on my deadline right now and my next target is getting my report in to the Commission. The next target date, or the next event that you would be looking for, is when the Commission makes its decision to go ahead with rulemaking. Then we will be in the preliminary stages of developing the record and that's when I would foresee us doing some of these studies you are talking about (on costs and so forth). So, this is pre-, pre-, pre-rulemaking.

Audience: What kind of expertise and training do the staff members of the FTC have in this area to make intelligent rules to handle an industry like this?

Taylor: No different than the experts at HEW.

Audience: My question relates to the issue of inflation allegedly arising from various property transactions, whether at arm's length or otherwise. It seems to us who have been working in reimbursement for some time that this ground has been trod rather well and most of the remedies lie in the area of reimbursement methodology. The states are doing a variety of things now which are addressing that issue. What does the FTC propose as an approach to that alleged problem which would be distinctive in any way from the kinds of things that are already underway?

Taylor: I don't think the FTC is in a position to be saving the day on inflated related-party property costs, though it is proper for us to bring attention to it. I am not sure that I agree with you that there are a lot of things being done to curb it. I hear an awful lot of people claiming that there is a lot going on to curb it, but I continue to see accounts of the same problems over and over again. To the extent that it has an impact on the cost of nursing home care, it is of concern to me.

Audience: I am not suggesting that it is not a legitimate issue to focus on. My suggestion is that an enormous amount of activity is being devoted to that area at the present time under the rubric of Medicare and Medicaid. I am curious to know whether you have any new and exciting ideas about what the FTC could do.

Taylor: No, I don't.

Audience: You mentioned that you have been receiving a fair number of complaints and in your preliminary review, you elicited certain areas where there seem to be more problems than in others. Can you give us an idea of (1) the number of complaints and (2) what you feel the Federal Trade Commission will consider as being a substantial number to provoke an industry-wide trade rule? The reason I ask is that we are just now beginning in the MMIS-type programs and through the ombudsman network to develop any data as to what type of complaints have come about, and whether they are significant or not significant. Our goal, of course, is to work with the Congress and with HEW implementing the laws that are already on the books. An interesting question from our standpoint is how do we defend ourselves (as providers of services) against old abuses—abuses for which the '72 and '77 amendments were intended?

Taylor: You've asked a couple of questions there. The things that were cited in my speech were very definitely complaints received in the last year, so they're not practices that occurred years ago and perhaps a lot has changed.

The other question I think you asked was how much of a complaint record do we need before we can justify looking at any industry?

Audience: Not looking at the industry—making the decision of a trade rule versus individual action against somebody in commerce.

Taylor: To a certain extent, the number of complaints is irrelevant. What we've done is collected information about the providers and then analyzed it that way. We haven't waited to get complaints; we have gone out and sought information to see what is being done as current industry practice now. I can tell you from this that I have a better idea probably of what most nursing homes have in their admissions agreements—better than if I'd waited for two or three individuals from around the country to complain about them.

Audience: At what point do you have a statistically significant sample, for instance, that it would say that in a content analysis of contractual agreements, you can cite *x* number of violations of what might be a deceptive practice? Is this sort of a quantitative thing, the thing that triggers a trade rule decision, or if in your content analysis of an agreement you see one provider within the marketplace, is that sufficient evidence to have a trade rule against everyone?

Taylor: First of all, it's not just one nursing home we have information about. What I have to do is give the Commission a reason to believe that a rule or a case would be in the public interest. At this point, on the basis of the contracts that I have received and contracts I haven't received because nursing homes have not wanted to provide them, I'm not sure it would be fair to go after one company. As I said, I really don't think people are not getting cost disclosures because industry is withholding the information on purpose. I think there has been a lack of experience dealing with the consumer movement. When we go in and buy a pair of shoes or a car, we all expect to get more disclosures than providers have traditionally been giving. I don't think the residents or their relatives are asking the right questions.

Audience: Do you have an alternative beyond the trade rule? There are things like consumer information or working with those in the provider field to do certain things. For example, we put out a consumer's guide to continuing care when we identified that as being a problem area. We realized most consumers were not asking the right questions. Do you have alternatives short of trade rules or formal proceedings where we can work together to educate the consumer rather than working from a premise of total dependency of the consumer upon government protection?

Taylor: We were considering this whole consumer education angle. Then, I began looking at all the consumer booklets out there that talk about how to choose a nursing home. It's a very curious thing why consumers are not better informed. I just don't think consumer education is the answer here. I think it's part of it, and I would say that it's very likely we would be involved in consumer education whether or not we do a rule. I would hope that we could be involved in that, but I don't think it's going to be the only thing we would want to do. And, there are other alternatives to rulemaking.